D0153605

THE PSYCHOLOGY OF READING

The
Psychology
of Reading
an introduction

Robert G. Crowder
YALE UNIVERSITY

OXFORD UNIVERSITY PRESS
New York   Oxford
1982

Copyright © 1982 by Oxford University Press, Inc.

Library of Congress Cataloging in Publication Data

Crowder, Robert G.
The psychology of reading.

Bibliography: p.
Includes index.
1. Reading, Psychology of. I. Title.
BF456.R2C73   153.6   81-22358
ISBN 0-19-503138-5   AACR2
ISBN 0-19-503139-3 (pbk.)

Printing (last digit): 9 8 7 6 5 4 3 2 1

Printed in the United States of America

153.6
C 953p

212936

11-9-82 - Bradbury $9.25

For
Julie, Edward,
Bruce, and Lorial

Preface

This book is intended to provide a solid, but highly accessible, introduction to what is known about the psychology of reading. It is written on the expectation that the reader has had a background equivalent to the introductory course in psychology. The context for this book is the virtual stampede of experimental psychologists during the 1970s into research areas that can be grouped loosely around the term reading. Such an interest in reading is completely natural as an extension of the "boom" in cognitive psychology that began in the early 1960s: Reading is a splendid natural laboratory for cognition, one that can be linked to almost all cognitive processes from sensation and perception on up to comprehension and reasoning.

Many books have been coming out that represent state-of-the-art research in this specialty, written by cognitive psychologists by and large *for each other*. Often, these volumes present contributed chapters by leading experts who gathered at a conference of some kind or other. This book is intended to be very different from that model. It is written for people who are not cognitive psychologists.

The guiding purpose is to give a comprehensible answer to the question, "What have we learned, so far, from this decade of mounting interest in the psychology of reading?" For this reason, there will be fewer citations of the scholarly literature than professionals are used to finding in books about their area. There will also be no attempt to review the literature, or even to provide comprehensive balance, on theoretical controversies. (This is not to say the book will be slipshod and biased! I will refer to the relevant literature in the References and Notes at the end of each chapter and I will also indicate where I am making a generalization with which others would likely argue.)

Specialists in the field of education will be startled to find little that has passed for the psychology of reading in their discipline. I am, after all, a psychologist and I have written a book about the work I know. So neglect of traditional educational psychology is not an act of imperialism on my part. I hope students of education will approach this book, therefore, with an open and skeptical mind, asking themselves whether this major effort from a sister science has or has not been worth the effort.

Acknowledgments

There are many people who have helped me in various ways in the preparation of this book. I am at a loss to decide where to stop singling them out for mention, but at least there is no question where to start: Professor Alvin M. Liberman, with his colleagues at Haskins Laboratories, was instrumental in first getting me interested in the subject of reading, over a decade ago. (Perhaps I should say he helped me to see that without realizing it I was already interested in reading.) Another important stimulation came from Ms. Amy Walker, formerly a reading specialist in the Martin Luther King Elementary School in New Haven. For several years, she arranged for me and for students in my undergraduate reading course at Yale to spend time tutoring individual children with difficulties in learning to read. A third major influence were the successive groups of students who participated in that course over a period of several years. They helped shape the book by reacting with lively intelligence to a point left hanging here, a botched explanation there, or a missing connection to life outside the laboratory and classroom. To all these people I want to extend my thanks.

New Haven   R.G.C.
April 1982

Contents

THE PSYCHOLOGY OF READING

CHAPTER 1

What This Book Is About

Nothing would be easier, in these opening pages, than to become tangled in a long and practically useless set of arguments about the proper definition of reading. It would soon develop that reading is a term including a very wide range of different activities and that we would never achieve much agreement about the exact boundaries around them. Is it reading when we enjoy a poem or when we sweat blood over the pages of a FORTRAN programming manual? Do we read the string $30 = 50 - (4 \times 5)$? What about the string of characters that used to be popular in comic books, $%#&&*&%$? Does reading necessarily include comprehension? If so, what is it we do when we pronounce the letter string, hyperphractic?

We would be better off, in this matter, if the language had two different words, one to cover *reading* in the sense of translating print into speech and the other to cover *reading* in the sense of understanding language that happens to be written. In earlier times, the first skill was sometimes referred to as the "ABC's" and kept separate from the comprehension process.

Reading may be one of those "fuzzy concepts" that we can't define exactly by drawing boundaries around its members. The concept of "table" is such a fuzzy concept: Would we want to include all forms of telephone tables in a strict definition of this concept? Would we want to include certain types of desk? All desks? Fuzzy concepts are better defined by a prototype example than by strict boundaries; we all agree readily that a standard, plain, dining room table is just about a perfect example, or prototype, for the concept "table."

We don't want to become paralyzed trying to define reading exactly and so we neatly bypass the problem, defining reading, instead, in terms of a prototype—a target activity that everyone would agree is surely absolutely central to what reading is. Our goal in this book is finding what goes on when a normal adult reads a newspaper article silently.

Gathered into this mundane activity are three stupendous achievements: First, there is the evolution of language within our species, which some (not all) consider to be the quantum leap in biological history that separates us from our subhuman ancestors. Second, in human intellectual history, there is the slow and meandering evolution of written language, which marks real civilization. Finally, the development of literacy within the early school years is the third of these achievements. In a few months of breathtaking progress, the typical child recapitulates, all by himself or herself, this entire biological and social evolution.

READING AND COMPREHENSION

Although hairsplitting on what is and what isn't reading would be wasted effort at this point, there is a serious question about comprehension that will come up in Chapter 7 (which is about the comprehension process). The question is whether the term reading should include comprehension, and all the mental processes that go with it, or not. Because this issue affects fundamentally what different people may be expecting to find in this book, it is worth some preliminary discussion now.

It goes without saying that reading without understanding is no more than a cheap trick. But it is also true that comprehension occurs very often in the absence of reading—especially when we understand speech. The way comprehension works is sure to have a lot in common whether language comes in over the visual or the aural channel; this much can hardly be denied. The position taken in this book, which is argued formally in Chapter 7, is that, therefore, the proper subject matter of reading leaves off more or less where comprehension begins. The book includes a chapter about comprehension, to be sure, because it would be abrupt to provide no glimpse of where effective reading leads the reader. However, this particular book, unlike some others, does not take comprehension as a primary responsibility, or even as a coequal responsibility next to the process of coping with print.

If a book were titled *The Psychology of Understanding Braille,* what would one expect to find in it? If it contained chapters on how people understand metaphors, how people analyze stories, and how people make inferences, we would surely be startled. "What do metaphors and story understanding have to do with Braille?" we might ask. Well, people who read Braille do understand stories and metaphors and do make inferences while they are reading, of course. But this response would confuse a particular mode of getting language into the mind with what goes on in the mind once the language has become available. The same confusion occurs when people say that metaphor and story comprehension are integral parts of the subject matter of reading: They are confusing the destination (comprehension) with the particular mode of getting to that destination.

Reading, like Braille, sign language, and speech, is one communication channel over which we receive messages in our language. Comprehension of language is a tremendously important topic and no one in his or her right mind would deny that. But comprehension is likely to have much in common whichever communication channel is employed. So, therefore, this book does not dwell on comprehension. These matters are discussed in Chapter 7. In the meantime, the reader is urged at least to keep an open mind on the possibility that reading, as conceived here, can take shape as a coherent topic, amenable to psychological analysis.

THE PLAN OF THE BOOK

Chapter 2 is about eyemovements and speed-reading. These two topics give a broad view of the subject of reading and they also help show the need for the more analytical and systematic approach taken in the remainder of the book. In Chapters 3 through 7, we consider reading as a deeper and deeper analysis of printed marks, starting with how patterns of any kind are recognized (Chapter 3) and continuing with single letter and word recognition (Chapters 4 and 5, respectively). In Chapter 6, we consider contextual influences that converge on the individual word from the rest of the sentence. In Chapter 7, the focus is on how even larger units of organization influence sentences and sentence fragments.

Chapters 8 through 11 emphasize reading as a developing skill, on both the individual and the social scales. The story begins with the evolution of writing in history and how writing represents language (Chapter 8). Chapter 9 continues the latter investigation and applies it to the developing reader, which then becomes the main topic of Chapter 10. Chapter 11 treats the topic of *dyslexia*, the most severe form of reading disability. There is information in all of these chapters that can be read independently of the others. However, the sequence of chapters in both parts of the book is meant to form a coherent argument and the reader is encouraged to go through them in sequence.

CHAPTER 2

Eyemovements and Speed-Reading

The first lesson to be learned about reading is both very important and ridiculously easy to appreciate with a simple experiment: Watch someone's eyes from up close as he or she reads something. (The best way is to face the person from a couple of feet away and peer over the book he or she is holding.) You will see immediately that one intuition we have about reading is wrong: Although it seems to us that our eyes travel smoothly across the line of print, the facts are different—the eyes travel from left to right in quick jerky movements. There is a technical name for these jerky eyemovements, they are called jerks. But some scientists have a tendency to conceal simple concepts behind fancy terms, so it has become traditional to call these jerks by their French name, *saccade*. Saccadic eyemovements come between successive periods in which the eyes are steadily directed at a single position. These periods of constant gaze are called fixations.

During a saccade, little or no useful information can be picked up. Their speed is about 100 or 200 degrees per second. (One hundred-eighty degrees per second would be equivalent to sweeping the gaze from directly left to directly right in 1 second.) At this speed, visual experience is just a blur. The saccades are ballistic in the sense that once initiated there is no way to change their direction, just like a bullet's direction can't be changed once it is fired from a rifle. Saccadic movements take only about 10 or 20 milliseconds (thousandths of a second) to complete and so their ballistic nature is understandable—it takes about 200 milliseconds to start a voluntary movement of any kind. Therefore, we may consider the pickup of information from a page as being a succession of still snapshots, each superimposed on the last one.

GROSS ASPECTS OF EYEMOVEMENTS. We continue now to examine reading from the point of view of what the eyes do. Table 2.1 shows descriptive information on eyemovements in children and adults of various school grades. These observations come from a major study by Taylor, Frackenpohl, and Pettee (1960) involving 12,143 young readers grouped under the wings of 39 reading specialists, all carefully diversified on educational, geographic, and sociological factors. The readers were in all cases dealing with materials at "midgrade" difficulty level (texts at an average difficulty for typical students halfway through the school year) with 70% comprehension.

Notice that certain of the measures in the table change considerably and that others change very little, as readers develop. For example, beginning readers make about three fixations per second while college students make about four. Thus, the time spent gazing at the target of a fixation changes only from about 0.33 seconds to about 0.25 seconds, which is not much change considering how vastly better the reading of a college student is in other ways. (The time spent during the saccade itself is very short, by the way, only about 6% of the total time by some estimates, and so we can safely disregard it in these gross estimates.)

Changes in the number of fixations are a different story (see the third column of the table): At the youngest age, 183 fixations are required for a 100-word passage whereas only 75 are required at the college level. The number of regressive saccades, which are backward, right-to-left eyemovements, also changes considerably (column 2). However, the percentage of all eyemovements that are regressive (column 4) remains quite constant at about 20% across all ages.

Table 2.1 Gross Data on Eyemovements

Grade	(1) Average duration of fixation (seconds)	(2) Regressions per 100 words	(3) Nonregressive fixations per 100 words	(4) Percent of all fixations that are regressive	(5) Words per fixation	(6) Reading rate in words per minute
1	0.33	42	183	0.19	0.55	80
2	0.30	40	134	0.23	0.75	115
3	0.28	35	120	0.23	0.83	138
4	0.27	31	108	0.22	0.93	158
5	0.27	28	101	0.22	0.99	173
6	0.27	25	95	0.21	1.05	185
7	0.27	23	91	0.20	1.10	195
8	0.27	21	88	0.19	1.14	204
9	0.27	20	85	0.19	1.18	214
10	0.26	19	82	0.19	1.22	224
11	0.26	18	78	0.19	1.28	237
12	0.25	17	77	0.18	1.30	250
College	0.24	15	75	0.17	1.33	280

Note. After Taylor et al. (1960)

An important quantity in reading is the number of words seen in one fixation. One way of estimating this is through the calculation of a simple ratio. If the first graders require 183 fixations to read 100 words, they must be getting 0.55 (100/183) words in each one. By the same method we conclude that adults are getting 1.33 (75/100) in each fixation. Converting these figures into reading rates based on words per minute (last column) shows that adults read on the average at a rate of about 300 words per minute.

The gross descriptions in Table 2.1 do not, of course, represent all readers or all reading material. Common sense tells us that the figures would be different for reading poetry, light fiction, or a microbiology textbook.

VISUAL ACUITY AND THE SPACING OF FIXATIONS. The data of Table 2.1 show that adults gain about 1.33 words in each fixation.

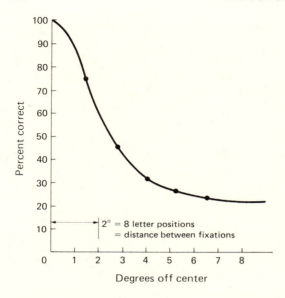

Figure 2.1   *The change in visual acuity as a target is moved away from the central point of fixation toward the periphery. (After Feinberg, 1949)*

Figure 2.1 gives an idea of what information is clearly available during this fixation. It shows the relationship between our ability to name a letter that is flashed briefly on a screen and the distance that letter appears "off center" with regard to where we are looking.

We need first to keep in mind that a spacing of 1.33 words means that successive fixations are falling about 2 degrees of visual angle apart. (The size of a visual target has to be measured in degrees rather than in real units like centimeters. Two things that are a centimeter apart might be distinguished easily if they are close to the viewer but they might have to be moved apart if they were several yards away.) In terms of letter positions, including spaces between words, this spacing of 2 degrees corresponds to about eight character positions. The data displayed in Figure 2.1 show that the clarity of letters—measured by success in identifying them—falls off rather rapidly as the letters are spaced further away from the point of fixation. This is because of the structure of the retina in the eye, which contains densely packed receptors only in a small area of about 2 degrees called the *fovea*. The denser the retinal cells are, the sharper the detail that can be resolved by the visual system. (Please consult any introductory treatment of the visual system in a psychology text-book if this does not make sense to you.)

If each new forward fixation is spaced about 2 degrees beyond the previous one, the letters in a typical word will all be more or less clearly available to the system at once. This is probably not just a lucky coincidence; we may guess that the spacing of fixations is guided by the need to resolve most of the print on a page clearly. In the next section, we ask whether the precise point where a fixation lands is determined only by overall considerations of spacing or by more local features of the text a reader is looking at.

THE GUIDANCE OF EYE FIXATIONS. There are two opposed ideas on how it is determined just where the eyes will come to rest in a new fixation. One is that the target of a fixation is decided on using specific features of the text. Hochberg (1970) has, for example, suggested that the visual system guides fixations toward early word positions (the first few letters) and away from very short words, punctuation marks, or spaces. These rules would work toward getting the most informative part of the text into the region of the retina with the highest resolving power. Fixating on the word *a*, for example, would be a bit of a waste, because it carries little useful information and it takes up three letter positions if you count the spaces on either side. A system capable of this sort of intelligent guidance would have to depend on peripheral information. That is, while the eye is resting in one position, calculations would have to be made about word structures off in the right periphery in order to capitalize on this information in the next saccade.

The other viewpoint (Kolers, 1976, for example) is that the occurrence of fixations across stretches of print is random with regard to local information, although rhythmic and evenly spaced across larger segments. According to this hypothesis, the average spacing might very well change with the difficulty of the material, but once this setting is made, the eyes are allowed to "fall where they will."

It might seem obvious that the first theory—that eye-movements are specifically guided—is the smart way to run the system. However, this is not necessarily so: Of course, it is true that we would be better off avoiding uninformative parts of the page (blank spaces and so on). But on the other hand, the guidance necessary to bring this off would take up some mental capacity. Even if this expenditure of mental capacity were unconscious, it could detract from other important kinds of work during reading—figuring out the meaning, for example. We might be better advised to let the eyes fall in locally random positions but reserve our full attention for concentrating on the message.

What evidence pertains to this issue of guidance in eye-movements? In the first place, the matter is considerably more complicated than this treatment suggests so far. The two hypotheses identified—specific guidance and random spacing—are really the end points of a whole range of hypotheses (see Rayner, 1978, for a full discussion). What experimental evidence we have seems to favor some guidance in the system, however. One method for determining the facts is to record the locations of fixations during fluent reading of a passage of text.

(This record is made possible, among other methods, by reflecting a source of light off the surface of the eye and onto the text that is being read. When the eye moves, so does the reflected spot of light across the line of print. By careful calibration the reflection system can be adjusted so that the reflected point lies just where the person is looking. A fast camera then records the fixation points as they move across.)

If the cognitive guidance hypothesis were true, then we would expect that the location of fixations would be strongly related to the structure of the targets being fixated. There should be few fixations on short words or on blank spaces but relatively many on the initial positions within longer words. If the random spacing hypothesis were true, we should expect the same probability of finding a fixation across all positions in the line, be they letters or spaces. That is, if there are 60 spaces in a line of print, and if we know that a person made six fixations on this line, the probability that any one particular location received a fixation should be 6/60 = .10, no matter whether it was a space, a letter in a short word, or whatever.

But there does seem to be a relation between where fixations land and the word-length pattern. Positions in longer words receive more than their share of fixations. The word THE has, furthermore, been shown to receive reliably fewer fixations than one would expect, even fewer than other three-letter words (O'Regan, 1979). Also, it has been shown that the length of a saccade is greater when a long word is to the right of the previous fixation point than when a short word is. This, too, shows that what is off toward the side (periphery) during one fixation has an effect on where the next fixation will land.

Another method for establishing the role of guidance in eyemovement behavior is to tamper with the quality of information available from outside the "window" of clear vision that surrounds the fixation point. In experiments to be described more fully, McConkie and Rayner (1975) have arranged that this peripheral region—which is where the information used for guidance is supposed to be coming from—contain either legitimate words from the next part of the passage or, alternatively, contain words with the spaces filled between words filled in (likexthisxforxaxshortxexample). If information about word length from the periphery is important in planning eyemovements, we would expect to find some disruption or change caused by filling the spaces. This is what happened—reading was slowed down by filling in the spaces and the saccades were observed to be shorter. Thus, it looks like the evidence favors some type of guidance for saccadic movements, although some of the details remain to be worked out.

If we accept that fixation targets are somehow calculated from peripheral information, it is natural to ask this question: How far away from the current fixation is this influence felt? That is, how far to right of the current fixation point can we use information about where to go next? That question is the subject of the next section. It should be understood first, however, that this loose talk of "intelligent planning" in the guidance of eyemovements is only a convenient metaphor: Whatever guidance there is going on is unconscious and we are no more aware of it than we are of how we calculate the product, 9×7, how we remember the tune of Dixie, or how our kidneys function.

The Span of Fixation

We concluded that information is acquired largely or entirely during the stable fixations lasting normally a quarter second. These fixations are separated by rapid saccadic movements that may be subject to guidance. Now we ask what information is available during the fixation; in particular, we are interested in how far to the right of the fixation point there is useful information.

Two approaches to this question have already been taken up. From Table 2.1, we can estimate the fixation span, in words, by counting the number of fixations necessary to read a 100-word passage. The table shows that college students required 75 fixations; therefore, they gained 1.33 words per fixation (100/75). If the average length of words were about four letters, which is not far from the truth, then a fixation seems to be delivering five or six letters to the college reader. This indirect estimate is a good ballpark figure but there are reasons for wanting better information. For one thing, we know only that the subjects of Table 2.1 were reading with at least 70% comprehension. This is not particularly high. Furthermore, it is hard to know what kind of reading it was—skimming, reading every word, or what.

The second estimate of the fixation span we saw in Figure 2.1, which showed the sharp dropoff in peripheral acuity for individual letters. This figure documents the decline in clarity as information deviates from "dead center" in the visual field. But the stimulus material was neccessarily unconnected in these measurements and we cannot estimate the importance of this.

THE FIXATION MONITORING TV SYSTEM. A far more direct way of determining the information available in a fixation has become possible recently. The key to the system is a constant measurement by a computer of where the eyes are looking, on a TV screen. This computer can, in turn, change the display on the TV screen almost instantly in response to the subject's eye-movements. The current position of the reader's gaze is determined by bouncing (infrared) light off the eyeball and measuring just where it is reflected on the TV screen that he or she is looking at. The computer that is registering these measurements can then make changes in what appears on the screen. For example, the computer could be programmed to erase whatever word the subject has fixated at any moment—rather a dirty trick.

It is more useful to make the opposite arrangement: Imagine a screen filled with X's but stored in the computer is a normal page of prose whose letters and spaces correspond to the X's; the normal material waits hiding behind the X's, as it were. It can be arranged so that whenever the reader fixates a particular X, as measured by the eyemovement monitor, the computer obliges by exchanging that particular letter for the "real" letter or space of the text that was waiting behind the mask of X's. The first letter, in the upper left corner of the screen, might be the letter *t*. By moving his or her gaze one position to the right, the subject might then see *h*, while losing the original *t* back to its X. If the third letter turned out to be *e*, the reader could then surmise that the first word of the text was *the* (provided he or she got a blank on the fourth fixation). This is not a very efficient way to read, to be sure, but now consider a modification in which not only the X in central fixation, but also the surrounding two positions, were revealed as a result of fixating on a position. We would expect reading to become easier as the window size is increased in this way.

Up to a point, at least, reading should get easier with increasing window sizes. Perhaps there would come a point of diminishing returns when nearly whole lines of print are exposed at a time. One measure of the span of fixation might be when this point of diminishing returns is reached. However, for technical reasons, McConkie and Rayner (1975), have preferred a slightly different way of estimating the span.

TEXT MODIFICATION IN THE McCONKIE AND RAYNER STUDY. In one of their studies, McConkie and Rayner varied both the size of the window and the nature of the information outside the window.

Table 2.2   Stimulus Materials Used by McConkie and Rayner (1975)

```
        Graphology means personality diagnosis from hand writing.   This is a

XS      Xxxxxxxxxx xxxxx xxxxonality diagnosis xxxx xxxx xxxxxxx.   Xxxx xx x

XF      XXXXXXXXXXXXXXXXXXXXXXXonality  diagnosisXXXXXXXXXXXXXXXXXXXXXXXXXXXXXXXXXX

CS      Cnojkaiazp wsorc jsnconality diagnosis tnaw kori mnlflrz.   Ykle le o

CF      Cnojkaiaqpewsorcejsnconality  diagnosisetnawekoriemnlflrqcecYkleeleeo

NCS     Hbfxwysyvo tifdl xiblonality diagnosis abyt wfdn hbemedv.   Awcl cl f

NCF     Hbfxwysyvoctifdlcxiblonality diagnosiscabytcwfdnchbemedvcecAwclcclcf
```

Note. On each line a window of size 17 is shown, assuming the reader is fixating the letter d in *diagnosis.*

Key:
XS = X's with spaces intact
XF = X's with spaces filled
CS = Similar (confusable) letters with spaces intact
CF = Similar (confusable) letters with spaces filled
NCS = Dissimilar (nonconfusable) letters with spaces intact
NCS = Dissimilar (nonconfusable) letters with spaces filled

Recall that what we mean here by window is the region of true, unaltered text available on either side of the current fixation point. In Table 2.2, the first line shows a passage of unmodified text and the third line shows a window of 17 spaces surrounding a hypothetical fixation on the *d* in the word *diagnosis.* This condition is similar to the one described in the last section. That is, a fixed window is established around the position of the subject's gaze at each moment.

The other lines of altered text in Table 2.1 show a constant window size, but they all differ in the sort of information offered outside the window. For example, the condition called "X's with spaces" in the second line differs from the condition called "filled X's" only in that the first one offers information about word length whereas the second one does not. Likewise, there are two "similar letter" conditons in which the letters exposed outside the window are shaped similarly to the true letters. In one of these, and not in the other, the spaces are left intact to carry word-length information. If word-length information is useful from eight or nine positions to the right of the fixation point (half the window size we are considering) then it should be easier to read the versions of altered text that keep the spacing intact than to read those versions that destroy spacing by filling in. However, at some large window size, where people can't see anything at all outside the window, then it shouldn't matter any longer.

The conditions shown in Table 2.2 allow other comparisons of interest. Consider the two conditions retaining spaces that are labeled "similar letters" and "dissimilar letters" (CS and NCS, respectively). In both, there is equal information from outside the window about word length. However, in the condition with similarly shaped letters (i.e., the substituted letters resemble the correct letters) there is also potential information in the fringe of vision about the shapes of words to come. Thus, the second word of text—means—is visually more similar to its replacement in the similar condition—wsorc—than it is to its replacement in the nonsimilar condition—tifdl. If general word-shape information can be used as far to the right of fixation as eight or nine letter positions, then the similar condition should be easier than the nonsimilar condition. By varying the size of the window, McConkie and Rayner were able to trace the usefulness of different kinds of information by observing when these specific comparisons (having spaces filled or not, having useful word-shape information or not) ceased to be reliably different. That is, we may assume that when the window is widened to the point that some factor like spacing no longer affects performance, then, at that distance, the particular kind of information being varied is not being registered by the reading process.

One experiment using this technique (McConkie & Rayner, 1975) tested six high school seniors who were reputed to be the best readers in their school. There were many results of interest and we can only summarize here, of course. Evidence for use of specific letter and word-shape information was obtained only for about 10 or 11 positions beyond the fixation point. This specific letter information would be suggested by comparing the true text condition with the condition where outside-window information consisted of similar shaped letters with spaces provided (lines 1 versus 4 of the table). Word-length information was apparently useful as many as 15 positions beyond the fixation point. Thus, McConkie and Rayner found that eliminating word-length information (spaces) reduced the length of saccadic movements from about 8 letter positions to about 6. These are the major results to remember: As our eyes are fixed on 1 position, we are registering information of a specific sort for about 10 letter positions (somewhere just over two words) to the right. As the same time, information on word length may be coming in from another word or so beyond that.

Research by Rayner, Well, and Pollatsek (1980) has shown that a symmetric window is of no use to readers: Only the information on the right side of the fixation point is useful. For example, a window of 16 positions on either side of the fixation point is no better than a window of 8 positions extending only to the right. This situation is *reversed* for readers of Hebrew, which is written from right to left.

CONCLUSIONS ABOUT THE SPAN. There are two major messages to be gained from this elaborate treatment of the fixation-monitoring TV system. First, the method itself is an exciting breakthrough in technology for finding out about the behavior of the eyes in fluent reading. Whereas clever investigators around the turn of the century were able to generate data on eyemovements that have withstood the test of more modern techniques, this new method allows the raising and answering of questions that were simply not subject to test before. The second message to come from the McConkie-Rayner research is a pair of numerical estimates of the fixation span. The 10 letter positions or so to the side of the fixation point that give useful information on specific letters and words set out quite a *narrow* band of clear visual information for the reader. The narrowness of this band of clear vision makes the claims of speed-reading specialists—seeing a whole line of print in one glance—ridiculous. On the other hand, information about word length seems to be useful from a wider band, perhaps 15 or more positions to the side. Since the normal saccade spans about 8 positions, this means the reader can see word-length information a word or two beyond of where his or her eyes will be thrown next, on the average. This suggests that guidance systems responsible for determining the next fixation point might very well rely on word-length information.

Integration of Succesive Fixations

The fixation-monitoring TV system has been used by Rayner and his associates to investigate another important aspect of eye-movements in reading. We have already commented that information is gained in reading from a series of fixations. The fixations provide frozen snapshots of where the fovea is directed at each particular moment, before a saccade shifts to a new fixation down the line. The problem is this: How is it that information gets combined, so to speak, from one fixation to the next? We have no impression that the *page* is jerking—or that new information is being superimposed on old information. Instead, the page we are looking at seems to hold steady; what we see in one fixation builds on what we saw in the previous one. How is it, then, that information is integrated across visual fixations in reading?

McConkie and Rayner performed several experiments on this question. In an early study (Rayner, McConkie, & Ehrlich, 1978), they compared two different explanations of how information gets integrated. According to one, there is a record kept in memory of how far each saccade travels. With this information, each new fixation could then easily be lined up with the previous one. By analogy, it would be like scanning any scene in the dark with a flashlight: If one knew how far the flashlight traveled each time, it would be easier to figure out the overall structure than if not.

However, this explanation was rejected by evidence: In one of their experiments, Rayner et al. (1978) compared two conditions. In one, people made normal saccadic movements as they read and in the other they kept their eyes fixed on a single spot. The new information came in batches of about as much as people would have been grasping in each fixation if they had been reading normally. Furthermore, it came at the same rate as saccades occurred in time. Very simply, results showed that the condition with no eyemovements at all was just as easy as the control condition; integration was not damaged by depriving people of information about saccadic travel distance. Therefore, we turn to the second explanation of integration:

According to this explanation, some sort of memory store is used to hold information from the previous fixation until it can be aligned with the new fixation. McConkie and Rayner called this memory store the *Integrative Visual Buffer*. The simplest analogy would be to a photographic transparency. If a person had a pair of these transparencies from two successive fixations, he or she could move them around over each other until the images "fit." The same kind of comparison process could occur mentally. This second hypothesis, like the first, has the great virtue of being testable experimentally. Also like the first, it did not turn out to be strictly true.

In one experiment, McConkie and Zola (1979) had people read paragraphs from a TV screen. On certain lines, the computer would change how words looked during a saccade. In particular, the computer would detect when the subject began a saccade, and during the time the eyes were in motion—when the subject was not receiving any information—the computer would exchange the cases of letter in the words about to be fixated. (A change in case is from capital to small letters or the other way around.) Thus, the subject was reading a text where some lines were written in mixed typography (LIkE thIs).

Consider those two words in parentheses from the last sentence: Assume the subject was fixated on the letter *L* in the first word. In the McConkie and Zola experiment, the computer would detect when the subject started to move his or her eyes toward the second word—*thIs* and change it to *THiS*. What if the subject had placed information from the second word into a Visual Integrative Buffer while being fixated on the first letter of the first word? Then the change in case should make it harder to match the new information from the following fixation than it would have been if the letters had retained their appearance during the saccade. In other words, with no change the subject would have *THiS* from first saccade and *thIs* from the second. With no change during the saccade, the subject should have the pattern THiS from both fixations, which should be easier to integrate.

However, the result in the McConkie-Zola experiment was that there was no difference between the condition where cases were exchanged and the control condition where everything remained stable from one fixation to the next. Therefore, the information that is used in integrating two fixations must be from a higher level than Rayner and McConkie (1977) originally thought. Perhaps there is some form in which the letters themselves can be identified independently and compared across fixations. We cannot take the time to fill in the details of such a level of comparison. The thing to remember is that some progress has been made with this technique on the problem of integration of fixations. We know that the memory for the distance of eyemovements is not crucial. We also know that the integration is not just a matter of lining up the two visual patterns from before and after a saccade. Knowing how something *doesn't* work is not as good as a definite answer, of course, but it is much better than guesswork and speculation, most of us think.

SPEED-READING

The information about eyemovements and fixation spans that we have been reviewing so far can be used to make intelligent estimates of how fast reading could possibly occur. In this section, we make such an estimate, consider claims of speed-reading programs for more impressive performance, and try to resolve the discrepancy. The examination of speed-reading is a useful way to conclude this chapter for it brings us back to issues in the definition of reading as well as in oculomotor control.

HOW FAST SHOULD IT BE POSSIBLE TO READ? Using what we now know about normal reading behavior, let us make generous estimates of how much the process could be speeded up. Begin with the frequency and duration of forward fixations: (We will ignore regressive saccades, which are about 20% of all fixations normally, and also ignore the negligible time during the saccade itself.) Table 2.1 suggests that the normal fixation is about 240 milliseconds long. Given our simplification as to regressive movements and time spent in the movement itself, this suggests about four fixations per second. Let us be generous and propose that one might make five fixations every second.

How much information can be grasped during each of these five fixations? Depending on just how the fixation span is determined, we saw above that there were estimates of from 4 or 5 positions (Table 2.1) to estimates of about 10 positions to the right of the fixation point (the Rayner-McConkie method). But some information (length, for example) gets in from even farther out. Perhaps a liberal estimate is then that the subject has about 15 letter positions available in some form during each fixation. Notice how much more generous this is than what we might conclude from Figure 2.1, which suggests that acuity is very badly deteriorating by about 8 letter positions from fixation. In any case, a span of about 15 letter positions might contain information sufficient for the identification of about three words.

If five fixations per second are each yielding 3 words' worth of information, the subject might have access to 15 words every second, or 900 each minute, as an outside estimate. True, we have been anything but conservative in these calculations, but the data reviewed earlier in this chapter come from normal people and perhaps some individuals can do a lot better.

CLAIMS OF SPEED-READING PROGRAMS. Advertisements for speed-reading courses typically state correctly that an average adult is reading at about 250 words per minute. The customer is guaranteed that this rate, or whatever his starting rate happens to be, will be tripled at least, with no loss in comprehension. Case studies are usually cited with more staggering gains. Sometimes graduates' rates are quoted at 40,000 to 50,000 words per minute. (This would correspond to covering *Gone with the Wind* in around 12 minutes.) These fabulous reading rates are not claimed to be within the grasp of most people, but rates in the thousands of words per minute are. One advertisement I saw myself suggested that for academics, the average gain is on the order of 5,000 words per minute.

A reading rate of just 3,000 words per minute implies about 7 to 10 pages each minute, depending on the book. This, in turn, allows for about 10 to 15 seconds for each page, a time in which up to about 50 fixations could conceivably occur. Since there are often about 50 lines on the page, this implies that the reader is making one fixation per line of print. Each line contains about 50 letter positions.

At this point, anyone who has kept up with these simple calculations should be raising his or her eyebrows. If the average reader is fixating each line only once, there is no chance of seeing many of the words printed on that line. Assuming a window size of 20 or even 30 positions around the fixation point (which goes drastically, wildly, beyond the just-cited evidence), many words could not be seen. If our definition of reading, for these purposes, includes any requirement that the words on the page be processed, then, it just can't work.

How does the speed reading industry *say* it works? Many programs contain some or all of the following four components:

1. The student is taught to see larger areas of print in a single fixation than was possible before. The implication is that this is a visual process, in which the eyes can be trained to see in meaningful units rather than to rely on whatever happens to fall on the retina within the window-size limits defined earlier.

2. Subvocalization is eliminated, largely by pushing the student to move over print at a rate where internal speech can't keep up. It is easy to estimate the fastest people can talk to themselves. Just repeat some well-known cycle of words to yourself as fast as possible—perhaps the cycle "one-two-three-" and so on—until a friend has timed 10 seconds. Meanwhile, keep count on your fingers of how many times you have gotten through the full cycle. If you got through a 10-word cycle 7.5 times in 10 seconds, your fastest rate of subvocalization must be 7.5 words a second. This example (which is not far from the true result) would then give a rate of $7.5 \times 60 = 450$ words per minute. But this must be a large overestimation because this cycle is so well known; a stretch of unfamiliar words could probably not be handled this fast. In any case, reading several thousand words per minute could never work

even with the fastest rates of silent speech, if silent speech were engaged in while reading. Hence the desire of speed readers to eliminate it.

3. In order to get them to read large segments (Number 1) and to avoid subvocalization (Number 2), students are taught to use their index finger as a visual guide down the page. The most common pattern of finger guidance is a zigzag motion from the top to the bottom of the page. However, it is reported that advanced speed readers reach the point where they use vertical movements down the middle of the page (but still see the edges of both pages clearly). The most striking pattern of finger guidance reported is going down the left-hand page and then *back up* the right-hand page.

4. A fourth component is more "mental" than the first three. The reader is told to read aggressively, making inferences about the subject matter, relating it to what came before, and predicting what will likely come next. The student is supposed to be active, in this way, about what he or she is reading, but at the same time the student is not supposed to be obsessed about understanding and digesting every single point.

The evidence concerning the merits of such training can be presented under several headings:

VISUAL CHUNKING. The idea of chunking is that a group of pieces of information can be organized into a new unit that is easier to process mentally than the several individual units of which it is composed. For example, if we take the arbitrary letter string VCSCJ and remember it as "Very Courageous Supreme Court Justice" it will be easier to remember than the original string of letters.

Can the visual system somehow be taught to do this sort of thing? An experiment by Carver (1970) shows that visual chunking is not always helpful. He studied reading speed for normal readers on three kinds of specially prepared typographic layouts. The first closely resembled ordinary newspaper typography—paragraphs indented, right justified (right margin held constant for every line), with words hyphenated when necessary. The second typographic style was intended to build in all of the advantages of chunking that are instructional goals of the speed-reading programs.

Words that formed meaningful units
were written together
in chunks like this.
The grouping was done by typographic means
rather than relying on
the ability of people
to do it.

The third typographic style was intended to be very difficult. It resembled newspaper style, but all capital letters and punctuation marks were removed.

The results were in terms of reading rate and comprehension scores for the several passages tested this way, all of which were from a standard reading test. The deliberately difficult style did indeed produce slower reading rates and lower comprehension scores than the other two. However, there was no difference between the normal newspaper format and the specially chunked versions, either in reading speed or in comprehension scores. This negative conclusion was unchanged when Carver looked separately at fast and slow readers and when he looked separately at the accurate and inaccurate readers. (Although the chunking did not help readers objectively, there was evidence that the subjects in this study *preferred* the chunked version.) Previous studies showed that chunked typography is useful when people are skimming. There is also evidence from a recent experiment by Frase and Schwartz (1979) that typographic cues of the sort studied by Carver can help with highly technical documents. But for ordinary reading situations, we may conclude that artificial chunking does not help even when it serves up meaningful units in spatially distinct visual units. If getting meaningful chunks "on a silver platter" does not help, there is some cause for skepticism that the eyes can be taught to do it on their own.

EYEMOVEMENTS IN SPEED-READING. There have been a few reports of oculomotor behavior of people who are graduates of such programs as the Reading Dynamics Institute. Although these reports are not very extensive or systematic, it is established that speed readers do not differ from normal readers in the duration of their fixations; rather, they are different in their patterns of saccadic movements. These patterns have been described variously as erratic, zigzag, and, as we noted before, even down-the-left-up-the-right. One investigator (Liddle, 1965) concluded that speed readers are doing what is ordinarily called *skimming* when they use what they learned in commercial programs. This conclusion is supported by similar rates of speed and comprehension when people are instructed either to speed read or to skim.

The eyemovements patterns are also similar. S. E. Taylor (1965) reports little indication from eyemovement patterns that speedreaders actually do use much vertical sweeping. Furthermore, Taylor observed that those subjects who did show such vertical movements were those that scored the worst on a true-false comprehension test; in some cases these "vertical sweepers" did no better on the test than they would have by flipping a coin.

COMPREHENSION IN SPEED-READING. In most situations we can speed up what we are doing if we are willing to sacrifice accuracy. Conversely, we can achieve high accuracy by slowing down. The joint measurement of speed and accuracy in human performance is a difficult problem in psychology and it conceals abuses that border on outright hucksterism in speed-reading programs. The measurement problem is highly technical but we can put the questions in simple terms: What if a person can perform something with astonishing speed but only at the expense of many mistakes? Exactly how much should we revise our estimate of his or her speed if accuracy falls by 39%? How impressed should we be with fantastically accurate behavior if it takes inordinately long?

Some speed-reading programs play off this relation between speed and accuracy in a particularly vicious way: A new student is asked for his or her reading rate when beginning the program.

This is measured at home in a straightforward way and turns out to be in the neighborhood of 200 or 300 words per minute. After the course, what is usually measured is called the Reading Efficiency Index. This last measure is based on the plausible argument that rapid reading rates should be qualified by the percentage of the material that was comprehended by the subject. Comprehension is then measured with an objective test following reading of the critical passage. To compute the index, the reading rate is multiplied by a percent score on the comprehension measure. If a person reads 10,000 words a minute, but scores only 73% on a comprehension test, his or her Reading Efficiency Index is measured at 0.73 × 10,000 = 7300 words per minute—not bad.

But what we seldom know is how well people would score on the "comprehension" test without ever having read the relevant passage. If a true-false test is used, chance performance would of course be 50%. Should this "score" then be multiplied by some fabulous reading rate—say a million words a minute—to yield a Reading Efficiency Index of 500,000 words? Carver (1971) found that one widely cited experiment (Liddle, 1965) is greatly clarified by this reasoning.

In Liddle's study, graduates of the Reading Dynamics Institute were compared with readers who had signed up for the program but not yet taken the course. (This is just the right control group: People who elect to take such courses may differ systematically from other people.) All were tested for both speed and accuracy of comprehension in both fictional and nonfictional materials. The reading rates were from 300 to 1300 words per minute faster in the graduated group than in the control group. In comprehension, however, there was a significant decline for the graduates in the fictional test material. This outcome is not emphasized in the commercial publicity, of course. Instead, much is made of the fact that comprehension scores were not reliably different in tests of the nonfictional passages; the speed readers got 68% correct and the control group got 72% correct.

Carver administered the same comprehension test to a group of people who never had the benefit of reading the passage at all, fast or slow. These people achieved an average score of 57%

"correct." Common sense and guessing were apparently all that was needed to do respectably on this test. If we now take 57% as the zero point, against which to evaluate the results in Liddle's study, quite a different conclusion emerges. The control subjects got 15 percentage points above the chance level and the speed readers got only 11 percentage points above it. The speed-reading course can then be said to have caused a decline in comprehension of 4/11 = 27%. This difference would probably not be statistically significant, but it certainly qualifies the conclusion that there had been no comprehension loss for the nonfictional test materials. And, of course, we have already seen that the comprehension loss caused by speed-reading was statistically significant for the fictional materials.

This discussion, especially consideration of comprehension scores from people who never read the material to be comprehended, shows that the Reading Efficiency Index is a fishy measure, limited in theory only by the rate at which people can physically turn the pages.

THE GOOD NEWS. So perhaps at the outside, we can learn to read at rates approaching only 800 or 900 words a minute. Are we to conclude that promotion of speed-reading at rates considerably beyond this limit is a fraudulent practice without redeeming value to anyone but the promoter?

On the contrary, it can be argued that graduates of these programs have received training of very specific value. Skimming, after all, is a very important skill to the literate adult. In most career settings that depend on the written word, there is simply too much information to be assimilated thoroughly and one must be constantly seeking and selecting. Someone unable to shake the habit of word-by-word plodding through text would be at a distinct disadvantage.

Early in the 1960s there was a lot of publicity about certain government officials' use of speed-reading. We can see the importance, in such circles, for the skill of skimming. Imagine the circumstance of a high government official, perhaps an undersecretary of state, picking up a new book by a senior diplomat on foreign policy. Think of what information this hypothetical reader brings to the task: The reader knows the area of the world, perhaps the Near East, quite thoroughly, both its detailed history and month-to-month developments recently. Second, the reader knows the author of the book both personally and professionally, the author's background concerning the subject of the book, and his or her general views (perhaps the author has recently been on "Meet the Press"). The layperson, by contrast, brings no such wealth of prior background to the same book. The author would have written it for a general audience—for the layperson rather than for the undersecretary. The background necessary for the general reader would be worthless to the expert reader, who would be reading the book for occasional side comments and new analyses that might be contained in it. This is, then, a prime situation calling for skimming, for paging through to catch key words and section headings, and for jumping whole stretches that have little to offer this very special reader.

This example is not farfetched. All of us have pockets of highly specialized knowledge, whether in experimental psychology, in sports, in commodities futures, or in hairdressing. There is written information in all of these areas that is prepared for the general reader, necessarily, but that the specialist needs to consult for specific purposes. Without skimming, there would simply not be time to deal with the quantity of information that exists. With skimming, we can bypass the laborious word-by-word processing we learned as children.

Most educated people hit on skimming out of necessity. But a little systematic practice probably increases its efficiency. Who knows, pacing with the finger movements might allow more controlled skimming than depending on some voluntary control of the saccadic movements that are ordinarily almost unconscious. Thus, speed-reading programs may well be improving the quality of life, though not necessarily in the ways promoted in advertising.

THE BAD NEWS. But is the speed-reading movement, if we can call it such, necessarily always so benign? A case history from the *Journal of Reading* suggests not. This article described a "performance contract" between a firm called the Reading Foundation of Chicago and a school district near Los Angeles, California. The contract called for a dramatic upgrading of reading skills of the entire seventh grade of the school district in return for a fee of $110,000. The terms included a specification that, of the 2501 seventh graders in the district, 75% or more would quintuple their reading speeds, or better, and at the same time, these 75% would gain at least 10% in comprehension scores. In accomplishing this, the students were each to spend 24 hours in class instruction and 22 hours practicing outside of class. Performance on a reading test for this entire population of 2501 students, before and after the reading program, is shown in Table 2.3.

The first column shows a gain in vocabulary, which would be expected for children this age during a significant part of the school year. The second column shows a large gain in reading speed on the average, just about a quadrupling of the starting rates. This measure of words per minute is a raw, uncorrected, figure and not one of those Reading Efficiency Indexes we spoke of earlier. Finally, the table shows that comprehension was low, about one-third of the 15 items' being answered correctly. However, the decline in comprehension scores (pre- to posttraining) is probably not statistically reliable.

How did the outcome agree with the contract? Only 259 students both quintupled their reading rates and also increased their comprehension scores by 10%. This represents 13% of the total population and not the contracted 75%. Even at face value, this looks like a bitter blow for the Reading Foundation, but there is skullduggery even in these results.

For one thing, the leaflet that goes with the standardized reading test used in producing the data of Table 2.3 indicates that the speed results are not useful unless comprehension results are at 75% or better. Here, the obtained scores were much closer to 33% and so the reading-rate measures are not strictly interpretable. Furthermore, we have no idea how close to 33% comprehension we would obtain from a "no-read" control that had never seen the test materials in the first place.

Worse still, the measurement procedure was changed from the pretest to the posttest: The reading rates were supposed to be

Table 2.3 Results of Speed-Reading Program by
Reading Foundation of America

	Performance measure		
Test	Vocabulary	Words per minute	Comprehension[a]
Pre	21.5	155	5.2
Post	24.4	657	4.9

[a]Maximum possible = 15.0

measured on a 3-minute sample of reading. This was done in the
pretest. However, the foundation argued that a shorter span of
reading would have to be used in the posttest because the full
passages contained only 1000 words. This meant that anyone
reading faster than 333 words per minute would finish before 3
minutes were up and therefore his or her true reading rate would
be indeterminant. To solve this, the foundation proposed instead
to sample reading for 30 seconds on the posttest and then double
the obtained figure to get an estimate of words per minute. This
proposal was accepted by the school district, but they were mistaken to agree to it.

For one thing, a short test of anything is likely to be less
reliable than a longer test. More seriously, however, the test was
constructed so that the paragraphs became progressively harder
the further one got into the test. The posttest was thus based on
easier material than the pretest; small wonder there was an
improvement!

Later, outsiders tracked down 440 of the total population that
had participated in this program and made a direct comparison
of estimated reading rates based on either (1) a 30-second sample
of reading, or (2) a 3-minute sample. The short test gave a mean
rate of 780 words per minute and the long test gave a mean rate
of 205 words per minute, all tests taken from the same materials.
This places the dramatic "gain" shown in Table 2.3 in quite a
different light.

There were further abuses in this particular episode that

would require too much space to describe. It remains to be said that the school district settled for an award of $99,010 rather than the contracted $110,000. The rate of return enjoyed by the Reading Foundation was estimated to have been about $2500 for each $75 invested.

It may be argued that isolated dishonest, or even malicious, business marketing tactics should not discredit the value of the product being sold and this is partly true. The lesson is that we should be aware of exactly what can and what cannot be accomplished in speed reading programs. As always, the informed consumer is protected; it is just that in this area the intelligent individual is not likely to be armed with the kind of specialized knowledge necessary.

REFERENCES AND NOTES

A recent and comprehensive review of research on eye-movements in reading has been published by Rayner (1978) and it may be consulted for information on virtually all of the topics dealt with in this chapter. An up-to-date summary of the basic processes in vision can be found in Lindsay and Norman's *Human Information Processing* (1977). (Actually, any standard introductory textbook in psychology contains all you need to know about vision for the present purposes.) Figure 2.1 is from Feinberg (1949). The exact levels of acuity observed in his experiment naturally depend on details of the testing situation, the subjects, and so on. The basic form of the relation is the important thing, not the absolute levels.

THE SPAN OF FIXATION. A chapter by Rayner and McConkie (1977) gives good detail on research with the eyemovement-contingent text modification experiments. Being written somewhat later than the original experiments, this summary has the benefit of hindsight to assist its organization. Theirs is the newest and most exciting research in this area but they provide references to earlier approaches.

SPEED READING. Carver (1971) published a book called *Sense and Nonsense in Speed Reading*, which summarizes his experiences as an undercover student in the Reading Dynamics (Evelyn Wood) program. A popular summary appeared in *Psychology Today* (Carver, 1972). Articles by McLaughlin (1969) and by S. E. Taylor (1965) provide some information about eyemovements and reading. It is a shame that so little high-quality research has been published on what speed readers actually do and how it works. Various unpublished articles and dissertations are occasionally cited (see Gibson & Levin, 1975) but there is no substitute for research that has been subject to the same high editorial standards that are demanded for work in more conventional areas.

In closing, I must mention one exception to this, which seems to be a thoroughly professional piece of research by Marcel (1974). This is a very technical experiment with several crucial details that require considerable explanation, an explanation beyond the scope of this book. However, Marcel's method seems worth considering and the results could offer some comfort to those who want to believe that the eye can be taught to embrace a wider span of print.

As I was busy correcting proof for this book, I received in the mail a technical report by Just, Carpenter, and Masson (1982) on speed-reading. These authors compared eyemovements and other performance measures for normal readers reading normally, normal readers instructed to skim, and speed-readers. The results are quite consistent with what I have said in this chapter. What few differences they obtained between skimmers and speed-readers they attributed to conceptual, rather than visual, processes: The speed-readers are trained to be active and aggressive in making inferences from an "impoverished data base."

CHAPTER 3

Pattern Recognition

This chapter provides an introduction to ideas about how human beings perceive patterns. This coverage is strictly preliminary; the aim is to explain how pattern recognition *could work*, without for a moment suggesting that we have a complete theory.

It is important that any serious student of reading have some idea how patterns of print on the page could possibly be matched up with the language we have learned as children. At first, we tend to think that there is no problem there—"a person just sees what the word is and that's it." But that common-sense attitude is no explanation at all; it simply describes what it is we are trying to understand. We need instead to have some plausible explanation in terms of mechanisms.

WHAT NEEDS TO BE EXPLAINED

The main thing about pattern recognition is that a match occurs between two energy patterns in the brain, new information from the sense organs (the eyes in this case) and information stored in memory about some category. Consider a perceptual event in which you recognize a familiar word in its printed form, say, the word *horseradish*. The matching is between a pattern of light and dark areas on the retina (the letters and spaces) and the remembered knowledge about the concept of horseradish—how it is spelled, how it sounds when pronounced, what it means, perhaps how it tastes. Until that matching occurs, the word is simply represented as a visual pattern, not unlike the pattern formed by the string *hrswerntxgk*. But once the match has been made, what we are calling pattern recognition has occured and a whole lifetime of information is unlocked. There is obviously much more to reading than this but the categorization of a single meaningful word is at least a starting point for the analysis of reading.

LOGICAL STAGES NECESSARY FOR PATTERN RECOGNITION. As we study a person reading, all we can ever observe is the stimulus information that entered the two eyes and, later, some response the person might make showing that he or she understood or perceived the piece of information. In between these two "public" events, we are positive that pattern recognition occurred, provided that the response the person made is somehow related to the stimulus he or she saw, but we are not privileged to see it directly. To help think about the intervening stages, however, it is worth trying to sort out what must have happened. Figure 3.1 shows a breakdown of intervening stages that is the basis for the following discussion.

First, the normal limitations on visual acuity form a sort of preliminary information processing stage. If nothing else, the stimulus pattern gets simplified because of the relatively crude resolving power of the visual system. The letters you are looking at now, for example, if you looked through a powerful magnifying glass, are really made up of individual clods of dried ink that

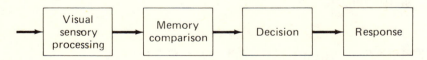

Figure 3.1 *The stages of information processing that are necessary in pattern recognition.*

cling to a tangle of hairy fibers that make up the paper. The paper is not smooth, as it seems to us, and neither is the ink spread evenly. But the limited resolving power of the visual system prevents us from seeing this detail without special aids. So in this limited sense, the eyes are passing on to later stages of information processing an image that is already abstracted to some extent.

Second, information that does survive its progress through the visual system must be compared against information stored in memory, information that defines the possible category states. This is the crucial stage in pattern recognition and this chapter concentrates on how it might occur.

Next, given some type of comparison of new stimulus information and permanent memory concepts (the possible categories), there must be a decision rule to determine what the item was. What if the stimulus had been ambiguous, perhaps a capital O with a bit of irregularity in the lower right that made it look slightly like a capital Q? There are two category states to which this item could be assigned and some process has to "break the tie."

Finally, the chain of processing in pattern recognition has to be completed by a response of some kind. Of course, we can recognize a word without moving a muscle; however, our interest as scientists must focus on cases where there is some assurance that pattern recognition did actually occur, for which we need to have a response. Others would break down this invisible history between stimulus and response differently, in some details. Everyone would agree, however, that the *memory-comparison stage* needs to be distinguished from the others. We shall now introduce two ideas on how this memory-comparison process could work. Neither is likely to be the whole story but together they form the basis for contemporary thinking about pattern recognition.

TWO THEORIES OF PATTERN RECOGNITION

The two main ideas about memory comparison are called the *template-matching* and *feature-comparison* theories.

Template Matching

The word *template* means outline and what this theory says is that we have, stored in our brains, a sort of cutout corresponding to the outline of each familiar pattern. The shape of this template corresponds to the prototype (most typical) shape of the pattern. The template for the letter *H* would thus represent a sort of average of all instances of this letter. The templates are stored in memory and get compared against new input. The new input, too, has a shape—defined by the pattern of excitation on the cells of the retinal surface as transmitted into later stages of the visual system. If the comparison of these two shapes matches by some criterion, the letter in question is perceived.

The template theory is notoriously wrong if we take the cut-out-matching metaphor too literally. Some well-known examples of the problem are shown in Figure 3.2. The figure shows that a rigid template system would fail to "recognize" instances that were even slightly deviant as to shape, size, or orientation.

NORMALIZATION (CLEANUP). The template theory can be improved by assuming that before comparisons of new input to stored templates occur the input is "cleaned up." This cleanup process would separate the essential information in the pattern from the nonessential information. It is easy to see how the sizes of potential letters could all be equalized before making comparisons from among the stored templates. Slightly more difficult would be the process of rotating all stimulus patterns to the upright position. It is very complicated to imagine how an automatic system could decide which parts of a new pattern were essential and which were nonessential before having recognized the pattern. Perhaps, however, we can believe that it would be straightforward to close up gaps and to eliminate fussy little squiggles. It is then not too large a leap to accept on faith that more subtle cleanup operations, *normalizations*, as they are called, could be possible.

Given machinery for normalization, the template model has a reasonable claim for plausibility. One particularly lucid metaphor, for which I am indebted to Peter Podgorny, compares the

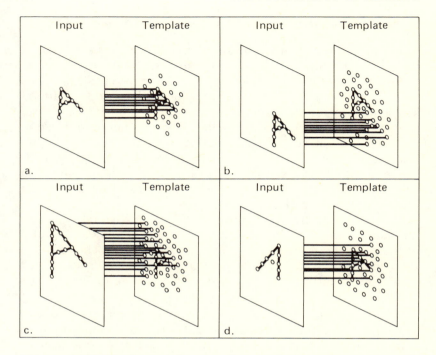

Figure 3.2 *Difficulties with a simple template-matching system for character recognition. (After Neisser, 1967)*

template-matching process with a test of photographic materials. Imagine templates stored in memory as transparent photographic negatives of simple outline figures such as letters. The normalized stimulus representations that are taken into this template storehouse are like positive transparencies. The two transparencies are held up together against some source of light and a measure is made of the light that passes through. If the positive and the negative match perfectly, the result will be a uniform gray—they will fit like hand and glove and no edges will show. If the negative and positive do not match, the result will be uneven, certain regions being darker or lighter than others, depending on the nature of the mismatch.

A popular word in perceptual psychology these days is *holis-*

tic. It means the handling of information in large organized packages rather than piecemeal. In this sense, the template theory is certainly a holistic theory. The opposite of holistic is *analytic*, where fragments of a large unit are handled separately before the entire unit becomes available. Thus the letter *F* can be described as a holistic pattern or as three line segments with certain connections. The feature theories of pattern recognition, to which we now turn, are analytic in this sense of the term.

Feature-Comparison Theories

The starting point for feature theories is the fact that there are many common elements in different characters. Consider the relation between letter pairs such as O-Q, R-P, and E-F, or the lowercase letter groups h-m-n and b-d-p-q, to name a few. These similarities make it tempting to describe these letters in a way that is more economical than just listing them one by one. The scheme shown in Figure 3.3 is one example of how the letters could be organized in terms of their *distinctive features*. In this type of system we can describe a letter in terms of its constituent parts. The important point about the feature theory of recognition is the assumption that we can also *recognize* the letters by analyzing their features.

This feature-analytic theory of pattern recognition of course assumes that we have stored in memory short lists of features that go with each possible letter. As an exercise, look at Figure 3.3 and work out the feature lists for H and Y. According to this type of system, the first step, when a new stimulus arrives, is to analyze it and prepare a list of its features. Then, this list of features is carried into memory and compared with the lists that are stored there. Once the list being classified matches exactly one of those stored in memory, the character has been recognized.

The memory comparison process in feature theory entails a search but it is not the same kind of process we proposed for the template theory. Now it is not any kind of coincidence between actual forms that we are looking for. Instead, lists of descriptive

Figure 3.3 An organization of the letters of the alphabet based on distinctive features. Each letter is described by a list of yes/no statements (pluses and minuses in the figure) about a strictly limited number of visual properties. (After Gibson, 1969)

Features	A	E	F	H	I	L	T	K	M	N	V	W	X	Y	Z	B	C	D	G	J	O	P	R	Q	S	U
Straight																										
Horizontal	+	+	+			+	+								+											
Vertical		+	+	+	+	+	+	+	+	+						+		+				+	+			+
Diagonal /	+							+	+	+	+	+	+	+	+											
Diagonal \								+	+	+	+	+	+	+	+											
Curve																										
Closed																+		+			+	+	+	+		
Open vertically																			+	+						+
Open horizontally																	+		+						+	
Intersection	+	+	+	+			+	+								+						+	+	+		
Redundancy																										
Cyclic change	+								+			+													+	+
Symmetry	+	+	+	+	+	+	+		+	+	+	+	+	+		+	+	+			+					+
Discontinuity																										
Vertical	+															+		+	+	+		+	+			
Horizontal			+		+		+													+						

statements about those forms are being compared. For either kind of comparison—feature lists or templates—there are certain ideal kinds of search process, or strategy, that need to be considered.

THE SERIAL VERSUS PARALLEL ISSUE. We have agreed that whether the information is stored as templates or as lists of features, there has to be some kind of comparison process between the new stimulus candidate and the many possible categories it may stand for. It is conventional to call this one-to-many comparison process a *search*. The issue is how the search is organized. In a *serial* search, the comparison is one at a time, in series. In a *parallel* search, the new sensory information is simultaneously compared against all possible categories stored in memory. Remember, either a template-comparison or a feature-comparison process can be either serial or parallel. This means there are four main varieties of the memory-comparison stage in pattern recognition—serial template, parallel template, serial feature, or parallel feature. Later in this chapter we look at evidence that is consistent with one of these possibilities.

WHY TAKE FEATURE THEORIES SERIOUSLY?

Most people find the template theory satisfying and reasonable, at first, and the feature theory farfetched. In this section, we pause to look at some of the factual evidence that favors a feature-analytic approach.

PHYSIOLOGICAL EVIDENCE FOR FEATURE DETECTORS. In lower animals there is quite a bit of evidence that feature detection machinery is wired into the perceptual system.

The best-known experiments are those begun in the 1960s by Hubel and Wiesel on the visual system of the cat. The experimental setup used by these authors is shown schematically in Figure 3.4. Electrical recordings showed the amount of activity (rate of firing) of individual cells in the visual cortex of the brain. The visual cortex is an area in the "back of the head" where

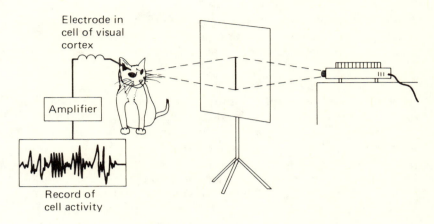

Figure 3.4   *The experimental arrangement used by Hubel and Wiesel (1962).*

information from the visual system is carried after leaving the optic tract and passing through various way stations. Hubel and Wiesel were interested in whether and how individual cells in this visual part of the brain would change their rates of firing depending on what the cat was looking at. As they recorded how fast the cell was firing, they projected points of light and more complicated patterns onto different regions of the retina.

In this way, it is possible to map out the receptive field for a cortical (back of the brain) cell—the cell might become very excited, or fire fast, when a point of light is put in one retinal zone but not when it is moved to another zone. The actual map obtained thus shows the whole retina and marks points on it where the cell being measured is either affected or unaffected by light. When light in a retinal location influences firing in our test cell, it is sometimes an excitatory effect—the cell speeds up—and sometimes an inhibitory effect—the cell slows down. Either type of effect is important, of course, for information is transmitted either way. Figure 3.5 shows a map of the receptive field for a simple cortical cell and for a more complex one.

Hubel and Wiesel discovered a variety of kinds of cortical

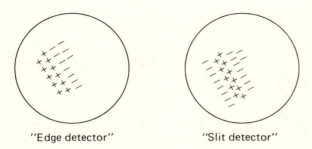

"Edge detector"   "Slit detector"

Figure 3.5 *A pair of hypothetical receptive fields investigated in the manner of Hubel and Wiesel. The circle represents the retina of the cat's eye. Pluses mean that when a point of light was shined in this location the cell in the visual cortex speeded up its rate of firing; minuses mean the cell actually lowered its rate of firing in response to the light.*

cells using this method. Some were more complicated than the one shown in Figure 3.5. Some, which they called "edge detectors," responded most by getting light along a line but were inhibited (fired more slowly) by light falling just to one side of this line. Other cortical cells responded excitedly to light falling, again, along a particular line, but were inhibited by light falling on *either side of that line,* rather than on just one side of the line, as in the edge detectors. Such a slit detector is represented in Figure 3.5. Still more cortical cells were responsive to lines or to slits but not just in a single position on the retina; instead, these units were responsive independent of the location of the feature they were specialized for. Even more abstract detectors were specialized for moving lines, but they had to be moving lines of a certain length.

The importance of these specialized cells in the cat visual cortex is that they show direct evidence for something like the sorts of feature detectors we should want for a character recognition system based on feature analysis. It is not hard to extend the edges and slits of Figure 3.5 to the features suggested for Roman letters in Figure 3.3. For true character recognition, you would need more complicated feature detectors, to be sure, but that is not too great a leap of the imagination for most of us.

AFTEREFFECTS. A second line of evidence that the nervous system is partly organized in terms of features is the existence of visual aftereffects in perception. The relevance of aftereffects to this question will be stated after we describe first what they are.

Anyone who has taken introductory psychology has had the experience of staring intently at a patch of vivid color for a minute or so and then looking away at a point on some neutrally colored surface, perhaps gray. The experience, if it is done carefully, without movement, is that we see the neutral surface laid over with a patch of "washed out" color, which matches the shape of the original patch and whose color is complementary to the original patch. This negative afterimage is instructive about how color perception occurs in the brain: Let us be very specific and say that the person fixated for one minute on a triangular patch of bright red laid against a dull gray or white background. Afterward, the red triangle was removed and the person stared at a faint dot on the same gray surface. He reports seeing a green triangle matching the original triangle but with a fainter color.

The standard explanation for colored afterimages is that our color receptors, in the eye, are arranged in pairs. Figure 3.6 shows this schematically. The color-sensitive retinal cells are arranged in pairs; a red-green pair is shown in the figure. As is generally the case in the nervous system, the units are always firing at some "resting" or normal rate. Information is carried by changes, up or down, in this normal rate of firing. (This is a change in how we understand the nervous system. It was thought previously that neurons lay more or less asleep, waiting to be stimulated by other units nearby.) The simple red and green receptors shown at the left of Figure 3.6 do not contribute to color experience directly. If they did, we would always be perceiving both red and green at the same time, since, as we just said, all cells are always active at some base rate. Instead, it is some *Difference Detector* that lies behind our experience of color. The job of this difference detector is to detect how much faster one of the simple receptors—red or green—is firing than the other one. If the red one is firing faster than the green one, we experience red; if the reverse, green.

The one additional piece of information we need for under-

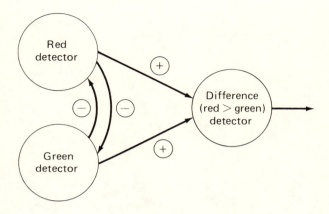

Figure 3.6 *The explanation of negatively colored afterimages. Pluses mean excitatory connection, minuses mean inhibitory connection.*

standing afterimages is that the simple red or green detectors *get tired* (become habituated) if they are stimulated repeatedly by their appropriate color of light. When this happens, they become less capable of firing rapidly. As long as a person is staring at something red, with no green in sight, however, the rate of red firing will exceed the rate of green firing and the experience will remain red. However, now consider what happens when the person looks away from the red and stares at a gray surface: Neither red nor green is now getting direct stimulation. The green detector will be firing at its "business as usual" rate but the red detector will be exhausted by the previous ordeal of receiving all that red light. Thus, without any relevant color present, the two will be unequal in their firing rates—the green one normal and the red one slower. The difference detector, at this point, will detect a surplus of green firing over red. Since its only job is to examine the differences between red and green, it will be "fooled" into the conclusion that the eye is looking at something green and send that message up into whatever part of the brain records experience.

The relevance of this digression into color for feature theories

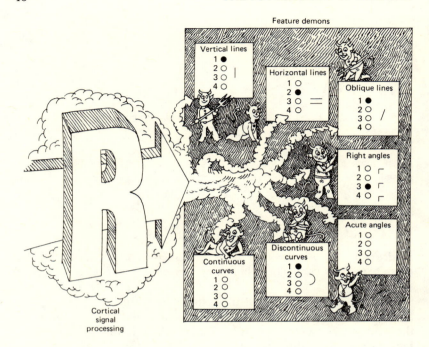

Figure 3.7 *A representation of Selfridge's Pandemonium model of feature-analytic character recognition.*

of character recognition is that color is a prime feature of visual stimuli. Perhaps color is not useful in telling letters apart but it shows clearly how some feature systems could work. Like other feature analytic systems, the color machinery in Figure 3.6 is a specialized set of equipment for abstracting one kind of information from events independently of other kinds of information.

PANDEMONIUM: A FEATURE SYSTEM FOR CHARACTER RECOGNITION

At this point, we pause to inspect a suggestion for how character recognition could work under a feature analytic system. This

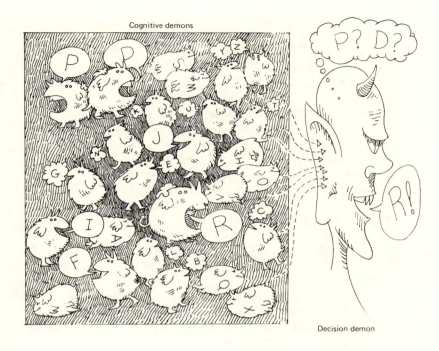

Cognitive demons

Decision demon

theory was first developed by Oliver Selfridge in England. The main assumptions of the theory are shown in Figure 3.7 (be careful not to let the charm of the drawings detract from its serious content).

The story begins in the left part of the figure, where two chains of events are set in motion. First, the cauldron called Cortical Signal Processing produces an image, which is appropriately called the Image Demon; this makes available to the nervous system something very much like a template. The model has nothing more to say about this visual representation. It stands for our experience that we can be aware of what a letter looks like *as a shape* without worrying about what it means.

The feature-analytic part of the Pandemonium model begins

with the connections between the original cortical processing and a set of feature detectors, the Feature Demons. These detectors resemble the sorts of units uncovered by the physiological work of Hubel and Wiesel in the visual cortex of the cat. The exact features used are a matter of speculation. Instead of moving slit and edge detectors, however, we should expect to see units specialized for the sorts of features elaborated in Figure 3.2.

Each Feature Demon is automatically aroused when his special target feature occurs. In the model of Figure 3.7, furthermore, the Feature Demons are able to count the number of instances of "their" feature, rather than just say whether it is present or absent. The drawing of Pandemonium has all the feature detectors within the same column: This conveys the important assumption that they all work at the same time, in parallel. This would not have to be true—you could have a serial feature extraction system where the demons look for their target one at a time.

The next stage of the system is also set up to operate in parallel. Each of the units at the next stage, called Cognitive Demons, stands for a candidate letter. Each contains a list of features (remember Figure 3.3) and is scanning the Feature Demons for entries on that list. Again, they are working in parallel, all scanning at the same time. For a Cognitive Demon, the more of his particular features are present, the more excited he gets. The output of each Cognitive Demon is to shout toward the next level of the system and the intensity of his shouting is directly proportional to the amount of positive information received from the Feature Demons. It is from this metaphor that the name Pandemonium arises. The Cognitive Demon shouting the loudest is the one most likely to capture the attention of the final stage of the system, the single Decision Demon.

The Decision Demon corresponds to conscious experience in the sense that it is a limited channel, operating on a one-at-a-time basis. In the simplest case, only one letter "gets through" despite the chaos evident in earlier stages of the machinery. This corresponds to our subjective impression that perception of a letter is direct and immediate and not chaotic at all.

Earlier in this chapter, we classified theories of character recognition as serial-template, parallel-template, serial-feature, and parallel-feature models. In these terms, the whole system corresponds to a parallel feature extraction model of character recognition. Recall that the serial-parallel and template-feature distinctions are made in respect to how the *memory-comparison stage* of character recognition works. It would be an outright lie to claim now that experts in the field have settled on the Pandemonium system as the "truth" on how character recognition is organized. Actually, there surely is no single truth but instead, a variety of proposals that apply in different situations. In the following section, we make the case that in at least one situation that is closely related to reading, the Pandemonium model makes excellent sense in terms of experimental evidence.

EXPERIMENTS ON VISUAL SEARCH

Beginning in the 1960s, Ulric Neisser performed a series of important experiments on *visual search*. Figure 3.8 illustrates this task. Look first at the left panel. The subject is suddenly allowed to see such a display on a stimulus card. Each line contains six letters. The task is to scan down the column searching for a particular letter, say the letter *J*. As in the display on the left of Figure 3.8, only one of the lines actually contains the target.

Standard condition Target = *J*	Nonconfusable condition Target = *Z*	Confusable condition Target = *Z*
RYVMKF	CBSOGS	VMWNMW
PTHSHG	UBSQOQ	WYLKWV
GTVCBH	BQOUDG	XMWLLY
HUIRYD	SCDOBC	YXZWXL
KJREGD	CZOQUS	NMWYMN
GBHTBN	OUBCCD	YNLXLI
POLKRF	DOQUCB	MNWXMH
FTIEWR	CCOQOU	LYXWLT
· · ·	· · ·	· · ·
· · ·	· · ·	· · ·

Figure 3.8 *Neisser's visual search task. A display is exposed and the subject must scan vertically, from top to bottom, until finding a target item. Time to reach the target is recorded as a function of the position of the target.*

When the person being tested sees the line with the target, he or she responds so as to stop a clock recording the total search time required to scan the list down to that point. The position of the line containing the target is varied, sometimes high in the list and sometimes low. As you would expect, people are slower to find the target when it is toward the end of the list than when it is high in the list.

What is the subject "doing" to the lines he or she rejects on the way down to the target letter? The assumption behind the research is that the subject is perceiving these letters to some minimal level—perhaps not fully enough to recognize what they are but still fully enough to know what they are not. Admittedly, this is not like a normal adult reading a newspaper, by any reasonable definition. However, it is a case of getting information from the printed page—information that is related to the meaning (categories) of the characters. And if we could understand how this and other simple tasks worked, we could begin to guess intelligently about how real reading works.

If we measure the time it takes the subject to read down through the list as far as the location of the target letter, we can estimate the time required to process a letter. This is because we know how many letters *had* to be processed before the target was reached and we also know how long it took. Thus we can see how much extra time was required, on the average, to find a target when it was 10 lines down the list and when it was 20 lines down the list. Whatever this extra time was can then be divided by 10 to estimate the processing time for a single line. The method is illustrated in Figure 3.9, which gives the result of a fictitious visual search experiment.

Each data point in Figure 3.9 shows how long it took people to find the target letter at a particular location in the list. On different tests, the location of the target was changed, of course. Naturally, the search times were slower when the target was buried deep in the list than when it was towards the top of the list. You can see that the dots on the left side of the graph are lower than those on the right—when the target is early in the list, the time to locate it is short. The solid line drawn through the graph is the "best fitting" straight line in that it lies closest, in a

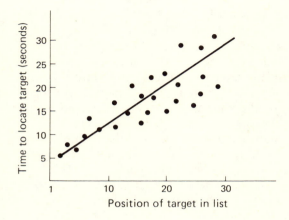

Figure 3.9 *Typical results from Neisser's visual search experiments. Results are shown for the condition whose stimuli are represented at the left side of Figure 3.8.*

technical sense, to the obtained data points. It is a sort of average for the points drawn in separately. The slope of this solid line gives the price, in terms of extra time, of having the target lowered by one line—the amount of extra time each line takes to process.

The results given in the figure are typical of Neisser's research: Every time the target is lowered by one line, the total reaction time increases by about 250 milliseconds; the people tested here can process about four lines in one second. There are six letters on a line, so this means about 24 letters get handled every second. By "handled" we mean here only that the letter is processed to the point where the person knows it is not a target; it is not necessarily "read" in any deeper sense. However, most everybody would agree that this is a form of character recognition.

The quarter-second estimate for the data shown in Figure 3.9 is far from inevitable. By changing the experiment slightly we can have a profound effect on this figure. For example, on the right side of Figure 3.8 we see a version of the visual search task that is logically equivalent to the one on the left. The display on the right shows the stimulus card for a subject asked to search for the target letter Z from among the nontarget letters V, M, N, W, Y, and L. These nontarget letters are quite similar, visually, to Z whereas the nontargets C, B, G, S, O, U, Q, and P (which are the nontargets for the middle panel of Figure 3.8) are quite distinct from the target. Not surprisingly, it is harder (slower) to locate the target Z from among the similar nontargets than from among the nonsimilar ones. Neisser has found that when there is a clear contrast between the features of the target and the features of the nontargets, as in the middle panel of Figure 3.8, people can search as fast as 0.09 seconds per line. That is, in this easy condition, searching goes on at better than 10 lines per second. However, when nontargets are deliberately chosen to resemble the target letter, as in the right-hand panel, the search is slowed down to about 0.50 seconds per line, or 2 lines per second.

RELATION OF VISUAL SEARCH TO FEATURE THEORY. It is not hard to apply the Pandemonium type of theory to Neisser's visual search result. In the condition where the target is highly confusable with the nontargets (Z versus X, M, and so on), a large number of the features relevant to the critical Cognitive Demon for Z will be active almost all of the time since nearly all are contained in the nontarget letters. The Decision Demon will be hearing Z shouting constantly, to speak loosely, and it will be difficult to determine when Z is louder than the other Cognitive Demons also responding to their critical features. On the other hand, when the nontarget letters share almost no features with the target (Z versus B, S, and so on), the Cognitive Demon for Z will be dead quiet almost all of the time and come alive only when the target actually appears.

A template theory could also be modified to handle Neisser's result without too much difficulty. You can probably think for a while and construct such a modification. Remember, we said above that no single theory is likely to be proven correct to the exclusion of others but that the purpose here is to show how at least one model could possibly work. The reason for mentioning visual search here is to show evidence that is consistent with the Pandemonium model but not necessarily proof of it.

NUMBER OF TARGETS. In some of his experiments, Neisser asked subjects to search for more than 1 letter at a time. Sometimes, they were asked to be looking for up to 10 different letters on one stimulus card like those shown in Figure 3.8.

The effects caused by having to look for more than one character at a time depended on how practiced the person was at visual search. For beginners, there was a slower rate of scanning when there was more than one target letter to look for. Specifically, the slope of the graph corresponding to Figure 3.9 was increased such that each additional letter in the display was more costly to process when several targets were in mind than when one was. As would be expected, the cost of having multiple targets was reduced with highly practiced subjects. What we might not have expected in advance was that after about a month's practice (an hour a day), people got to the point where they were looking for 10 targets *just as fast* as for one. In other words, people eventually overcame the initial slowing down caused by multiple search targets. Neisser cited highly experienced professional newspaper clippers, who commonly scan for articles on a large number of subjects (their clients) at top speed.

The multiple target experiments show parallel processing. People are doing several things at once and, since they are doing them just as fast as any individual one of those things, we may be assured that they are not just shifting from one to another. In the latter case—rapid serial alternation among targets—it would have to be slower to look for many things than to look for only one. The application of this result to reading is simple, at a low level: Normal adult readers are operating on a base of years of training and any change we see between beginning and mature visual search is likely to correspond to the sorts of things that get overlearned during this extended practice.

Now, can we go a step beyond this simple observation and talk analytically about how people might be changing with practice in visual search? The change in Neisser's experiment was truly dramatic: On the fourth day of the month-long experiment, people in the 10-target condition processed about 5 letters per second, in contrast to our rule-of-thumb average of 24 per second for single targets. On the thirtieth day, these same subjects were processing at a rate of about 30 letters per second for both single and multiple targets.

Although we cannot offer a complete account of this phenomenon here, the Pandemonium concept does offer a useful suggestion. First, let us simplify and reduce the scope of the result. Suppose that in the single-target condition the person is searching for the letter Y. The Decision Demon simply keeps track of the Cognitive Demon representing this one letter. Now when the task is made more complex by assigning the target letters R, X, Q, and K, the Decision Demon has four Cognitive Demons to watch. We remarked above that the Decision Demon is limited in his capacity to divide attention—he can pay attention to only one thing at a time. Therefore, searching for multiple targets ought to require more time than for only one, which it does initially.

During the long days of practice with the four-letter set, the system could somehow register the fact that the letters R, K, Q, X all have a diagonal stroke in the lower right-hand corner and that the other, nontarget, letters do not. If we allow Pandemonium the capacity to reorganize itself (which seems a necessary complication since children do, after all, start somewhere) then a new Cognitive Demon could be "grown," one whose sole feature is the presence of one of the critical diagonals. By the time this reorganization has taken place, then the single-target and the four-target conditions have become comparable from the point of view of the Decision Demon—in both cases he has to worry about activity in only one Cognitive Demon. It follows that performance should be the same after practice but different initially.

Of course, this illustration is too simple. We chose the four-letter set to be sure it included some one critical feature. Most would not happen to be such a lucky choice. But on the other hand, even single letters aren't usually defined by only a single feature. It is not too large a stretch of the imagination that over prolonged practice, the Pandemonium system might be able to invent a feature list that goes with a multiple-target set uniquely. As always, we are not trying to insist on a particular explanation, just to show that some explanation has potentially the power to cover a given phenomenon.

CONCLUSIONS

In this chapter, we intended to do three things. First, we identified a problem, character recognition, and showed that it depended on a matching process between a stored representation (the item in memory) and sensory input (the visual reaction to a configuration of print). The memory comparison stage of pattern recognition is the logical first step in reading even though it is an elementary process that seems automatic in real reading.

The second purpose of the chapter was to suggest a set of distinctions and concepts that provide a language for theoretical analysis of character recognition. Thus, we distinguished serial and parallel processing as well as template matching and feature analysis. We took some pains to establish the plausibility of feature analysis because it is the only one of these four concepts that is not especially intuitive.

Finally, the Pandemonium model was presented in order to give at least a glimpse of how one explicit character recognition theory works. Pandemonium works in two senses: It contains assumptions that do allow letters to be perceived accurately and it also provides a language for explaining results of experimental investigations of visual search.

REFERENCES AND NOTES

Character recognition is a vast and highly technical subject and this chapter only begins to scratch the surface. *Human Information Processing (2nd Edition)* by Lindsay and Norman gives a good survey at a somewhat higher level. Neisser's *Cognitive Psychology* was published in 1967 and is still an excellent source for the subject of character recognition as well as for his own research on visual search. A more recent contribution by McClelland (1979) is worth study for those with a special interest in the theory of character recognition. McClelland proposes stages of processing that work in *cascade,* that is, where each stage feeds information gradually into the next stage and that next stage goes on to make preliminary classifications based on early information.

It would be a mistake if this chapter left the impression that people turn into parallel processors in general after enough practice. There seem to be three relations between the number of

stimuli to be handled and reaction time, not just the one discussed here (parallel processing, or a flat relation). Furthermore,
the two other relations between stimulus numerosity and reaction time both imply character recognition systems different
from Pandemonium.

Saul Sternberg (1966, 1969) has performed experiments in
which people search through short lists held in their memories
rather than on a stimulus display. He gave people a list of digits
to learn, say 2-6-4-3 and then asked them whether some test
digit, say 8 had occurred on the list. The measure of performance
was how rapidly people could make this decision. The main
experimental variable was how many items were held in memory, usually from two to about six, for example, rather than the
four used in our example. Sternberg found that no matter how
well people were practiced at this task, there was always slower
performance with more items in the memorized list (in contrast
to Neisser's finding). Furthermore, the amount by which reaction
times were slowed down by additional items in the memorized
list was a constant for each new item. That is, going from three to
four items in the list has the same effect as going from six to
seven. The most straightforward interpretation of this pattern of
findings is in terms of a *serial-template* model of recognition. In
such a model, the templates are checked one by one and so the
more templates have to be checked, the longer the reaction time.

In another line of investigation, originally started by the
Dutch psychologist Merkel in 1885, still a different relation exists between the number of stimuli to be handled and reaction
time. Here, people were required to make a different response,
say pressing a key, to any of several different stimuli that could
occur, perhaps lights or words. Depending on the circumstances,
it was often found that the more stimulus-response pairs in this
choice reaction time situation, the slower the responding. Here,
the form of the relation is that it goes up fast at first and then
levels off, as might be expected from a *serial-feature* model of
recognition. It is a little harder to see why this pattern of out-
comes favors a serial-feature model than it was to accommodate
the other research in models. More discussion of these matters
may be found in Nickerson (1972).

CHAPTER 4

The Perception
of Unrelated Letters

Chapter 3 provided a look at how physical patterns—such as scrapings of a pencil on the rough texture of a piece of paper—might get connected up with our memories of conventionally defined categories, such as letters. This chapter provides an *information-processing model* of how people deal with a group of letters flashed briefly on a screen. If you like, we are moving gradually toward some halfway plausible version of reading: The problem of classifying a single character (Chapter 3) may be a necessary part of reading but it is too abstract to be applied directly to the kinds of questions raised in Chapter 1. Now, however, we turn to what may happen during a single visual fixation where there are several letters simultaneously within the sharp, foveal region of vision.

In the first section of this chapter, we develop a reasonably complete theory of how people deal with short flashes of unrelated letters. In later sections of the book, we look at the way in which this theory has to be modified to handle situations in which more realistic stimulus materials are used. In Chapter 5, we look at the perception of letter strings that form real words. In Chapter 6, we examine the influence of meaningful context, such as in a sentence, on the perception of individual words. Finally

(Chapter 7), we deal with the setting of language in a context larger than the sentence, in prose comprehension. The material here on unrelated letters forms an obvious base on which these wider analyses can be built.

It is legitimate to ask why we should spend time worrying about the processing of unrelated letters if the essense of reading is the extraction of meaning from print, as many people believe. The answer is based on a common strategy in psychology: We begin our analysis from a simple situation that we can understand rather well and then try to see how that understanding breaks down, if it does, when we work toward more complicated and lifelike situations.

Not everyone believes this is a good strategy for reaching an understanding of complicated psychological processes. Some scholars say, instead, that there are *emergent* principles found at the higher levels of complexity and that the only way to discover these is "to begin at the top." However, most experimental psychologists prefer to believe that the rules don't change radically as processing moves from simple to complex but instead the rules begin to interact and are more concealed than in the simple tasks. That is the kind of attitude that this book takes. If it is wrong, we will eventually be "found out" because then the application of elementary principles to complex situations will just simply fail to work.

SPERLING'S RESEARCH ON READING UNRELATED LETTERS IN A SINGLE FIXATION

Since the early days of psychology, investigators have been interested in the process of reading and in the question of how much information is gained from a single fixation (see Chapter 2). For this purpose, some form of *tachistoscope* (stress on the second syllable, which sounds like KISS) has been used. This is a device for producing a flash of some stimulus display for such a brief interval that there is no time to allow a person to shift his or her fixation. In the early research, a spark was generated to illuminate a box containing an otherwise dark display. Now, of course, we have fancy electronic tachistoscopes; however, some of the research results from the turn of the century have held up well on modern instruments.

One of these findings was of particular interest to George Sperling in his doctoral dissertation at Harvard University (Sperling, 1960). This was the observation that people could report only about four or five unrelated letters from a quick flash. It made little or no difference how long the display was exposed between about 15 and 500 milliseconds nor did it matter how many letters were displayed within the range of 4 to 15—people were always able to report about 4.5 letters. (Nobody reports half a letter of course! The 4.5 average means people got four half the time and five half the time.)

The people being tested in this way reported that they could *see* the letters all quite clearly for a while but that the display faded before there was time to identify more than a handful. Sperling's particular interest was in the possibility that the visual system was able to register and hold information briefly even after the physical display—on the screen—had gone off.

Iconic Memory

Sperling was interested in the possibility that the visual system registered and actually "remembered" the display information for a brief time after the physical display itself had disappeared. This kind of primitive memory—a fleeting trace of the visual display—has since been called *iconic memory* and we adopt that terminology. To demonstrate it, Sperling presented several rows of letters, say three rows of 4 letters. In a control condition, people were just asked to watch the brief flash and report as many letters as possible; the typical score was around 4.5 letters, as noted above.

The innovation in Sperling's experiment was the use of a *partial-report cue* in the experimental conditions. The partial-report cue he used was a tone of either high, medium, or low pitch. These three tones, by previous arrangement with the subject, were to indicate that the subject should report only the top row of letters, only the middle row, or only the bottom row. The tone was presented at various delays after the disappearance of the rows of letters from the screen. Sometimes the tone occurred just as the display disappeared and sometimes it was delayed by up to a second afterward.

If people have an iconic memory for the display, lasting longer than the display itself, then they should be able to use the partial-report cue to "read" the letters on whichever row was signaled by the tone. Think of it this way: If the tone were presented *before* the display of letters, it would be easy to fixate on the top, middle, or bottom position. Now the question is whether some comparable adjustment can take place after the display has disappeared. Notice that the subject would be responsible for only four letters on one of these partial-report trials (in the case where there were three rows of four each). This number of letters falls within the average capacity to gather information from a single glimpse, as we know from the conventional experiment with no tone cue.

What happened in the experiment was that the subjects tested were able to get over three letters correct, on the average, from *whichever* row was signaled by the tone. Since the subject had no way of knowing beforehand which was going to be the signaled row, it must have been possible for the subject to get over three letters from any one of the three rows at the instant the tone sounded. Since the tone coincided with the disappearance of the letter display, this information must have been registered in iconic memory. If the visual system didn't hold an iconic memory trace, then telling people which row to "go for" would be a useless instruction after the display went off. If people can report 3.3 letters from one row when it is signaled by the corresponding tone, then we have to assume that they have available in their visual systems a total of $3 \times 3.3 = 9.9$ items. (This is because we could have chosen any row at random and the score would have been 3.3 on the average.)

What accounts for the contrast Sperling found between conventional "whole report," where the total score is 4.5 items, and the new partial-report procedure, where the score for one row is around 3.3 items? To account for this discrepancy, we assume that iconic memory has a large capacity, perhaps around 10 items for a three-by-four letter display. We assume also that the rate at which people can "read out" or identify the letters is slow, perhaps on the order of about 3 to 5 items in a fraction of a second. If the 3 to 5 items are taken from the whole display, performance appears poor; however, if the tone instructs the subject that only one row is relevant, then the subject has time to read almost all of that row.

Sperling found that when the tone was delayed by one second, or even one-half second, relative to the offset of the display of letters, performance was no longer better in the partial-report condition than in the whole-report condition. For example, if the tone was delayed by one second, people got about 1.5 items in the signaled row. Making the same assumption as before, that they could have gotten 1.5 items from any one of the three rows, we estimate capacity in this case as 3 × 1.5 = 4.5 items—which is just the same result as when there is no tone signal at all. This kind of evidence is interpreted to mean that during the second that follows stimulus offset, the iconic memory trace *decays*. A careful series of experiments has suggested that iconic memory typically lasts about 250 milliseconds in these situations, about a quarter second.

The demonstration of iconic memory and of its main properties requires considerably more rigorous support than we have offered here. However, we have what we need now, conceptually, to go on to form a processing model of letter identification in this type of task. There are really two concepts, that of a large-capacity iconic memory and that of a slow rescue process operating on that iconic memory. People seem able to direct their attention to locations in visual displays *after the displays have ended*, when the tone signals which row is for partial report. We assign the performance limit of around 4 items to the rate at which information can be identified, or read off, the visual system. In Sperling's study, the display itself was visible for 50 milliseconds. Another 250 milliseconds is added by iconic memory. Therefore, people are "rescuing" about 4 items in about 300 milliseconds, or just slightly faster than 10 items per second. This estimate should be considered a ballpark estimate—the correct figure is not 1 item every second, it is not 100 items every second, it is, instead, about 10 items every second.

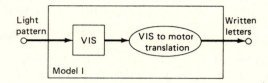

Figure 4.1. *Sperling's Model I for visual memory task. VIS = Visual Information Storage. The large rectangle enclosing the square and elipse represents the boundary of the subject's skin.*

A Process Model

A STRAW MAN. Figure 4.1 shows the simplest theoretical model we might be tempted to suggest from the two concepts used to summarize the last section. In this and similar models, the large outside box stands for the subject's external boundary—his or her skin, if you will. Thus, light enters the subject, on the left, from outside, and the subject's final response is in the form of written letters, on the right. (This doesn't mean that the subject looks with the left eye and writes with the right! Time flows from left to right, by convention.) In between, Model I suggests two parts, a Visual Information Storage (VIS), or iconic memory, and a process translating the visual form to motor information relevant to writing down the letters.

The limits on performance in Model I are the relation between the speed of the visual-to-motor translation and the life of the icon. According to this model, the subject can get only 4.5 letters from a display because the icon dies by the time the subject has gotten around to writing down the fourth or fifth letter—the subject goes back for the next and there is no icon left. But we can throw out this model after only a moment's consideration: It takes around three seconds to write a few letters whereas the icon lasts only about a quarter second (250 milliseconds). So by the time even the first letter has passed through the translation process, the icon has long since disappeared. This model is useful to present, even if as a "straw man," because it shows where the assumptions of the subsequent version begin.

SPEECH AS A MEDIATOR. Another reason for modifying the straw-man model was a pair of observations Sperling made during his original experiments: He noticed his subjects could be heard mumbling the letter names to themselves during delays between the stimulus items and a signal for report. Furthermore, the errors subjects made, when they were wrong about a particular letter, suggested they were somehow using speech as a memory format in the task. For example, if a subject were to make a mistake when P was the correct letter, he or she would be more likely to say "B" than "F." This type of *confusion error* in immediate memory has been a very important phenomenon in cognitive psychology over the last 20 years and we have a good deal more to say about it later in this chapter. British psychologist R. Conrad discovered it independently and was responsible for bringing it to public attention.

For now, the important point is that these two observations—mumbling subjects and errors based on something like rhyme—strongly suggest that there is more going on than a translation from a visual into a motor code, as Model I claims. It seems that some process related to speech is inserted between the iconic (VIS in Sperling's terminology) and written levels of coding. Even though the task requires no sound to come from the subject, or only the sound of pencil on paper, the subject seems to be using a form of memory that relies on the sounds of speech. Sperling suggested, accordingly, that the visual information in the icon gets translated into speech form in the process of categorization. The motor commands necessary for producing the written response would then issue from the general speech-language system. We will see that this suggestion allows a solution for the first problem with Model I, the problem that iconic memory is too rapidly lost to survive getting through the sluggish writing process.

MODEL II. According to Model II, the iconic traces are scanned by a "rescue process" consisting of internal naming. In response to the shapes in the icon, the spoken forms of the letters become available. This processing is seen in the second component of the model in Figure 4.2, immediately after VIS. The scanning

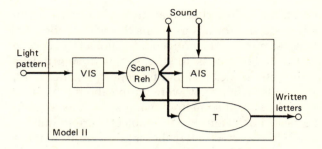

Figure 4.2.   *Sperling's second model for visual information processing. AIS means Auditory Information Storage; Reh means rehearsal; other symbols as before.*

process includes a "rehearsal" operation—rehearsal in its literal sense of rehearing. This rehearsal has three possible consequences. The first possibility is that the scan results in overt pronunciation, leading to external sound, shown in Figure 4.2 by the arrow leaving the rectangular "skin." The second consequence of rehearsal is a covert version of the same thing—the items are spoken by the person *to himself or herself*. In this case the information goes directly to the right, into Auditory Information Storage (AIS). The subject remembers the sound of his or her inner voice, as it were, scanning and reading the letters on the display. The third fate of information following the scan-rehearse operation is the familiar translation into motor commands necessary for written responding.

So, in summary form, Model II maintains that information is first held briefly in iconic memory, from which it is "rescued" by a scanning operation that leads to internal naming (rehearsal). The sound that results from this internal naming, or from naming out loud, is fed into a storage modality for auditory information—echoic storage, as it is sometimes called. Notice that Sperling claims that the same echoic storage results from internal and external vocalization.

Model II contains a "feedback loop" that greatly extends the flexibility of processing. When information gets to AIS, in the model, there is an arrow leading back to the scan-rehearse operation. This means the subject can listen to the contents of AIS and categorize them just as the scan-rehearse loop allowed categorization of VIS information. In simple terms, the subject can understand the sounds that his or her inner (or external) voice has placed into the AIS. There would have to be a scan-rehearse loop for regular speech perception anyway! The presence of the loop in letter-perception experiments means that we can keep information circulating back and forth through rehearsal—very much as we say a telephone number to ourselves if we need to remember it while crossing the room to make a call. This looping can thus be used to explain how it is that a 250-millisecond memory can be used to support written responses that may not come for three seconds or so; the "rescue" gets letters from VIS into a rehearsal loop that can go on indefinitely (if it is not too long).

ONE MORE MODEL. The objection to Model II has to do with timing considerations. We just concluded that whatever the "rescue" operation was, from iconic memory, it must go on at about a rate of 10 letters per second. There is reliable evidence from other sources that this 10-letters-per-second estimate applies to the maximum rates of both external and internal speech. Now, how could we estimate the rate at which letters get *scanned into* VIS? We would like an estimate that is independent of the naming process. Changing the exposure duration of a brief flash to see how fast those first four or five letters become available might seem like a good idea. However, we now know that no matter how long the original flash is, there will be an icon for about another quarter second. What is needed is a means of cutting short the icon so as to limit strictly the duration of the relevant visual experience. Well over 100 years ago, it was known that a bright flash of light seemed to knock out, or mask, iconic information (although it was not called iconic in those days). Sperling (1963) repeated one of these early experiments in which the delay was varied between starting the icon and then knocking it out with a mask. If scanning goes on at the same rate as naming, as Model II says, then Sperling should have found that increasing the delay by 100 milliseconds led to an additional letter, up to about 4 or 5. The results showed, however, that the first few letters were gained at a much faster rate than that—at about 100 letters per second, or 10 milliseconds per letter.

This means there is a huge discrepancy between the rate at which people can name letters to themselves (10 per second) and the rate at which the first few letters become available in the icon (100 per second). The discrepancy is a 10-fold difference, which is sometimes called an "order of magnitude" difference; it indicates something really fundamentally wrong, not just a quibble. Accordingly, Sperling (1967) changed the model. Let us be clear why: Because of the 10-to-1 discrepancy between naming speed and the speed with which the first few letters get registered in the icon, it was necessary to subdivide the scan-rehearse operation of Figure 4.2 into two parts—a fast scan and a slow rehearsal process.

Figure 4.3 shows the resulting model, Model III. The main change over its predecessor is that the scan-rehearse mechanism has been subdivided into three components: There is first a rapid scan of the icon that feeds into a "Recognition Buffer"; the slower rehearsal process follows, with very much the same consequences as in Model II. The Recognition Buffer will be explained presently.

We now trace the history of information through the mechanisms of Model III: Information registered in the icon is first

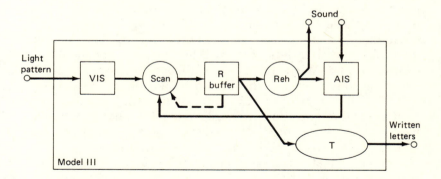

Figure 4.3. *Sperling's third approximation to a model for visual memory tasks. Abbreviations as before, except R-Buffer = Recognition Buffer.*

scanned at a rate of around 100 items per second. Sperling assumed that this rapid scanning could be affected by biases for certain kinds of *physical* features, such as an instruction to read only the top line or perhaps to read only the letter printed in red. However, at the scanning stage, there has not yet been contact between the stimulus information coming in and the stable categories defined in the person's long-term memory—no categorization, that is. In the language of Chapter 3, the scanning operation might result in the availability of physical features for the next stage of processing. This next stage, the Recognition Buffer, is the location where contact is established between the stimulus and its target category. More will be said about this recognition buffer in Chapter 6. There, the proposal is advanced that this important component contains individual units corresponding to each possible category state—each letter, word, or whatever. These units are capable of counting evidence from the scanning mechanism that is relevant to "their" category. When this evidence exceeds a certain level, the units become active and available to later portions of the system. This set of assumptions has been called the *logogen model* by John Morton (1969), its creator. The Recognition Buffer clearly accomplishes much the same thing as the Cognitive Demons in the Pandemonium Model of Chapter 3. Information from prior to the logogens or the Cognitive Demons may be organized according to physical features but not according to category states.

Sperling's assumption was that information contacted in the Recognition Buffer was in the form of speech-motor commands designed to control the pronunciation of the particular item or character presented. Categorizing some item, according to this model, amounts to having it in a state of readiness to speak. The important thing is that activating an item in the Recognition Buffer results in preparation for speaking it, not actual or internal speaking of it. This is so important because it allows Sperling to get the information recognized at a much faster rate than it can be named. This was the major purpose of going from Model II to Model III in the first place.

Once the information leaves the Recognition Buffer, the story is much as it was before. Notice that there are two modes of internal (silent) rehearsal shown in Model III: There is the feedback loop resulting from the scanning of AIS, as in the previous model. However, the dotted line allows another possibility here. Information can be recycled from the Recognition Buffer through a scanning operation without necessarily requiring the slow (10 items per second) rehearsal process. Sperling's model anticipates an idea that will be a central conclusion in Chapter 9, on speech coding in reading. Notice that his claim is that the use of speech in visual information processing *follows* identification of the items; the speech code is used for the purpose of holding information in some durable form of short-term memory (the rehearsal loop). This conclusion will not make much sense yet but it will be important later. In common language, you don't have to say an item in order to find out what it is—you say it to yourself to remember it.

CONCLUSION ON MODELING VISUAL INFORMATION PROCESSING. There have been later modifications of Sperling's model but they are not really necessary for our purposes here. The main conclusions from this story of an evolving theory are as follows: There is an initial iconic level of representation that probably holds a great deal of information in "raw" form, but only for about a quarter second. This information can be scanned and fed into a recognition system at a fast (100 items per second) rate by a "scanner" that can selectively attend to physical dimensions such as location. In order to "rescue" information from decay, people go through a covert naming process that is slow (10 items per second) but allows them to retain the information almost indefinitely through the use of overt and covert rehearsal loops. Since the information eventually written down on the answer sheet thus depends on the rehearsal and auditory storage systems, it is no wonder that errors made in these tasks reflect the sounds of the letters. It is this observation that we discuss now.

SPEECH RECODING IN SHORT-TERM MEMORY

As mentioned previously, Sperling noticed that his subjects' errors in a visual memory task often were rhyme substitutions (B for P, for example). He concluded that people may transform the visual items into some speechlike format in order to retain them in memory. R. Conrad, in Cambridge, England, made the same discovery independently at about the same time. It was Conrad who then went about studying this phenomenon systematically.

Conrad's first question (Conrad, 1964) was whether the errors made in visual memory were indeed similar to the errors that would occur in listening. Is it really like listening to an inner voice when we recall items from the sort of AIS, or rehearsal loop, proposed by Sperling in his Model III? Conrad's experiment could not have been more straightforward: He simply tallied the confusion errors made in remembering letters and compared them to the confusion errors made in listening to letters. (Confusion errors occur when the person writes down one item incorrectly where another should have been written; the other kind of error is an omission error, where the space is left blank.)

There were two separate parts to Conrad's 1964 report—a memory experiment and a listening experiment. In the former, people received *silently presented visual lists* consisting of six letters. They had to recall the letters in these lists, in order, by writing them down in spaces provided. Conrad looked at lists where exactly one of the six items was in error and where the error was a confusion rather than an omission. (Looking at just these "single substitutions" required throwing away, so to speak, a great deal of information from the experiment.) These errors were summarized in a "confusion matrix," a large table in which all of the possible stimuli are listed down the side, in the rows, and all the possible responses are listed across the top, in the columns. If the items are listed in the same order in the rows and columns, all correct responses would fall on the diagonal dropping from the upper left to the lower right. However, we are interested in confusion errors here, not corrects. The individual cells of the matrix, or table, show how often each possible letter was used in a confusion error in place of any particular correct letter. For example, when the letter V was correct, but the subjects recalled something else instead, it turned out that the most common confusion was the letter B, with C the next most common confusion; X was the least likely error to occur as a confusion to V.

In Conrad's second experiment there was essentially no memory involved: In that study, the subjects had to listen to single letters presented out loud and write down what letter was presented on each trial. Plenty of time was allowed for responding after each individual letter. In order to make people commit errors in this task, without which it would hardly have been a very interesting study, Conrad presented a burst of hissing noise simultaneously with each letter. This allowed him to construct a confusion matrix for the listening experiment. Again a table was constructed showing, for each possible stimulus letter, the letters people used in response (when they were wrong).

The main finding of the experiment was that the errors in listening were very similar to the errors in memory. For example, in the listening experiment, when V was presented in the midst of a noisy hiss, B was the most "popular" response, with C next and X last. The two confusion matrices, one from visual memory and the other from listening, were not *identical*; however, the correlation between them was + .64, which indicated a strong similarity. It is important to keep in mind that the memory confusions came from a strictly visual presentation arrangement, where recall of the letters was written. Thus, no sound occurred in the course of subjects' remembering these lists. Nonetheless, the sounds of the letters determined in large part which substitutions they made in recall.

In the same year, Conrad and Hull (1964) published a report showing that lists of items with high similarity in terms of speech are harder to remember than lists of the same length with low internal similarity. Thus, the six-item list B-C-T-Z-D-G is harder to recall in order than the list F-G-W-B-M-Q. We may distinguish this latter demonstration, which I have called the *similarity decrement* in another place (Crowder, 1978) from the *confusion effect,* with which we started this section. The similarity decrement is lower recall of lists with a high density of phonemically similar items than with a low density. The confusion effect is the high probability, given a substitution errors occurred, that the confused letter will rhyme with the correct one.

Both phenomena support the claim that visual memory is mediated by a speech-based transformation.

We can look in two directions with this generalizaton. First, it confirms the suggestion of Sperling, in Models II and III, that there is a speech-based intermediary between the visual symbols and the ultimate response. Second, we can realize that, among other things, visual memory tasks are partly *reading tasks*. The information comes from print, after all. Visual memory tasks are a degenerate form of reading, perhaps, but here we have a case where reading is indeed reliably associated with speech. The general relationship between reading and speaking is the "big" issue in the theory of reading; Chapter 9 is devoted to nothing else. The evidence discussed in this section is one solid point of departure for inquiring about speech in other forms—more realistic forms—of reading.

Extensions and Limitations of Speech Recoding in Memory

Table 4.1 shows the results of several extensions made by Conrad (1972) of the confusion effect. Each section of the table is a collapsed, or summarized, confusion matrix, in which the columns represent the type of stimulus presented (BCPTV or FMNS) and the two rows represent the same two sets of letters as they appeared in responses. So an error of B for V would be entered in the upper left quarter of the collapsed matrix and an error of B for F would be entered in the upper right, and so on.

Each matrix goes with a different comparison, or experiment. The Chance matrix shows what would happen if people chose their confusion errors randomly. If there had been equal numbers of letters rhyming with "EH" as with "EE" (there were only four of the former and five of the latter) then all cells would have an expected frequency of 50%. The Visual Matrix shows how errors would occur if people "chose" confusion errors based on visual shape (which they do not). The Immediate Recall Matrix is the one we have been talking about; this gives confusions, or substitution errors, from visually presented memory lists with written recall. Obviously more errors occur within the two rhyming

Table 4.1 Confusions Among Consonants for Various Testing Situations

Matrix source and rhyming class of response given	Rhyming class of stimulus presented	
	/i/ (BCPTV)	/ɛ/ (FMNS)
Chance matrix:		
/i/	50.0	62.5
/ɛ/	50.0	37.5
Visual matrix:		
/i/	35.6	79.1
/ɛ/	64.4	20.9
Immediate recall matrix:		
/i/	79.2	19.8
/ɛ/	20.8	80.2
Delayed recall matrix:		
/i/	58.2	58.1
/ɛ/	41.8	41.9
Suppression matrix:		
/i/	57.6	57.8
/ɛ/	42.4	42.2

Note. After Conrad (1972).

classes than between them, in direct opposition to what we would expect from the visual predictions.

The next two matrices show results that extend the confusion effect in theoretically interesting ways. In the Delayed Recall matrix, we see performance from an experiment in which recall was not immediate; instead, subjects had to perform a distractor task between seeing a list of four letters and trying to recall them in order. Specifically, the four letters to be remembered first popped up one at a time on the screen then, without interruption, there were digits appearing in the same position and the subjects had to read all items—the letters to be remembered and the digits providing the distraction—as they appeared, out loud. The digit naming continued for 7 seconds and then the subject was asked for the letters.

Performance was considerably poorer in the Delayed Recall experiment than in the Immediate recall experiment; that is not of interest here, however. What is important is *which* errors people made in the delayed condition, when they committed confusions. The table shows that the errors tended to move toward the direction of the Chance Matrix. One interpretation of the fact that the evidence for speech coding goes away in the delayed-recall condition is that the distractor task used by Conrad, during the interval, kept the rehearsal system "busy." If rehearsal were the source of memory confusions, then this would have prevented their occurrence. The idea would be that the subjects in that condition were naming the digits occurring on the screen and therefore couldn't engage the speech-based rehearsal processes which ordinarily produce the confusions. In the language of Model III, it would be as if there were some blockage of the loop containing rehearsal due to its being full of the irrelevant distractor material.

Much the same thing may be going on in the final experiment shown in Table 4.1, which produced the data seen in the Suppression Matrix. In this procedure, there was no delay between original reading of the stimuli and recall of them. However, people were required to pronounce the word *the* over and over during the time the memory letters were appearing on the screen. This senseless chatter (the-the-the . . .) adds nothing to memory but it does keep the rehearsal system occupied. With the rehearsal system occupied, it stands to reason that the to-be-remembered items can't be rehearsed. Obviously, this type of suppression of rehearsal or naming activity was enough to remove the evidence for speech-based coding in performance. In other words, the errors that did occur were as would be predicted from randomly "choosing" substitution or confusion errors.

It is very important that in the Delayed and Suppression matrices, overall performance was better than chance. If people were just wildly guessing, it would be as if they never even saw the stimulus list and so it would be no surprise that their errors were not related to anything. Instead, the people were scoring correct responses at better than guessing in these comparisons. Table 4.1 displays the nature of errors *given that an error occurred*. In this analysis we forget about how many errors were made and focus instead on how the errors distributed themselves among the four categories shown in each subsection of Table 4.1.

Since performance was better than chance in the Delayed and

Suppression matrices, it must be true that there is some other form of memory occurring besides speech-based coding. If the naming-rehearsal process were the only form of memory coding, then there would continue to be confusion errors like those in the Immediate Recall matrix until performance got so poor it dropped to chance. Experts do not agree on the nature of this other form of coding used in short-term memory, and it is too complicated a question to take up here.

THE DEVELOPMENT OF SPEECH ENCODING. At what age do children first begin to use speech to encode memory stimuli? That is, at what age do they begin to behave like Sperling's Model III? One might think that once children know the names of the things they are being asked to remember, they would use these names for retaining information in their memories. Conrad's research (1972) suggests otherwise: He tested children ranging in mental age from 3 to 11 years. In the task he used, the children saw a few colored pictures of everyday objects. Then, the response was to pick out the objects presented from among eight alternatives represented again by pictures. (Pictures were used, of course, because the youngest children tested were not old enough to read.) The objects were common enough so that even the very youngest children could easily supply their names. As each was presented in the series to be remembered, the experimenter named each aloud as he presented it.

There were two sets of objects pictured. In one set, the names were highly similar in terms of speech (CAT BAT RAT MAT HAT MAN TAP BAG) and in the other set they were not (FISH GIRL BUS SPOON HORSE TRAIN CLOCK HAND). The point of the experiment was whether children would have more trouble with the ones that were similar on the basis of speech. Now, of course, younger children aren't able to remember lists as long as older children can. Conrad tested each individual child to determine how many items the child could remember about half the time. For this purpose Conrad used the High Similarity (CAT RAT) set. So the older children, on the average, got longer lists than the younger ones; however, everybody got just enough of the High Similarity items to be correct about half the time.

Table 4.2   The Development of Phonological Confusion

Stimulus	Mental ages (years)				
Type	3—5	5—6	6—7	7—8	8—11
Homophones	52.4[a]	52.0	51.9	52.1	52.4
	(3.2)	(3.8)	(4.1)	(4.4)	(5.9)
Nonhomophones	52.8	59.1	64.0	69.1	75.3

Note. After Conrad (1972).
[a]The entries are percentage of correct responding. The figures in parentheses below the homophone data show the number of items that needed to be presented in order to obtain approximately 50% correct scores for the homophone condition at each age group.

The experimental question was whether it would make a difference when the children were given *lists of the same length* consisting of the Low Similarity (FISH GIRL) items. In other words, for a particular 5-year old, who perhaps gets 50% correct on three-item lists from the High Similarity set, we want to know whether he or she does better than 50% when the items are not similar. The result is shown in Table 4.2. Notice in that table that performance hovers around 50% at all ages for the High Similarity items; this is the result of adjusting the list lengths, as we mentioned. In parentheses are given the number of items presented, at each age, to achieve this uniform score on the High Similarity items. The last row of the table shows the amount of "relief" that occurred at each age when the subjects were switched from High to Low Similarity materials. Clearly, it began to make a difference only at around five or six. The younger children were remembering slightly more than three items but it made no difference, to them, whether the items rhymed or not. Remember, we stipulated that these youngest children *knew* the names but apparently they did not use the names for the purposes of memory in this task. The 8 to 11 year age group, on the other hand, who are normally fluent readers, showed a huge performance difference between the two similarity conditions.

Thus, Conrad's experiment with children seems to say that even young children who have the names of items available do not use these names for the purposes of memory until they are around 5 or 6 years old. This is of course the same age at which children first normally become able to learn to read. It may be sheer coincidence that using speech for short-term memory and reading begin to show up at about the same age; on the other hand, many think it is a profoundly significant fact. These matters are discussed in Chapters 9 and 10, in our surveys of speech in reading and of the teaching of reading. For now, we conclude the chapter with several more limited observations:

SUMMARY. First, we saw that the reading and reporting of unrelated letters from a brief flash is a reasonably well-understood process. The information first is registered in a high-capacity but short-duration iconic memory. From that iconic store, information is scanned by a high-speed process that leads to a contact, in the Recognition Buffer, with memorized category states. Normally, the information is then cycled through a naming process that can be looped repeatedly. It is somewhere in this naming-rehearsal operation that the letters become coded (defined) in terms of their speech properties, which, in turn, leads to confusion errors based on speech. This process begins to appear in children around 5 to 6 years old. Finally, it can be broken up by concurrent distraction that keeps the speech system occupied. We see in the next chapter how well this story holds up when we begin to change the displayed items from unrelated letters to meaningful words and phrases.

REFERENCES AND NOTES

Early work on tachistoscopic presentation can be found summarized in Huey's (1908/1968) book, *The Psychology and Pedagogy of Reading,* and in the chapter on reading in Woodworth's (1938) *Experimental Psychology.*

In Chapter 2 of my book, *Principles of Learning and Memory,* I have provided a thorough and careful development of the logic and evidence necessary for the concept of iconic memory. The interested reader is urged to consult that source for more information on Sperling's work and related topics. For present purposes, only the general ideas are necessary. One current controversy is about whether the iconic memory system is located on the retina, as Sakitt (1976) claimed, or not; For a recent review of this literature, see Wingfield and Byrnes (1981, pp. 163–169).

Philip Gough made the strong claim about a decade ago (Gough, 1972) that word perception could indeed be understood by reference to the Sperling model for unrelated letters. Evidence since that time has forced a softening of that position, but see Gough and Cosky (1977) for a thoughtful review of the matter.

The information-flow diagrams shown in Figures 4.1 through 4.3 are a convenient way to set out logical distinctions among processes but they should not be taken too literally. One dangerous attitude that is suggested by these diagrams is that of strictly serial, left-to-right processing—as if a tiny bug were walking from box to box along the lines. The mechanisms represented in flow diagrams might well be occurring partly or entirely in parallel; the distinctions among functions are the important representations.

Much of my own research (Crowder, 1976, Chapter 3) is concerned with how Sperling was *mistaken* about the equivalence of overt and covert presentation of auditory information. It has absolutely no bearing on the issues at stake here and so I resist trying to work it in. There is now a good deal known about the concept of the rehearsal loop. A recent article by Baddeley, Thomsom, and Buchanan (1975) shows with great care and cleverness that this form of internal speech is really very speech like: Long words, and words with long vowel sounds, fill up the loop more than shorter words. For a somewhat different attitude on the maintenance of information in short-term memory, see Estes (1980).

There are interesting data on the issue of how the deaf code information for immediate recall. The answer seems to depend on how deaf people have been trained to use language; for example, those trained to use speech in as normal a way as possible seem to show the same confusions normals do. This set of questions is covered in Chapter 4 of my *Principles of Learning and Memory*.

In Crowder (1978) I discuss the evidence that speech coding is not the only form of coding used in short-term memory. The circumstances that favor speech coding seem to be (1) memory for order is required, not just memory for the identity of items, (2) the kind of order is temporal order not spatial position, and (3) the items are familiar linguistic units. Work by Healy (1975) can be consulted for details.

There is a body of research from the 1970s by John Locke and his associates that approaches speech coding from another direction. Locke has measured tiny muscle potentials on the surface of the skin with recording electrodes. He has found that these little electrical responses are more vigorous during the speaking of words that require vigorous movement of the lips (BOMBER WAFFLE) than during the speaking of words that do not (LICENSE CORDS). We look at this type of research in Chapter 9. The important result is that these electrical lip responses occur also during "silent" rehearsal of the corresponding words as well as during their overt pronunciation. Studies with children suggest that this rehearsal does not appear until around the same age as Conrad found significant changes. See reviews of this work in Garrity (1977).

It is perhaps smug to claim we "understand" the Sperling situation, where unrelated letters flash on a screen for immediate report. The fact is we may be wrong! But understanding in this sense refers to a level of explanation where we can relate the complex situation to a collection of simpler processes that we have reason to accept on other grounds. It is no explanation to invent magic new processes that enter the picture at each higher level of complexity. Thus, we understand the Sperling task in that we can build from plausible simple mechanisms a model (Model III with some amplification) that would be sufficient to produce the behavior we observe.

CHAPTER 5

Word Perception

Why is the letter string BURGUNDY easier to perceive than the letter string YRUUDGBN? Why is the word BURGUNDY understood more rapidly when we are reading about France or about wine than when we are reading about kangaroos? Why is it that word perception is sometimes really automatic (try not to perceive the word that comes at the end of this phrase—FOOTBALL)? These three questions stand behind this chapter and the next.

As usual, our purpose is not to summarize an enormous research literature from cognitive phychology nor to wind up with conclusive answers to the questions posed. The first of these goals would take a book of its own; the second would be grossly arrogant at this stage in our knowledge. Instead, the effort will be to look at some of the factual information that bears on these questions and some of the theories that have been proposed to cover them. A few classic experiments will be covered in detail; many more will be left out.

WORDNESS AND THE UNIT OF ANALYSIS IN READING

We begin with the promise that was the basis for Chapter 4—that we would examine whether and how the models developed there for perception of unrelated letters broke down when the letters formed meaningful words. The comparison of words and non-words was made very early in the history of experimental psychology, using the first tachistoscopes (see Chapter 4). James McKeen Cattell (1886), among others, gave people 10 millisecond flashes of stimulus displays and determined how many items they could read in that brief exposure. He found that people could name 3.5 unconnected letters (a little poorer than Sperling's subjects did in comparable circumstances, but Sperling's shortest display time was 15 milliseconds). When Cattell changed the items from letters to short words, which were each 3 or more letters long, people were able to get about two words correct. In terms of letters, there was obviously better performance on related than on unrelated letters. When the words were connected themselves, in a sort of phrase, people got about four items correct. These observations have not been challenged by subsequent work; it is only their interpretation that has been a topic of lively debate.

The Reicher (1969) Experiment

It is interesting that, until very recent times, nothing particular occurred to explain Cattell's findings. The main question is whether the advantage he found for words comes from the visual system or from "later" stages of information processing. A doctoral dissertation by Reicher (1969) was largely responsible for bringing this question into modern focus. Reicher began with the observation that Cattell's findings are not really as analytical as we would like: For one thing, words serve to group together several letters under a single name. Consider Sperling's model; the advantage of letters forming words over unrelated letters *could* come from the fact that the rehearsal loop gets "crowded" with individual letters sooner than with short words. If the rehearsal process can handle about four items, for example, then it would be better to have four words in rehearsal than four letters. By this interpretation, words would not really be any easier to see than unrelated letters, just easier to hold in some form of short-term memory.

Another interpretation of the Cattell comparison is that there is predictability in words that is not present in unrelated letter strings. Say the subject were given a four-letter array, the word GULP in one case and the four-letter string GUKL in the other case. Suppose furthermore that the subject didn't see the second letter. In the word condition, assuming the subject knows each item is a word, it is easy to guess that the second letter must be U; however, the subject who missed seeing the second of four *unrelated* letters has no chance of making an educated guess. Again, the word would not have been handled any better than the nonword in the visual domain. The result would be explained by some late stage in our information-processing system.

Reicher tried to improve on Cattell's experiment by eliminating the possibility for these alternative explanations of the word advantage. In Reicher's experiment, people saw a single-item display, either one letter, a series of four unrelated letters, or a common four-letter word. Thus, the display might contain the letter H, the letter-series CSAH, or the word CASH. The special feature of Reicher's technique was use of a forced-choice test. Instead of asking subjects what they had seen, Reicher presented them with a choice of two letters, say H or T. The subject's task was to select which of the two had been in the display. Notice that for the word condition, both of the two choices make up a legitimate word (CASH or CAST), therefore the guessing advantage for the correct item in the word condition is lost. Guessing will help no more in the word condition than in the single letter condition or in the nonword (four unrelated letters) condition.

The use of the forced-choice test (H/T) not only eliminates the guessing bias favoring words, it also greatly reduces the force of the rehearsal-loop explanation. Subjects never have to report the whole stimulus, for one thing. Second, the two alternatives were presented exactly when the original stimulus display was erased, so there was no appreciable time over which the subject was required to depend on memory.

Reicher found that the mean percent correct choice, where 50% would be chance guessing between H and T, was 89% for the word (CASH) condition, 76% for the nonword (CSAH) condition, and 78% for the single letter (H) condition. Words were significantly better than nonwords *and better even than single letters.*

The Word-Letter Effect

Let us discuss the advantage of words over single letters first, because it forces the most dramatic modification of the Sperling model: If, as that model states, visual displays are processed letter by letter, then no matter how fast they are processed, something with more than one letter absolutely must take more time than something with only a single letter. It would have been only a small concession to add to the Sperling model the assumption that letters forming words work the same way as unrelated letters, only faster. But that concession won't save the model! The first letter of a word display should take the same amount of time as a single letter display. No matter how rapidly the other letters in the word might be processed, owing to their "predictability" or something, there ought to be at least some extra time added. To find, as Reicher did, that the word takes *less* time to process than the single letter, must mean there is something decidedly different about the way words are processed than single or unrelated letters. The suggestion is offered in what follows that words may be perceived as distinctive, overall shapes.

We pause here to raise an important clarification about how Reicher's effect was measured and how it is described. Reicher showed an 89 to 78% advantage in accuracy, for words over letters, and yet we have been talking about the speed with which these items might be processed. The underlying assumption is that measures of percent accuracy and processing speed go together. When processing time is consistently cut off sharply, as it was in Reicher's experiment, then the more rapid processes will have had time to complete but the slower ones won't.

There is not room here for a full discussion of the subsequent history of the word-letter comparison. Wheeler (1970) demonstrated, for one thing, that the result could be repeated in another laboratory and showed that it was not a consequence of several plausible but basically uninteresting factors. Thompson and Massaro (1973) argued, however, that the guessing problem had not really been eliminated in Reicher's technique. The gist of this argument is presented in the References and Notes at the end of this chapter. Smith and Kleiman (1979) argue with persuasive force that part of the confusion about the word-letter effect may come from the fact that subjects are flexible in their use of strategies. The story is thus not yet completely written about the word-letter effect. But what is our interpretation of it at face value? What hypothesis do we adopt *in place of* the Sperling letter-by-letter model?

THE WORD AS A "SUPERCHARACTER." One obvious alternative theory is that the word is perceived more or less as a distinctive shape itself. In earlier discussions in this book, we inquired how the letter R, for example, is perceived as such. For a partial answer, the Pandemonium model was enlisted; it assumes that the image is sorted out into primitive shapes, or features, and that these feed automatically into Cognitive Demons representing each possible character. The Cognitive Demons, in turn, shout for the attention of the central processor (the Decision Demon) in proportion to how much feature input they receive. The Pandemonium reasoning will be used from time to time in this and subsequent discussions and you should review it (see pages 46 to 49) now before going on.

The modification is as follows: There could be Cognitive Demons representing words, as well as single characters. The demon for the word NO might carry a list of features (left angularity, right curvature, two upright lines, one diagonal, and so on) that would be sufficient to tell it apart from other familiar items. Naturally, these Word Demons would have to be learned; people wouldn't even have one for some items, perhaps words they seldom encounter, like XEBEC and GLEDGE.

Now why should words be faster than letters if they are both represented by their own Cognitive Demons? Here is a speculative answer: The system might be organized so that a particular demon starts shouting sooner if the demon represents a very common item than if he represents a rare item. So the demons for the words THE and THY might have very similar feature lists. However, the demon for THE might require fewer of these features to be stimulated before he starts shouting toward the Decision Demon than the demon for THY. This would make sense— THE is occurring all the time whereas one might want to have plenty of extra evidence before concluding that one had read THY.

Now, of course, we encounter the individual letters all the time too, more often than any individual word. However, it is rare indeed that we are asked to perceive letters by themselves as units. We go through months, perhaps, reading almost constantly but never having to respond that a particular symbol is a W. (People who participate in some psychology experiments are exceptions.) Thus, in a certain sense, common words are indeed "more frequent" than single letters. Although they will tend to have long feature lists relative to letters, they swing into action more readily, or, in technical terms, they have lower thresholds. We return later in this chapter to the kind of theory being outlined here. For the moment, the supercharacter idea is offered just to show how one rationalization of the word-letter effect works.

The Word-Superiority Effect

Reicher's other major finding was that four-letter items that were words were perceived much better than four unrelated letters. This finding, sometimes called the Word Superiority Effect, has attracted considerable attention. Before presenting some ideas on the cause of the word-superiority effect, we describe one further experimental demonstration of it, this time a report by Johnston and McClelland (1974) with the charming subtitle "Seek not and ye shall find."

THE JOHNSTON AND McCLELLAND EXPERIMENT. These authors examined four main experimental conditions in a setting much like Reicher's—a four-letter item was flashed and then erased by a second display that contained two letters, one from the original item and one not. In one condition the item was a word (say COIN) and in the other it was not (say CPRD). However, the fact that COIN was a word did not give away the correct choice in the two-alternative test (C versus J, perhaps). So far, we have nothing more than conditions replicating Reicher's work. In each stimulus situation, however, there were two instructions that were

Table 5.1 Percent Correct Responses in the Study by Johnston and McClelland (1974)

Instruction	Stimulus	
	Nonword	Word
Whole item	70.0	79.2
Letter position	76.5	72.5

compared: In one, subjects were told to pay attention to the first letter; this seems like good advice, because this is where the critical information for the test was to be presented. In the other condition, people were told to pay attention to the overall shape of the item rather than to any particular region of it.

The results of the Johnston and McClelland study are shown in Table 5.1. There was an *interaction* between the two experimental variables, instructions and wordness. That is, the effect of one variable depends on which level of the other variable one looks at. For the Whole Item instruction, there was a 9% word superiority effect; however, for the Letter Position instruction, it was actually reversed, with words being poorer than nonwords. With nonwords, as you might expect from Sperling's work on iconic memory, knowing where to look in an item helped. However, with words the result was the opposite.

The Johnston and McClelland study makes two points that we want to underline here. First, it shows that the word-superiority effect does not occur inevitably whenever we compare a word and a nonword. Instead, the word-superiority effect depends somewhat on the strategies that subjects bring to the task they are performing. Second, the result of Table 5.1 *is consistent with* the following explanation (but it does not prove that explanation, of course).

AN INTERPRETATION. Under instructions to look at the whole item, words were better than nonwords because they have a familiar pattern. That is, common words, at least, possess a category representation at the level of Cognitive Demons. Nonwords do not, and thus the letters in them have to be perceived independently à la Sperling. Thus, one Cognitive Demon can be activated in the word case but several, four in this example, have to be activated in the nonword case. This is a way of understanding the advantage of words over nonwords in the Whole Item condition. Now, how do we account for what happened under the Letter Position instruction? With nonwords, first, it is unsurprising that performance improved when subjects knew where to look; some explanation like the one used in Sperling's partial-report conditions would be used here. The real question is why the same explanation would not apply to the word stimuli and lead to the false prediction that with words, too, knowing where to look would help.

One account would go like this: It is possible that the same focusing of attention to one position does occur in the word condition as it does in the nonword condition. However, in the word condition there is an extra Cognitive Demon competing— the one that is associated with the word identification of the target item COIN. This demon is activated *automatically* whenever a sufficient number of its features occur in the visual field. So the automatic activation of COIN's unit should compete with the unit, the demon, corresponding to the target letter C, at least in the word condition. However, in the nonword condition, there is no such competing demon, for CRPD has no unit corresponding to it, therefore the classification of the target letter C, in the designated position, can go on without competition. In other words, with attention focused on the relevant letter position, the Cognitive Demon corresponding to COIN would provide competition for the attention of the Decision Demon; however, when the item displayed is CRPD, there is no such competition. When attention is focused on the whole shape, of course, it is helpful that there is a unit, a Cognitive Demon corresponding to that shape in the case of COIN.

In this interpretation, we meet for the first time an important idea in information processing—automatic processing. Recall that the presence of the familiar word COIN actually hurts the subject in the Letter Position condition. There is nothing the subject can do about it; if the features sufficient for the word COIN appear in the visual image, that unit will simply be activated and will feed information (shout) to the next level of the system. In the next chapter, we have more to say about automaticity, both its costs and benefits.

IS IT REALLY WORDNESS? The comparison of words and non-words depends partly on what we use as nonwords. Comparing PINCH and FULCH will not yield as big a difference favoring words as comparing PINCH and GKUYQ. FULCH is what we call a "legal nonword"—it obeys rules of English spelling and can easily be pronounced, whereas GKUYQ is not, in this sense, legal. Baron and Thurston (1973), among others, showed that performance on legal nonwords is very good indeed, relative to true words, and vastly better than performance on illegal non-words. In fact, there has been some controversy about whether there is any remaining advantage of words over nonwords when the latter have been made as wordlike as possible. Most experts (for example Allport, 1979, and Baron, 1977) now concede that there is a genuine wordness advantage, although small, whatever nonwords are chosen. We take this for granted here and go on to display other evidence favoring a theory that recognition can sometimes occur on the basis of words' overall shapes.

WORD SHAPE

The idea for inspection in this section is that words may sometimes be perceived in terms of their overall shapes. This notion has been anticipated above, when the term "supercharacter" was used. Now we turn to the examination of evidence favoring it. Let us be clear on what this means: Some writers mean by word-shape cues only those patterns formed by ascending and descending letters, usually most conspicuous in lowercase printing. As a matter of fact, there is some evidence that lowercase words are easier to read than uppercase (see below) so the ascending and descending strokes may be significant. However, we intend here to include the *internal* shape of words, not just their

outline. The words POOL and KILL do not have especially different overall outlines, as printed here, but they have distinctive
patterns internally. This is best explained by reference to features and the Pandemonium model: A letter's shape, in this
model, is really just the list of features that each Cognitive Demon has waiting as he scans the Image. Now if we imagine a
Cognitive Demon acting on behalf of a whole word, not just a
letter, the word's shape is defined by the collection of features on
that particular demon's list.

It was explained in the previous section that legal nonwords
(FULCH) are perceived very well, almost as well as regular
words. This suggested to some workers that it was the orthographic regularity or the pronunciability of words that caused
their advantage, and not the fact that they were in the dictionary.
One study by Henderson (1974) added important information on
this point. He showed that in a perceptual matching task (deciding whether or not two letter strings were identical) familiar
letter strings such as FBI and YMCA were at an advantage over
unfamiliar strings such as OBM and YSSU. Now these are all
nonpronunciable strings. They do not obey the laws of English
orthography at all! Henderson also found that if the familiar
strings were presented in mixed typography (Fbi or ymCA), there
was no advantage for them. These results point to the sheer visual familiarity of these letter combinations as the key to their
perceptual advantage.

The mixed typography operation was introduced by F. Smith
in the 1960s to make a point about word perception. Although
his experiments showed minimal disruption, subsequent experiments have shown it to be a significant hindrance to perception.
For example Coltheart and Freeman (1974) compared pure uppercase words (SNAPSHOT), pure lowercase words (snapshot),
and mixed words (SnapSHoT) in a tachistoscopic perception experiment. Percent correct responding for these three conditions
was 60.4, 64.8, and 47.9, respectively. (Notice the advantage of
lower- over uppercase alluded to previously.) Quite clearly, the
mixed typography was detrimental to word perception. This result, by the way, argues against a simple application of Sperling's
letter-by-letter model to word perception—the integrity of indi-

vidual letters is, after all, preserved in mixed typography. The evidence from mixed typography does not by itself prove that words are perceived as whole units but it fits very well with that hypothesis.

THE BROOKS EXPERIMENT. An impressive experiment by Brooks (1977) uses the mixed-typography technique to argue for the whole-word shape hypothesis. The task was to search through a list of 16 words for either names of places or for common first names. The method was much like that used by Neisser in his studies of visual search (see Chapter 3). Brooks found that the time required to process a word was about 30 milliseconds slower when the items in the display were mixed case than when they were all lowercase, in conformity with the Coltheart and Freeman result. However, with continued practice, people improved with the mixed typography to the extent there was no longer much difference between the two. The initial segment of Figure 5.1 shows this convergence.

This much is preliminary; the real interest in this experiment comes from what Brooks did next. He reasoned that there were three explanations of why people first had difficulty when forced to deal with mixed typography, and then overcame that difficulty. One possibility is that they were simply being cautious with the unfamiliar-looking print, and therefore slower. As they got used to it, so to speak, the caution would have disappeared.

Two more interesting possibilities are that the mixed type required specific new learning. There would be two forms of this new learning: People might have learned, during the practice shown in the left segment of Figure 5.1, to accept either upper- or lowercase features as evidence for target items (names). This would be a very general kind of learning. The second kind of new learning that might account for the recovery in Figure 5.1 is that people learned specific shapes of the target and nontarget items. That is, they would have learned, by this second explanation, that HArvEy is the way that name looks and that KItcHEn is the way that word looks, at least for the moment.

These hypotheses were tested in a transfer phase of the experiment. Transfer is a strategy in learning experiments whereby

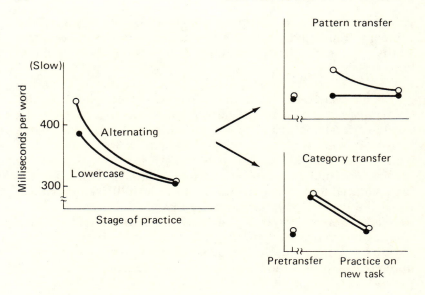

Figure 5.1. *A schematic representation of performance in the Brooks (1977) experiment. Each panel shows processing time per item in a visual search task as a function of practice. See text for an explanation of the two transfer conditions.*

we understand what someone has learned in one situation by seeing it applied (or not applied) in another. After the practice shown in the left part of the figure, there were two kinds of continuation tasks. In one, Pattern Transfer, people were instructed that they should continue to search for the kind of target—place names or people's names—as in the initial phase. However, although the targets and distractor words remained the same, the upper- and lowercase letters were reversed, so that where HEnRy appeared in the first part of the experiment, heNrY appeared in the second part. In the second version of the continuation task, Category Transfer, the visual stimuli remained identical but the subjects were switched with respect to which category they were looking for—those looking for place names before the switch looked for people's first names after, and vice versa.

If the first explanation were true, that people just got cautious when they first saw the mixed type and got over this caution during the first phase of practice, then people in both conditions should be unaffected by the transfer task; they would remain as fast as at the end of the first phase. If the subjects had learned a very general adjustment during their practice with the mixed type, then this adjustment would still be in effect, as it were, after the transfer, and similarly, there should be no decrement caused by either, except for having to switch search categories in Category Transfer condition. However, if the subjects had learned to overcome the mixed type by learning specific patterns (i.e., HEnRy, and so on) then the two transfer conditions would give different results. Consider first the case where the type of search (names or places) remains the same, in Pattern Transfer, with each individual word rendered in complementary form with respect to its initial version—all lowercase to uppercase and vice versa. In this situation, the subject would be in trouble; his or her having learned to say "yes" when he or she saw HEnRy would not transfer perfectly to heNrY. On the other hand, such a subject, who had learned shapes specially in the first phase of the experiment, would have little trouble with the Category Transfer condition because he or she would still be dealing with the same word shapes. (It would be as if, during the first phase of the study, people had "grown" new Cognitive Demons, with feature lists appropriate to the mixed type.)

The results are given in the right panel of Figure 5.1. Control groups continued on unaltered typography, and their data are shown in the closed symbols. In the upper panel, we can see that the group continuing practice on regular, lowercase type continued at the same rate of processing as before, of course. The group with mixed typography, however, suffered badly from the Pattern Transfer operation (HEnRy to heNrY). This fits with the hypothesis that they had learned specific word shapes. Both groups suffered a loss when they were switched to searching for a different category, in the Category Transfer condition in the lower right-hand panel. But the degree of slowing was the same for the normal and the mixed typography groups. In short, as long as the two groups were looking at the same visual shapes, there was no difference between normal and mixed typographies in the amount of transfer. It was when the group with mixed typography was switched to unfamiliar specific shapes that performance suffered.

Naturally, one can always question whether visual search is a good enough analogue to "real reading" to put great weight in the results. However, at least as far as individual word perception—which is the subject of this chapter—the Brooks study does show that individual word shapes *can* be a powerful factor in perception.

HEALY'S EXPERIMENTS. Healy (1976, 1980) has performed a series of experiments that are also highly consistent with this idea of overall shape in word perception. She gave her subjects a passage like that printed in Figure 5.2 with instructions to read it normally and cross out all occurrences of the letter *t*. Try it now yourself, before reading on.

This passage contains 40 *t*' s and people typically miss 6.9 of them, having spent 47 seconds finishing the task (these figures come from Experiment 1 of Healy, 1976). The main outcome of this experiment is not only that people are inclined to miss occurrences of the target letter but that they are most especially inclined to do so when this letter occurs in the word THE. Of the 40 targets in the passage in Figure 5.2, 11 occur on the word THE. If people distribute their errors (misses of the target) randomly among each of the 40 possibilities, we would expect 11/40 = 27.5% to fall on the word THE. In reality, Healy found that a full 62% of the errors made (of which there were an average of 6.9) fell on that word.

Thus, over 60% of missed *t*' s occur on the word THE even though it accounts for only 27.5% of the possible misses. To help interpret this finding, Healy offered another experimental condition. In this condition, all of the punctuation marks, spaces, and occurrences of *t* remained identical to those in Figure 5.2. However, within regions of five words, the *other* letters were scrambled randomly. The average time to complete this passage was 55 seconds, rather than 47 seconds for the one in Figure 5.2. However, people were quite a bit more accurate overall, missing only

Smoke was rising here and there among the creepers that festooned the dead or dying trees. As they watched, a flash of fire appeared at the root of one wisp, and then the smoke thickened. Small flames stirred at the bole of a tree and crawled away through leaves and brushwood, dividing and increasing. One patch touched a tree trunk and scrambled up like a squirrel. The smoke increased, sifted, rolled outwards. The squirrel leapt on the wings of the wind and clung to another standing tree, eating downwards. The fire laid hold on the forest and began to gnaw.

Figure 5.2.   One stimulus passage from Healy (1976); the task is to cross out all occurrences of the letter t.

a total of 1.5 occurrences of the letter t, rather than 6.9. The main question is how they did on occurrences of the letter t, which matched those where the context was the word THE. The results showed that only 5% of the errors occurred in these locations, rather than the 27.5% expected by chance or the 62% observed in the condition of Figure 5.2. Apparently, having the target letter in a short letter string actually helped people find it provided that letter string was not the word THE. In any case, we cannot explain the high preponderance of t-missing in the main condition by the positions on the page or the spacings in which these targets occurred in Figure 5.2.

One might think that t is hard to see in the word THE, because this word is so very redundant—that is, it gives us little information. Perhaps people can just do without this word and when the context suggests it is coming up, people are able to skip over it. So, for example, if you read the words ". . . on the left side of . . . ," you can predict with quite good accuracy that the word THE is likely to be next; if so, why not skip on to the next informative words, which might be "gunpowder chamber"? If we often just skip that redundant word, it is no wonder we fail to see individual letters in it.

One way to test this idea that people see THE coming, from the sentence structure, and skip ahead without looking at it, is to destroy the linguistic structure that ordinarily lets us predict where there will be a THE. In another experiment, Healy presented the passage of Figure 5.2 in a word-by-word-scrambled version, leaving punctuation and occurrences of THE unchanged, but all other words interchanged haphazardly. The results for this Scrambled Word passage were very similar to those for Figure 5.2—53 seconds reading time, 5.3 errors on t overall, of which 67% fell on the word THE. However, in this passage, the other words give no clue that the "uninteresting" word THE is about to come up and therefore we cannot appeal to redundancy to explain why so many errors fall on t' s occurring there. There is more evidence that skipping over THE's is not the basis for failing to detect T's: In a recent study, Healy had people looking through intact passages, like that in Figure 5.2, for misspellings. They were to encircle words that were spelled wrong; if there were a tendency to skip over THE, then misspellings ought to be missed in this word (i.e., when TEH is substituted for THE). The result showed just the opposite! People were actually better at detecting misspellings in the word THE than in other words. This result, too, discourages the view that people skip over THE as a routine strategy.

Another possibility is that when t occurs in THE it is not pronounced "normally" as it is in the word TEA. Healy tested this by looking systematically for errors on the word THEY. There was no disproportionate t-missing, however, when it occurred within the word THEY. What remains is the hypothesis favored by Healy, that the word THE is read as a unit, as a shape of its own, if you will, and that therefore the individual elements of the word are concealed. Much the same thing seems to go on when the individual letter R is perceived—we are aware of the diagonal line only after the unit has been perceived by its familiar category. A consequence of this hypothesis is that the tendency of people to miss the target letter should increase as the word in which it is included becomes more frequent. Healy has shown that this is the case.

This research program is one of the strongest that exists favoring the idea that at least highly frequent words can be recognized by their global patterns rather than by their constituent letters. Naturally, no single source of evidence can ever be conclusive on so great a question as this one. However, when we place side by side the evidence on the word-superiority effect, the word-letter effect, the research on mixed typography, and this work by Healy, it gets nearly impossible to hold on to the sort of letter-by-letter model proposed by Sperling. At the same time, it gets difficult to resist some form of theory that claims the overall word shape is the critical cue for the perception of at least some words.

REFERENCES AND NOTES

The Reicher experiment has been greatly simplified in the exposition here. It contained several aspects that are important for theory but beyond the scope of our discussion. For example, Reicher compared the conditions described above with others in which the two stimulus alternatives (H/T) occurred *before* the stimulus display. This led to the same advantage of words over nonwords and over single letters. It also led to worse performance overall, which has been a provocative finding for workers in this area since. Sometimes it has been found that presenting the alternatives before the stimulus eliminates the word advantage (Estes, 1977; Thompson & Massaro, 1973). This outcome is obtained under conditions of very heavy practice and few alternatives. It is quite likely that subjects under these special circumstances cease to process words in a "normal" way (Baron, 1977).

Thompson and Massaro (1973) suggested that the Reicher method does not really eliminate the contribution of guessing: Their argument requires a preliminary identification decision before the subject checks to see what the two alternatives are. If the subject reaches such a preliminary decision, and if the subject knows that a word is coming on a particular trial, then he or she might be able to combine these two kinds of information and eliminate some possible letters in the word condition in a way that would not be possible in the letter condition. For example, if the subject sees a very curved letter at the beginning of a word whose last three letters are UIT, he or she would be able to eliminate O as a possibility for the initial letter and might decide it was Q. However, the same information in a single-letter condition, that the letter was very curvy, would leave both O and Q as viable candidates.

The Thompson and Massaro hypothesis makes the crucial assumption that visual information is not used in deciding between the forced-choice alternatives but rather information coming from a preliminary identification effort. If this were true, then it should make little difference overall whether the alternatives are visually similar. In our example here, it should not matter whether the two choices given the subject are Q and O or Q and X. This was in fact the result of the Thompson-Massaro study and other experiments that have made this comparison. But of course this explanation requires that subjects know an item is indeed a word, otherwise, the educated guessing mechanism couldn't work. The data necessary to resolve this controversy do not yet exist.

The controversy on wordness effects whether words are better than legal nonwords is a fascinating part of experimental psychology and I am tempted to devote several pages to it. But frankly, I think that this research is not a part of the *psychology of reading*, at least not yet. For up-to-date and excellent review chapters on these matters, see Smith and Kleiman (1979), Baron (1978), and Allport (1979).

CHAPTER 6

The Word in Context

Recall the second question with which we began Chapter 5: "Why is the word BURGUNDY understood more rapidly when we are reading about France or about wine than when we are reading about kangaroos?" This was, of course, a leading question, a question whose phrasing itself sneaks in a claim. But the fact is, words *are* easier to perceive in a meaningful context than "out of the blue." Any theory of reading that stopped at the point we have reached now—a partial theory of how individual words are perceived—would be missing an enormous part of the point of reading. Words are very seldom perceived in isolation but occur instead in their natural habitat, in meaningful sentences and phrases.

There is a popular distinction, these days, between two types of information processing in perception—bottom-up and top-down. For example: If you pick up a piece of paper with writing on it, from the ground, you might be faced with the following printed words: "Fourscore and seven years . . ." and then a word badly smudged with mud. Now there are two kinds of information that might be helpful in perceiving that last remaining word. There is first of all the kind of information we have been talking about so far in this book. The word AGO is a highly familiar shape with such features as curviness on the right and center, angularity on the left, short crosspieces on the first two letters, and so on. This type of information, called bottom-up because it starts with the most elementary sensory processes, is obviously sufficient for the perception of the target word if it happens to be printed clearly (which is not the case in our example).

However, consider also that when a person has read the "Fourscore and seven years . . ." he or she is likely to have made contact with a memorized piece of prose, stored somewhere as Lincoln's Gettysburg Address. *Whatever* appears on the page, there is a strong possibility that the next word is going to be AGO. This is a top-down source of information, in the sense that it comes from "higher" mental processes such as memory, reasoning, recognition, and so on. In plain language, bottom-up processing is identifying the item itself whereas top-down processing is figuring out what it is likely to be.

It would be a mistake to approach reading and leave out either the top-down or the bottom-up part of the skill. Just imagine eliminating top-down processing: The reader would be plodding along like a robot, working just as hard on each word, perhaps including THE, as on a list of randomly selected words. Furthermore, it would be hard to account for certain facts without top-down processing, such as the greater speed with which people read connected text than scrambled words, or virtually all of the evidence to be presented below. Equally ridiculous is the idea that one could get along without bottom-up processing. If we paid *no* attention to the print before us, in reading, we would float away from the text on an endless stream of consciousness. The result would be daydreaming and not reading.

Morton's Logogen System

In this section of the chapter, we present one solution to the problem of how top-down and bottom-up processing are blended in reading. This is the logical next step in our progression: We started with elementary pattern recognition, then the perception of unrelated letters, and, most recently, the perception of words. Now we go beyond the individual word to examine how the larger context of a meaningful sentence can affect word perception. The theoretical presentation here is based on two sources, the Pandemonium model, which was introduced in Chapter 3, and John Morton's (1969, 1979) *logogen* model; the term logogen comes from *logos*, for word, and *gen*, for source—it is a model for how words come to be available in information processing.

THREE KINDS OF INPUT. Morton's starting point is the essential similarity between the following three kinds of event: (1) One sees the written word FORK, (2) One hears a voice saying "fork," or (3) One understands the beginning of a sentence "The table was set except they forgot one knife and one. . . ." There is something quite similar about what happens to us in those three cases—the word FORK is somehow *activated*, somehow made available as a response. The word FORK seems to be on the tip of the tongue in each of the three cases. Morton's way of laying out the information processing system is shown in Figure 6.1. The first thing to do with Figure 6.1 is to note its similarities to the familiar Pandemonium model: The demons have not been drawn in here, but they could have been. There are levels of the Figure 6.1 model that correspond more or less exactly to the Feature Demons, Cognitive Demons, and Decision Demons. The heart of the system is at the level of Cognitive Demons, that is, the level at which individual units—letters, words, familiar FBI-like combinations—are each

2 /2936

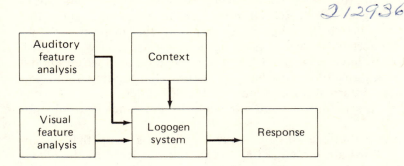

Figure 6.1 *Morton's logogen model of word perception, freely adapted to emphasize similarities to Selfridge's Pandemonium model.*

represented by a logogen. The logogen itself may be thought of as a demon standing there with a list of features.

The main difference is that now each logogen-demon is receiving information from three sources. The same logogen, perhaps the one representing FORK is receptive to visual feature information, to auditory feature information, *and* to information from context suggesting the occurrence of this word. The logogen itself is a "dumb" counter; it does nothing but count how much activation is feeding into it, from whatever source. When that incoming activation reaches a certain threshold, the logogen fires and it makes no difference whether that threshold level was reached by strong contextual information (top-down) or by strong stimulus information (botton-up) or any blended combination of these.

The top-down and bottom-up mechanisms are thus obviously in a coalition with regard to a given logogen unit. Let us say one is reading about (or listening to a speaker tell about) the French wine country, to return to the initial example. By this very circumstance, a large number of logogens are receiving activation, perhaps those corresponding to BURGUNDY, CLARET, BORDEAUX, ST. ESTEPHE, RHONE, TAVEL, APPELATION CONTROLEE, and many dozens more. These logogens have received no real *stimulus information* yet but their corresponding logogens are being aroused as if they had. Then along comes a word beginning BUR with a Y at the end and about eight letters long—and off goes the BURGUNDY logogen. If the context had not so strongly begun the perceptual process for that logogen, more visual information would have been necessary. The word could, after all, have been BURGLARY. This is how the logogen model provides an orderly explanation of how the top-down and bottom-up information are combined. They all result in the same effect, the arousal toward threshold of the same logogen unit.

THE ORGANIZATION OF LOGOGENS. Morton assumed that semantic features are the most important ones in governing the organization of logogens. For example, the written forms "TABLE" and "*table*" must feed into the same unit, even though their shapes are very different. However the two words CHOP (as with

lamb or pork) and CHOP (as with karate or axe) must have different logogen units. Indeed, these are different words that happen
to have the same spelling and the same pronunciation. The two
words WRITE and RIGHT have identical pronunciations but are
obviously different words as well. Thus, some different logogens
will have identical or highly similar feature lists with respect to
either auditory or visual input. This is as it should be: After all,
if someone says IRON to you, out of the blue, you have no way of
knowing whether he or she is thinking of the household chore or
of the metal! The context in which linguistic units are usually
presented tells us which logogen is the speaker's target.

The criterion value for a particular logogen is not always the
same: It is assumed that once a logogen fires, it returns only
slowly to its prior state. Until it has returned to that normal state,
it is easier to fire again than it normally would be. Thus, since
the logogen for BURGUNDY has been used several times in this
chapter, the corresponding logogen will be easier to activate, it
will have a lower threshold, for you now than it does ordinarily.
Furthermore, the model assumes that high-frequency words
(THE) have a uniformly lower threshold (easier to fire) than low-
frequency words (THY).

SOME FACTS THAT FIT THE LOGOGEN MODEL. In some experiments
on word recognition, an item is flashed on the screen briefly and
the subject must say what it was. In such experiments, a word
that has occurred previously in the experimental session is perceived at a lower threshold than a comparable word that has not
been presented yet in the session. That is, the repeated word
does not need to be presented at as high an intensity or for as
long as a completely new word. This result simply corresponds
to the assumption made earlier, that activated logogens return
only gradually to their preactivation threshold levels. However,
according to the hypothesized organization of logogens, the prior
occurrence of the word FRAYS should not affect perception of
the word PHRASE, which turns out to be the case. The lowered
threshold for repeated words fits well with common experience
that many of us have in writing: We use a slightly unusual word
in one sentence and then find ourselves using it once again in

the same paragraph, even though good usage would avoid such repetition.

If no logogen is fired in a presentation, according to Morton's assumptions, the thresholds for all logogens are lowered uniformly. It is as if the Decision Demon hears no particularly loud shouting coming from the Cognitive Demons, and so he turns up his hearing aid! This predicts that when there is actually no stimulus there to be perceived, it should eventually be a high-frequency word that the subject comes up with, rather than a low-frequency word. This follows from the assumption that the former have permanently lower thresholds than the latter. Research like this has been done, under the enchanting title of VIXIERVERSUCH by Goldiamond and Hawkins (1958) and the predicted result does occur. A general form of the same prediction is that the frequency of incorrect responses will be higher than that of correct responses. This is because the chronically lower thresholds of the high-frequency words will sometimes be reached actually sooner than the high threshold of a rare, correct, word. So, for example, we might read ALTERATION for the correct item ALTERCATION. We go months, years even, between encounters with ALTERCATION while ALTERATION is quite common.

Rare words, however, should be more easily perceived if there are no common words with highly similar feature lists. For example the word TERN is just about as rare as the word XEBU; however, since TERN shares feature lists with so many other items (FERN, TORN, TERM, to name a few) these other items will be going off by mistake and slow down correct recognition.

THE COALITION IN ACTION: LOGOGENS GETTING IT FROM BOTH DIRECTIONS. A landmark study in word perception and *context* was published by Tulving and Gold in 1963. They measured the amount of time a stimulus word had to be flashed on the screen before people could identify it. The main variable was how much context people had read just previously to being tested on the target word. For a target word PERFORMER, a long (8-word) contextual lead-in would be "The actress received praise for being an outstanding. . . ." Then there would be a pause and people's

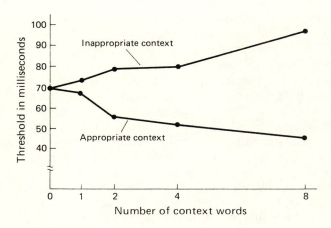

Figure 6.2 *Thresholds in milliseconds for words in the Tulving and Gold (1963) experiment. The length of context was varied, as was its relation to the target word.*

thresholds for perceiving the target would be measured. The length of this contextual word stream was either 0, 1, 2, 4 or 8 words. On the average, the more words provided the more strongly the target would have been implied in a "top-down" manner. There was, however, another set of conditions in which the targets and their various-length context strings were *interchanged*. So the word POTATO might have followed the lead-in for PERFORMER.

The results are shown in Figure 6.2, which gives numbers of milliseconds required for correct perception as a function of the amount of context and its appropriateness to the text. The higher the number the harder it was (the longer it took) to perceive the word. Clearly, the more context was added, the less time was required provided the context was appropriate to the target; the opposite was true of the inappropriate context. This is just the pattern we would expect from the logogen model. If the context feeds activation into the correct logogens, then less stimulus energy from the feature system is going to be necessary for the logogen to reach threshold. If the context is misleading, then all the wrong logogens are getting this extra boost, as if the word BURGLARY really did occur in an article on French wine.

This experiment is an excellent demonstration of the cooperation that exists between relevant context and stimulus features in promoting perception of a correct item. There is obviously a vast and complicated system that supports the top-down component of this system. A sentence on the same subject as the target word, with appropriate syntax and highly associated words in it, is only a mundane illustration of top-down processes. We should also have to say that idiosyncratic "flights of fancy" can also work to reduce bottom-up responsibilities in word perception. A poet may indeed capitalize on unconventional relationships of sounds, concepts and associations to produce his effect. This poses quite a problem for the psychologist: "All of thinking" is really connected to top-down processing in reading. Where can and should we draw the line? Is the psychology of reading no different from the psychology of thinking with a little visual perception thrown in?

Our answer has to be that we can illustrate only how the higher cognitive mechanisms—complicated thought processes— could connect with the more strictly visual aspects of reading. The connection is definitely a part of the psychology of reading; however, the content of the higher thought processes themselves must be left to investigators and scholars with a different agenda. Yet, in Chapter 7, we introduce a few ideas on the comprehension process—not because we can offer anything like a balanced survey of that area (any more than Chapter 3 offered a balanced survey of pattern recognition) but so that the reader will get at least some idea of the normal end goal of perceiving written language and how it could work.

AN INTEGRATIVE MODEL AND THE IDEA OF AUTOMATICITY

In this chapter so far, we have made several assertions about how various mental machinery fits together. It is time to make these assertions explicit in a descriptive model. As with earlier models presented in this book, this one should not be taken too seriously: It is a way of organizing our knowledge and a way of thinking analytically about the things that might be going on in reading. It is not a hypothetical picture of the layout of part of the brain. But before unveiling any such model, there is one more concept we need—automaticity.

The Idea of Automaticity and Its Role in Reading

THE STROOP EFFECT. One of the most useful results in all of experimental psychology is the interference in color naming first reported by Stroop (1935) and named after him. The Stroop effect is demonstrated by asking people to name the color of ink in which words are written. In the experimental condition, these words are themselves the names of colors, incongruously colored; so the word BLUE might be written in green ink, and so on. In the control condition, the words printed in colored ink are either unrelated to the color names or are just series of X's (XXXXX). It is much harder to name the ink color in the experimental than in the control condition. The items are typically presented on a page and one must read down the page as fast as possible. Both reading speed and accuracy are severely impaired when the incongruous color names are used.

The logogen model gives us a framework in which to understand the Stroop effect: The only additional assumption needed is that there is a connection between the logogen for a color (its Cognitive Demon) and the *actual hue for which it stands.* Earlier, we had assumed only that orthographic or sound features fed into the logogen system. But it is reasonable that the actual color red might also have some direct access to the appropriate name as well. Given this extra assumption, it is easy to see that an incongruously colored color name (RED written in green ink) would tend to excite two logogens, one for the spelled-out word (RED) and one for the pigment (GREEN). But only one of these two is correct, the first. To the extent that the second source of activation is exciting its logogen, there will be conflict. Not to harp too persistently on the Pandemonium metaphor, it is as if the Decision Demon were in trouble when there is an incorrect Cognitive Demon shouting as well as the correct one.

The interesting thing about Stroop interference is that we can't help it. One might think that in a well-organized system of processing machinery, it would be possible to arrange for turning off the connections between spelling cues to colors. If we were building a computer to do this task this feature would be easy. If the spelling-to-color connections were deactivated, the system would be left free to pay attention to only the pigments. But the fact is, even substantial practice leaves the interference intact. *The Stroop effect is a perfect example of automatic reading.* The connection between the spellings and the word units are so strong they cannot be ignored.

This way of putting it is a subtle change in emphasis from what we have been dealing with so far in this book. Our concern up to now has been with how in the world the system can struggle to achieve the category state that was intended by the writer. The Pandemonium model is like a boisterous competition in which the correct item wins due to overcoming all the competing category states. The logogen notion adds to the survival value of the "correct" message. It shows how context can come to the rescue to help achieve the end result that fits the intended meaning. But now we are talking in different terms: However we might wish that the word-recognition system would turn itself off, during the Stroop task, it goes right on. Perceptual mechanisms that are only going to hurt performance—that is, systems recognizing words that will conflict with the ink-naming responses—simply can't be turned off. The fact is, an illiterate would do the Stroop task better than a literate.

THE LaBERGE AND SAMUELS (1974) EXPERIMENT. Figure 6.3 shows a hypothetical segment of the information-processing system in which letter features are organized into their letter categories. Four features are shown including two letter units. This figure comes from LaBerge and Samuels (1974) who were especially interested in how *perceptual learning* might affect the visual information processing in reading. This figure is meant to capture the beginning reader in a transitional state: He or she has

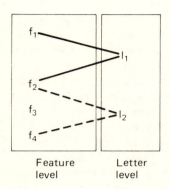

Feature
level

Letter
level

Figure 6.3 *A section of the organization of features into letter concepts according to LaBerge and Samuels (1974). The solid lines represent automatic connections and the dotted lines represent more poorly learned connections.*

learned very well the features that make up one of the letters (i.e., that f1 and f2 together produce l1); however, this beginning reader has only partially mastered the identity of the second letter, l2, as a combination of f2 and f4. This partial learning is represented by dotted lines. The child really does know this letter, but not without paying attention. In this figure, the solid lines represent information so well learned that it is automatic, requires no attention. The dotted lines stand for information that requires deliberate attention. Thus, we might be able to come up with the product ($3 \times 5 = X$) quite without attention but for ($8 \times 12 = X$) we might have to concentrate.

Provided the child is paying attention, either l1 or l2 can be perceived without error. The strong claim of the LaBerge-Samuels approach is, however, that if attention is directed elsewhere, then only l1 can be perceived readily. It is a widely accepted assumption in psychology that attention can be directed at only one thing at a time. We may be able to perform two tasks together, but not if both require sustained attention. The experimental procedure of LaBerge and Samuels was designed to capture this division-of-attention situation experimentally:

There were two experimental tasks, a cover task designed to control attention, on the one hand, and the task we are really interested in, on the other hand. Participants thought their main job was a *successive letter-matching* procedure. They first saw a single letter projected on the screen; the main task was to decide as rapidly as possible whether it matched a second letter that appeared after a short delay. So, if the first letter was *a*, they were to respond "yes" if the second letter were *a* and "no" if it were *m*. On the average, 57% of all trials were "yes" trials, where the second letter matched the first. On 21% of the trials a different letter occurred, requiring a "no" response. On the *remaining* trials (another 21%) something totally different happened: Instead of getting a matching letter, which was by far the most likely outcome, or a single nonmatching letter, the subject saw a pair of forms. In this latter case, the correct response was "yes" if the two forms were identical, otherwise "no." The subject knew this would happen from time to time, and he was warned what to do—disregard the first letter and respond only on the basis of the two forms. This second same-different task, which occurred only 21% of the time, is the one we are interested in. Figure 6.4 shows what the experiment was like.

Put yourself in the subject's shoes, having just seen the first stimulus, which was always a single letter, say *a*. By far the most likely thing that will happen next is another instance of the same letter. On 57% of the trials, it will be the same letter and on 21% it will be a different letter but, in total, the second item will be another single letter on 78% of the trials. We may assume then that attention is directed to that outcome most likely to occur; in simple language, people sit there waiting for the second stimulus, thinking about the letter they saw first because that is overwhelmingly the most likely thing to happen next. But on 21% of the trials, there is a surprise—two letters appear unexpectedly. The assumption behind the research is that these *unexpected* stimuli allow us to measure perception when attention is directed elsewhere.

The unexpected forms were either letters (b,d,p,q) or letterlike forms (,   ,   ,   ). With LaBerge and Samuels, we may call these "old letters" and "new letters," respectively. This was in-

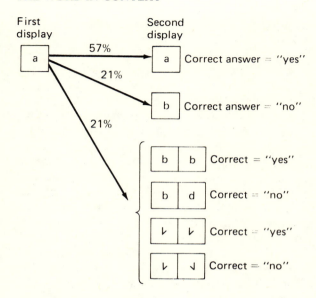

Figure 6.4 *Schematic representation of the LaBerge and Samuels (1974) experiment. The percents refer to the chances of getting a matching or nonmatching single letter as the second stimulus, or a two-item test.*

tended to insure that the people participating in the experiment had mastered some forms automatically, the letters, and that they had not mastered other forms, the "new" nonletters. In short, this opposition of "old" and "new" letters sets up artificially the problem facing the new reader (according to LaBerge and Samuels)—some well-formed connections and other shaky ones.

The hypothesis was that same/different processing of the "old" letter should go on well without attention. Stable categories exist for these letters and, even though their shapes are highly similar and confusing, they should be sorted into their proper categories without any trouble and without even the intervention of attention. The situation on same/different matching on the 21% "surprise" trials would be different for the "new" letters, however. Here, there is no automatic processing that will sort the forms out, at least when the experiment begins; it should require active attention to compare the two.

The results supported these expectations. Initially in practice there was a very large difference in secondary-task matching time between the "old" and "new" letters, with the latter much faster. This difference persisted even through several days of practice, although by the sixth day, the difference was beginning to disappear. It was as if the subjects, who were college students, were learning the new forms in a way that allowed them to be processed automatically almost as rapidly as the familiar letters.

In a control experiment, LaBerge and Samuels showed that when the unfamiliar letters were used as the *primary* task, the items people were expecting to receive, then the unfamiliar shapes were at no disadvantage. This last result is important for the theory: It wasn't just that the new shapes were harder inherently, for in that case they would have been slower even with the help of attention. Instead, the difference between the familiar and unfamiliar letter patterns occurred only when attention was guided in some other direction. It was then that familiarity was so important; however, extensive practice could compensate for the lack of familiarity.

THE LESSON FOR READING INSTRUCTION. The LaBerge and Samuels experiment is one of those that seems farfetched—the vast majority of people will live a lifetime of reading without ever doing anything remotely like the participants in this experiment. However, although this is true, the application of the principle from this experiment is rather direct: Children learning to read are also faced with a divided attention problem, especially at the early stages. They are struggling to learn and remember connections between the visual symbols on the page and the units of their language, what we call the "decoding problem." This decoding problem corresponds to the feature-to-letter associations of Figure 6.3. At the same time, children are expected to pay attention to the meaning of what they are reading. We would be horrified to produce a classroom of zombies, chanting the sounds of the words they are looking at but not understanding a thing.

So there is a divided-attention conflict in early reading *to the* extent that both the decoding and meaning analysis require at-tention. The point of the LaBerge-Samuels argument is that if the decoding half of the conflict could be made truly automatic, then attention could be reserved for where it belongs, in real reading, with the meaning. As long as the channeling of features and letters into their proper logogens is going on without attention, then the child can be directed to read thoughtfully in respect to the meaning.

This suggestion has a paradoxically old-fashioned implication for reading instruction (see also Chapter 10): The first priority ought to be ensuring that the bottom-up decoding mechanisms go on automatically. It might indeed be a mistake to try to set the child out to read meaningfully at first because it requires the attentional conflict of which we have been speaking. How can we make decoding automatic? Well, probably there is no better procedure than good old rote drill!

FINALLY THE MODEL. Figure 6.5 shows a composite drawing of some of the ideas that we have been explaining in this and in the earlier chapters. The portions of the model that come out of the Pandemonium and logogen formulations should be familiar and need not be explained again now. Notice one of the main fea-tures of this model is that there are alternative routes from the visual input to meaning. In some cases, features are connected to letter units, as in the previous figure. However, in other cases, there are direct connections between the level of features and words. This is intended to represent our assumption earlier in this chapter that some frequent words are perceived as units by their shapes, and not mediated by such intervening stages as letter identification. But not all words, of course, get processed this way. An unfamiliar word such as ADIPOSE is likely to get more analytic treatment than the familiar item THE.

A second observation to make about this model is the "pho-nological" stage. Chapter 9 is devoted entirely to the question of how speech mediates reading. For now, we can anticipate the result that in some readers, at least, some words are likely to be "sounded out" on their way to recognition. Other words, per-haps again the more familiar ones, may gain access to their

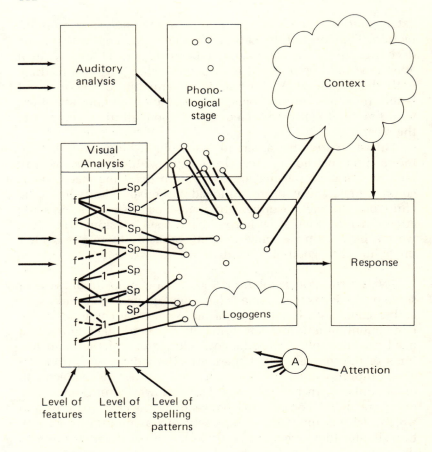

Figure 6.5 *A schematic model of word perception in reading.*

meanings without an intermediate speech-related stage. Both routes are clearly anticipated in the model.

The influence of the LaBerge and Samuels idea is also seen in Figure 6.5. First, there are both dashed and solid lines connecting components of the system; this represents the situation assuned for the new reader, where some but not all of the necessary recognition mechanisms are automatic. Second, there is an attentional source shown in such a way as to suggest it can be trained on only one part of the system at a time. This component is like a flashlight.

Remember not to take this model too seriously. Its main purpose is to show a way of getting all our discussion in this chapter "under one roof" conceptually. In the next chapter, we discuss comprehension processes that are involved in the top-down influences on reading.

REFERENCES AND NOTES

The distinction between top-down and bottom-up processing has taken a curious form, recently, in which some workers have seemed inclined to champion one *at the expense of the other.* This has occurred, for example, among those who study reasoning during comprehension of language. To some of those investigators, the bottom-up perceptual mechanisms seem little more than an annoying necessity. In Chapter 7, in the section "Auding and Reading," we provide some perspective on these attitudes, which make only a minimal distinction between reading and comprehending oral language. For the moment, it is enough to comment that the either-or approach to bottom-up and top-down processing could hardly be more wasteful. Both directions simply have to be occurring in normal reading and the only questions of interest are three: (1) How do the bottom-up systems work? (2) How do the top-down systems work? (3) How do they coordinate? Up to this chapter we have been concentrating on (1). Question (2) is mainly the burden of Chapter 7. This chapter has largely been about (3).

The material on Morton's logogen system here fails to convey the full complexity of that system and, particularly, fails to do justice to the recent modifications in the system (Morton, 1979). Morton now believes that there must be separate input logogen systems for hearing and vision. This is because of evidence that having just heard a word pronounced does not lower its threshold for visual presentation as much as it ought to according to the 1969 theory. The priming effects described here in the section "Evidence that Is Consistent with the Logogen Model" are much stronger in the case where the earlier presentation of an item is in the same modality, visual or auditory, than in the mixed-modality case. The evolution of the logogen idea makes a fascinating story (see Morton, 1979) and I urge you to look at it if you are the least bit interested.

The logogen model is not, however, without competitors: It is obviously a passive model of word perception—information from all sources is automatically fed into the relevant channels and units until threshold is reached, then the unit fires automatically. There are active models that try to account for the same domain of facts. Some of the most successful of these take the general form of analysis-by-synthesis devices: The context is used to form a short list of hypothetical candidates for what the target word could be. These candidates are then actively compared one by one to the available stimulus information until a match occurs or a new set of hypotheses must be generated. At the hands of theorists such as Kenneth Forster (1976) or Curtis Becker (1980) these models deal very well with the facts of word perception—according to them, better even than the logogen model. I have to resist the temptation to delve into this controversy; like so many others, it has little payoff at present for our understanding of reading. The logogen model covers many facts elegantly, it is easily explained, and many people find it has the "ring of truth." These reasons justify using it here.

It is hard to exaggerate the interest now shown by cognitive psychologists in how various forms of information get integrated in reading. During 1981, two prestigious journals had whole issues devoted to information processing in reading (*Quarterly Journal of Experimental Psychology*, November, and *Journal of Experimental Psychology: Human Perception and Performance*, June). While this book was in proof, another collection of invited contributions on the subject of interactive processes in reading appeared (Lesgold & Perfetti, 1981).

I have long thought the Stroop-interference task would be a perfect test of reading level—it really ought to be an index of how words automatically make contact with their meanings. Surely a nonreader would suffer no specific interference in color naming whereas we know that fluent readers do. Furthermore, the advanced reader would be scoring more poorly in the main performance measure than the beginning reader, which would rule out statistical artifacts and confoundings that plague conventional reading tests. Unfortunately, the data are not as clearcut as they might be on this procedure (Golinkoff & Rosinski, 1976; Shadler & Thisson, 1981): Nonreaders do indeed perform without interference from color words but the interference effect seems to reach a maximum at around the fourth grade, diminishing somewhat in later stages. There must be something else going on (strategies, general speedup, or whatever) that counteracts the interference effect in the more advanced readers. Still, applying the Stroop task to developing readers probably is well worth more research.

CHAPTER 7

Comprehension

This book began with the claim that it was a waste of time to worry about the definition of reading. That was an overstatement, although a useful overstatement at that point in the story. Before talking about comprehension—which is, of course, the single main goal of reading—it is important to make a couple of distinctions that are going to sound suspiciously like parts of a definition.

Reading is *connected with* almost all mental activities that there are! (For that reason, it has been called "visually guided thinking.") But we can't have this book be *the psychology of mental activities;* we have to decide, instead, which topics belong centrally to reading and which are important connections to other psychological processes. In basketball, dribbling and shooting are very closely connected activities, often smoothly integrated into an overall manner of play. But this does not mean that dribbling and shooting are the same thing or that they should not be considered separately.

AUDING AND READING

In this section, we borrow some ideas from Thomas Sticht (1978, 1979) concerning the relation between the two major lan-

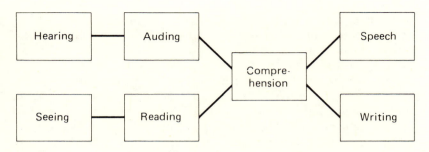

Figure 7.1 *A classification of language functions by the aural-speech and the reading-writing channels. The word "auding" refers to the categorization of language sounds in terms of one's own language system.*

guage systems people have—one concerned with hearing the spoken language and the other concerned with reading the written language.

A MISSING WORD IN OUR LANGUAGE. The two language channels are drawn crudely in Figure 7.1 to emphasize a curiosity about English. We have no word that corresponds to READING for the spoken language channel. The French *entendre* is very close to what we lack in English, for it means both "to hear" and "to understand." There is a separate French verb meaning "to listen" as to music (*écouter*). To see this point clearly, we need to fill in the logic of the whole diagram. One assumption Figure 7.1 makes is that the essential part of comprehension is the same whether language comes in through the ears or through the eyes. So if we read the sentence "Pythagoras was a Greek," we understand it in a way that is very close to the way we understand the spoken version of the same sentence. Furthermore, normal, literate people can respond to that information in either written or spoken form, independently of how they received it.

Now we look at the left side of Figure 7.1. The first stage of the information flow is either HEARING or SEEING. The main point here is that hearing and seeing do not depend on knowing the language in question: A total illiterate can see writing if his or her vision is normal. Similarly, someone with normal auditory function can hear the sounds of a foreign language of which he or she doesn't know a word. These stages are thus precategorical; they come before the system has sorted out sensory information into the *meaningful* units of the language. Our attention now turns to what lies between (1) the HEARING-SEEING stages that are precategorical and (2) the postcategorical comprehension stage. For the visual channel, we have the word READING but nothing corresponds to that word for the auditory channel. (LISTENING is no good—it merely means paying attention to sounds, not getting them transformed into meaningful language categories.)

AUDING is the term Sticht and others have proposed to fill this gap. It is a sort of shorthand term for speech perception, in which the input is understood to become classified with regard to meaning units. Perhaps auding is so thoroughly natural to us, we do not even think of it as a separate stage, distinct from hearing and from understanding. This would account for the lack of a term in the normal English lexicon. It seems to be such a natural and direct transformation from sounds to meaning that we don't even give the intervening process a name.

Auding is not the subject of this book. It is brought in to clarify some logical distinctions—mainly distinctions among the terms AUDING, READING, and COMPREHENSION. In the terminology of Chapter 6, the COMPREHENSION stage provides the top-down influence on reading and auding both. In other words, the expectations set up by receiving the phrase "Fourscore and seven years ago" are the same expectations whichever channel was used to get the phrase in. The bottom-up mechanisms are totally separate, of course.

APPLYING THE AUDING-READING ANALYSIS. Since auding and reading have a common comprehension stage, we can compare the two processes simply by varying the mode of input. Let us take a simple illustration: We give a child of 12 two different vocabulary tests, one with spoken words and the other with printed words, all equated for difficulty. Assuming normal vi-

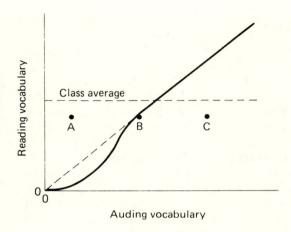

Figure 7.2   *An application of Sticht's (1979) AUDING-READING distinction. An individual's two scores, one for reading vocabulary and one for auding vocabulary are entered as a single point. The heavy line shows normal development and individuals A, B, and C represent individual cases used for illustration.*

sion and hearing, any discrepancy between them would indicate a selective problem in either auding or reading. There might be more complicated measures of auding and reading than simple vocabulary size, but the point can be made without wondering what these measures might be. Figure 7.2 shows a way of comparing auding and reading vocabularies.

As we follow the heavy line in Figure 7.2 from left to right, we can trace the normal course of development. At first, both the auding and reading vocabulary are at zero—perhaps for up to a year in the infant's development. Next comes a progressive growth in auding vocabulary with no corresponding growth in reading vocabulary; children normally have a good command of their language before being exposed to print in any systematic way. At about age 6, there begins a sudden increase in the reading capacity through school. Then, by and large, the reading and auding vocabularies grow hand in hand. Most of us understand roughly the same words in either form.

Consider now three individuals, A, B, and C, whose reading and auding vocabulary sizes are entered on Figure 7.2. They are, let us say, all in the same fifth-grade class. Furthermore, on the "reading test" (which we have simplified to be a reading vocabulary test) they all receive the same score, which is below their class average. Without knowing anything about their auding capacities, we would be tempted to conclude they are all backward in reading; after all, they are the same age and are all behind in their class.

Knowing their auding scores puts their performance in a different light, however. Individual B is just where he "ought to be" in reading, given his performance in auding. That is, he falls on the heavy line representing normal development. This youngster is not *auding* as well as he should be, at his age, nor is he reading as well as he should be. But since his slowness is shared by both the auding and the reading systems, neither one of those components is itself really at fault! It could be that individual B simply doesn't *know* very many words, whether they are spoken or written. This would be a comprehension difficulty. Or, alternatively, this individual might be inattentive or distractable, but in a general way, applying to both modalities.

Individual C is another story. This child has a relatively large auding vocabulary but her reading vocabulary is on a par with A and B's, below normal. Here, we have a true "reading problem." This child shows that her comprehension system is better than normal; she understands many words if they are spoken to her but not if they are written. It is here that we are justified in speaking of a reading problem. Thus, by this logic, the assignment of poor performance to a reading difficulty should be reserved for cases where an appropriate test of auding shows that the difficulty is specific to printed language, not coming from some other part of the system like comprehension, attention, or whatever.

Individual A is included for completeness and is undoubtedly less common, in real life, than B or C. One reason that reading vocabulary might be better than auding vocabulary would be a hearing impairment. A slightly more interesting pattern would be a child who had only recently learned the language and had learned it through written rather than spoken channels. Quite possibly, severe dialect differences could produce cases like Individual A, as when a family moves from the rural Deep South to New England.

Auding, Reading, and Comprehension

We have apparently just defined the title of this chapter out of the book. If the comprehension process is common to reading and auding, why does a chapter about it belong in a book on the psychology of reading?

One reason for not throwing out comprehension from a book on reading is that the lesson of Figure 7.1 is slightly oversimplified: There are at least some different demands on the comprehension process during auding and reading. In language comprehension by ear, in auding, that is, there are *heavier demands on memory* than in language comprehension by reading. It is obvious why this is so, once the point is made. You just can't go back to clear something up when someone is talking to you. But you can look back, obviously, when some point needs clarification and you are holding the text in your hand.

In the section immediately following this, we examine research by Carpenter and Just (1977) on eyemovements in reading, showing just such a process—a process where the comprehension mechanisms coordinate with the visual processes. It may be that interrupting with a rude WHAT? in conversation has a comparable function, but in many or most cases, the ability to look back makes reading easier than auding in terms of comprehension.

Another difference between comprehending the written and spoken languages is in untangling the syntax. In the spoken language, we ordinarily use a rich set of hints about sentence structure called the *prosodic* cues. The prosodic cues include pitch, intonation, stress, and timing and they give us much information about the underlying structure of sentences. Consider the different meanings conveyed by these three sentences:

1. WE rejected the offer.
2. We REJECTED the offer.
3. We rejected the OFFER.

Many questions are identified as such only by a rising intonation on the last word. The written language conveys this prosodic information only partially and only clumsily, through punctuation. It may be that readers reconstruct the prosodic information when they read, through internal speech (see Chapter 9) but, in any case, here is another sense in which the comprehension demands differ for writing and speech.

If one were bent on incorporating this consideration into the design of Figure 7.1, one might do so by drawing auding comprehension and reading comprehension as two separate areas, but with a very heavy overlap.

A second reason for dealing with comprehension here, in spite of our arguments separating it from auding and reading, is that comprehension is an absolutely integral target component of almost all reading. In our basketball analogy, it would be next to impossible to discuss dribbling and then cut off the discussion abruptly from that of shooting, all in the context of a layup shot. Our aim has consistently been to see how reading connects internally and externally to its various constituent parts. The earliest aspects of visual pattern recognition (Chapter 3) surely generalize farther than just to pattern recognition in reading. Yet we discussed these questions in order to see how reading could work, visually. Similarly, we have just finished saying that comprehension in reading is almost surely very similar to comprehension in other modalities. Recall that in Chapter 1 we said that the reader of Braille probably uses much the same comprehension machinery as the reader of print. Yet we continue discussing comprehension in general, anyway, to see reading through to its destination, so to speak.

COMPREHENSION EFFECTS ON EYEMOVEMENTS

In Chapter 2, we laid out some basic information on eyemovements for readers of different skill and also on the theory of how eyemovements are guided. Now we want to show two influences of comprehension activities on eyemovements. In the first of these, we will see that the duration of fixations in fluent reading can be affected by linguistic ambiguity. In the second, we will document the foregoing comment that reading differs from auding in its demands on memory. Specifically, we will see an experimental demonstration of the "looking back" process in reading, allowing the reader to supplement his or her memory with a repeat of earlier information.

Local Control over Fixation Durations

Research by Frazier and Rayner (1982) suggests that eye fixation durations are sensitive to extremely sophisticated comprehension processes. Recall that Rayner has a technique for displaying text on a TV screen and automatically recording exactly where the eye is fixated at any moment. This allows measurement of how long a person looks at any particular word, for example.

Now consider the sentence: "While she was sewing the sleeve fell off her lap." This is called a *garden-path* sentence because, as it is pronounced by a talker, it requires a reinterpretation in midstream. At first, it is clearly implied that the subject of the sentence was sewing a sleeve. But then comes the word FELL. This word in this position would be nonsensical if indeed the person were sewing a sleeve. Instead, we are forced to conclude that the subject of the sentence might very well have been sewing something else when the sleeve fell off her lap. Specifically, the words "While she was sewing . . ." now have to be interpreted as a prepositional phrase. It is called a garden-path construction because the first portion of the sentence, up to the word SLEEVE, is misleading with respect to what has to be the final interpretation of the whole sentence.

Frazier and Rayner found that people look longer at the word FELL in such a sentence than in a control sentence where there is no garden-path construction ("While she was sewing the sleeve it fell off her lap."). Now we know from Chapter 2 that the average fixation for normal readers is about a quarter second, or 250 milliseconds. In order for people to extend that duration in response to the grammatical problems raised by the word FELL, a lot of very high-level analysis must already have occurred within that brief period. That is, during the time the eyes were resting on the word FELL, people in this experiment must have *understood it* and understood it to the point that they realized it didn't fit with their tentative interpretation of the earlier part of the sentence. If the comprehension process lagged far behind the location of the eyes, then by the time the "alarm signal" sounded in response to the word FELL, the visual system would already have passed on to a new location.

Carpenter and Daneman (1981) have made a similar observation for materials like the passage printed below:

> The young man turned his back on the rock concert stage and looked across the resort lake. Tomorrow was the annual one-day fishing contest and fishermen would invade the place. Some of the best bass guitarists in the county would come to this spot . . .

The garden-path element in this passage is found in the word *bass,* which is strongly biased by the context coming just before it to mean a kind of fish. Of course, the word *guitarist* then immediately shows that the "fish" interpretation of *bass* had been a garden-path setup. The only meaning allowed by the word *guitarist* is the kind of *bass* that means low in the musical scale.

Carpenter and Daneman showed that people show normal fixations up through the word *bass* but then pause for considerably longer on the key word *guitarist.* Typically, they then regressed back to the ambiguous word *bass.* In other words, the process of looking back was successfully brought under experimental control through the garden-path construction. In this study, the subjects were reading aloud. This made it possible to determine which interpretation of the ambiguous item was used (because the two meanings of words like *bass* have different pronunciations). The results showed that the first time through, *bass* was pronounced to rhyme with *pass* and the second time, to rhyme with *face.* Thus, this research shows, like Frazier and Rayner's, that fixation durations are affected by issues of semantic interpretation and ambiguity. It also shows that such a "crisis" in comprehension can actually cause regressive saccades.

THE COGNITIVE LAG HYPOTHESIS AND WHY IT IS WRONG. The main point of the Frazier-Rayner and Carpenter-Daneman studies is that very fancy linguistic analysis happens very fast in reading. By very fancy, we mean the detection of semantic anomaly—the detection of a crisis in meaning caused by the garden-path situation. By very fast, we mean within a quarter second or so.

Until quite recently, many experts had the attitude that comprehension occurred at a considerable delay relative to visual processing. This Cognitive Lag hypothesis makes excellent sense, for example, in understanding the relation between reading and speech (see Chapter 9): We have seen that, in reading aloud, the voice lags behind the eye by several words. One might have supposed that understanding depended on contacting the spoken language and that the delay of the voice behind the eyes measured that lag. It is well known that grammatical forms sometimes, as in this very sentence you are now reading, involve delaying the interpretation of some words pending a digressive interruption (sometimes . . . involve). For this reason, it would be useful to have the interpretation or comprehension process delayed relative to the initial pickup of information in the visual system.

What these two experiments have shown is that this plausible theory is wrong—the comprehension system works fast enough to detect high-level problems all within the 250-millisecond fixation and to extend the duration of the fixation to make things right. We cannot minimize any longer the role of eye fixations in comprehension. The fixation is not just a time when visual information is scooped up and placed in the icon to await processing later by higher levels of the system. Instead, the quarter-second fixation on a word contains at least preliminary analysis at high levels of understanding.

Comprehension Effects on Visual Processing

Garden-path constructions are somewhat artificial. What evidence is there that the visual system is sensitive to meaning in more normal language passages? Carpenter and Just (1977) have been investigating other cases where relatively high-level comprehension processes affect the "behavior of the eyes" in reading.

Carpenter and Just measured, as before, how long the readers' eyes remained fixed on sentences and words within sentences as a function of linguistic structure. In one set of experiments, they looked at the problem of *pronominal reference*—that is, the problem of knowing to whom or to what a pronoun refers. The basic idea is to demonstrate that when a pronoun reference is ambiguous, the eye will go looking for the noun to which the pronoun should be assigned. There is no problem, for example, in the sentence WHEN JOHN SAW MARY, HE WAS DISTRESSED. However, there is an ambiguity in the sentence WHEN JOHN SAW CLYDE, HE WAS DISTRESSED. The possibility being investigates in this research of Carpenter and Just is that, in the latter case, people's eyes will scan back looking at JOHN and CLYDE to find the proper referent. (Of course, in this example, there is no correct answer; it is inherently ambiguous.)

Carpenter and Just, to their credit, used entire paragraphs in their research. Consider the following list of sentences forming a paragraph:

1. The guard mocked one of the prisoners in the shop.
2. The one who [sic] the guard mocked was the arsonist.
3. He had been at the prison for only one week.
4. It was the warden who never went to the shop.
5. He was busy with other activities.

The question is how we assign meaning to the first word in sentence 3. The hypothesis under test was much more sophisticated than in our simple example above. Carpenter and Just suggest the notion of a *discourse pointer*, a sort of figure-ground relationship in ongoing reading. As the person finishes with sentence 2, the ARSONIST is supposed to be in the foreground—it is the last word in the sentence and it is also in some sense the word that the whole sentence structure emphasizes. Carpenter and Just supposed that if the discourse pointer is stuck on AR-SONIST, when the subject sees HE at the beginning of sentence 3, the subject will assign the pronoun to the ARSONIST, and not to the guard. If this were the case, one might expect people to look at ARSONIST and ONE OF THE PRISONERS but not at THE

GUARD. In other words, the eyes should go back to the potential referents that are implied by the paragraph structure.

In a second condition, people saw exactly the same five sentences but their order was changed by exchanging numbers 2 and 3. Now, when the person reads HE at the beginning of sentence 3 (which is occurring second in the paragraph) it could refer either to THE GUARD or to ONE OF THE PRISONERS. The subject of sentence 1 was THE GUARD but on the other hand, ONE OF THE PRISONERS is the more recent noun phrase. Each of these alone would draw the eyes but together they might cancel out.

The measure in this experiment was where the eyes were directed when they came to the critical pronoun HE in sentence 3. Let us consider only cases where the eyes were directed to one of the words in sentence 1, which was the same for both groups. When the sentences came in the order listed above, where HE is likely, because of foregrounding, to refer to THE ARSONIST but not to THE GUARD, people were over twice as likely to look back at the former than the latter. However, when sentences 2 and 3 were reversed, there was a tendency to look at THE GUARD more frequently than at THE ARSONIST.

In the condition where sentence 3 comes before sentence 2, in other words, there is more ambiguity in pronominal reference—it could be either of the two sentence-1 nouns that is the target of HE. And in this condition, people divide their looking back fairly evenly, with some preference for the noun in the last position. However, when the paragraph structure implies that the ARSONIST is in the foreground—when people are likely to be thinking about the ARSONIST just before looking at the critical pronoun—they show the opposite result and direct their gaze at the ARSONIST.

KINTSCH'S PROPOSITIONAL THEORY OF READING COMPREHENSION

The ideas presented so far in this chapter on comprehension have been set in the context of small linguistic fragments—individual sentences or groups of simple sentences. The logic of the first part of this book requires something more ambitious than that: Recall, we started with pattern recognition in Chapter 3 and then advanced to individual letters in Chapter 4, individual words in Chapter 5, words in context in Chapter 6, and, just now, comprehension processes that are engaged by coherent text. It is time to face the organization of sentences and even longer texts in comprehension.

But opening a topic of this magnitude amounts to opening a Pandora's Box of new theory, data, and conjecture. Because our coverage has to be limited in order to keep this book in proportion as a text on *reading*, we discuss mainly one contribution. As so often before, the emphasis will be on showing how one possibility could actually work rather than on mentioning all possible approaches in too little detail to understand any one of them reasonably well.

The research of Walter Kintsch at the University of Colorado treats the comprehension process in a way that deliberately relates to reading. Much of his theory is surely applicable to the comprehension of the spoken language as well as the written language; however, Kintsch has focused on reading experiments. There are several distinct parts to Kintsch's argument: First, he is concerned to develop a form of memory representation *that could be used to store meaning.* His solution is a so-called propositional representation. Given that this representation is the goal of reading—a form of representation that holds the meaning—Kintsch is concerned to show that the difficulty of reading is related to the complexity of the propositional representation that the text stands for. Once the underlying propositions are achieved, however, he argues that it makes little difference what the actual sentences originally were, even whether the propositions were stated explicitly or implicitly.

To get at least some of the flavor of Kintsch's system, we look at these issues in turn—the nature of a propositional representation for meaning, the dependence of reading time on propositional complexity, and the indifference of the eventual comprehension process to how the information was originally presented.

A Propositional System for Carrying Meaning

According to Kintsch, all our personal knowledge can be identified as either (1) abstract concepts, which have no particular correspondence to words, or (2) word concepts, which do, of course. The word concepts themselves define our lexicon (mental dictionary) and they may be combined into propositions. The abstract concepts—the ones that do not match words—are interesting and important. Our understanding of mathematical principles and of certain visual knowledge (the way a Teddy Bear looks) are highly likely to be organized apart from words. However, Kintsch proposes to focus attention on verbal knowledge and propositions. For one thing, these are most likely to be the type of comprehension that results from reading, ordinarily.

The distinction that is important in understanding Kintsch's use of propositions is between the *text* and the *propositions on which the text is based*. This distinction is not logically necessary: There could be a theory, for example, that says knowledge is stored in the form of sentences, the same sentences that had presented the information in the first place. Thus, the sentence "Mary did not wash the coffee cup" would be represented in the mind more or less in just that format. But this would be an inefficient system. Consider the sentence "The coffee cup was not washed by Mary." It seems wasteful to require a totally different meaning representation for these two sentences that really seem to mean about the same thing. Essentially all theorists who worry about these problems have reached the conclusion that at least some abstraction in the representation of meaning is necessary. Kintsch suggests that these two sentences about Mary be mapped onto the same propositional representation—(NOT, X) & ((WASH, MARY, CUP) = X). Now we back up to where these representations come from.

HOW PROPOSITIONS STAND FOR TEXT. There is a persistent belief among many psycholinguists that the meaning of a sentence is more centrally attached to the verb component of the sentence than to any other part. Thus, if we distinguish the subject and predicate of a sentence, it is the latter that cues the meaning best.

In Kintsch's system for representing meaning by propositions, this assumption is included by the fact that the predicate comes first in the proposition. Thus the sentence "Norman built a boat" would correspond to a proposition (BUILT, NORMAN, BOAT); the predicate BUILT forms the first part of the proposition and there are two *arguments* that follow.

A proposition consists of a predicate and one or more arguments. The sentence "Jason conspires" would be written (CONSPIRES, JASON) and the sentence "A vulture is a bird" would be (BIRD, VULTURE). Notice in the second example that the predicate need not be the same as just the verb itself; the predicate is what the sentence expresses about the subject. The arguments include the subject of the sentence and also any other parts of it that are not predicates. The number of arguments depend somewhat on the type of verb used in the predicate. The sentence "Marcia opened the wine with a corkscrew" would get the propositional representation (OPENED, MARCIA, WINE, CORKSCREW), for example. A full discussion of this dependence of the number of arguments on the type of verb takes us into "Case Grammars" in linguistics, which is too far to digress; perhaps it is obvious that verbs like KILL and UNLOCK more or less require an object, at least, as well as a subject, whereas other verbs, like DIED and SLEPT do not.

A sentence from a text may require several propositions to represent its meaning. For example, one of the sentences discussed by Kintsch is "The snow melts slowly" and it receives the representation (MELT, SNOW) & (MELT, SLOWLY). There are really two assertions in this sentence, that the snow melts and that it does so slowly. It is not that a writer or speaker is obligated to say how the snow melted (rapidly or slowly); this is just another idea conveyed by the sentence. But there is a sort of obligation with a verb like UNCORKED. You just have to say what was uncorked; it is no afterthought or separate idea at all—you can't say "Harvey uncorked" and let it go at that!

EMBEDDING AND NEGATION. The main point of this section is that Kintsch's propositional system has sufficient power to represent the meanings that are conveyed in text, that is, in sentences we might read. Consider the sentence "If Carolyn betrays Paul, she will be foolish." This really represents three ideas—the betrayal part, the foolishness part, and the contingency between them (i.e., if the former, then the latter). The propositional representation of this sentence would be as follows: (IF, X, Y) & ((BETRAY, CAROLYN, PAUL) = X) & ((FOOL, MARY) = Y). This shows how propositions can be embedded in one another. The first proposition expresses a relationship between two other propositions; it is not a relationship between verbal concepts themselves, as the previous examples have been. Without going into more detail, we can see here how the propositional form of memory representation gains considerable power by being able to use embedded propositions.

The same power to represent subtle shades of meaning is contained in the representation of negation in Kintsch's model. The main idea is that a negation is asserting something about a proposition, essentially a predicate with respect to the proposition that is the subject. So if we say "The cat is not thirsty" we are, according to this idea, saying "The sentence 'The cat is not thirsty' is not true." Thus the propositional representation would be (NOT(THIRSTY, CAT)).

Very subtle shades of meaning in negation can be expressed differently in this system. Consider the two sentences "The baby didn't spill the milk" and "It was not the baby who spilled the milk." One might expect these to be so close that the two meanings would show up the same in a propositional representation. However, study the following two expressions and you will see this is not the case: (NOT(SPILL, BABY, MILK)) versus (NOT(SPILL, BABY, MILK)) & (SPILL($, MILK)), where the symbol "$" stands for "somebody." It is understood, in the second but not the first sentence, that the milk was indeed spilled but the baby was cleared of the crime; in the first sentence there is no evidence that milk was spilled in the first place.

PROPOSITIONS AND THE MACROSTRUCTURE OF A TEXT. Kintsch's theory is meant to include written language in packages larger than the single sentence. He refers to a Text Base as an ordered list of propositions that could be expressed many different ways in actual sentences. Here is an example from Kintsch (1977):

(LOVE, GREEKS, ART) & (BEAUTIFUL, ART) & (WHEN, (CONQUER, ROMANS, GREEKS), (COPY, ROMANS, GREEKS)) . . .

This set of propositions could serve as the text base for either of the following miniparagraphs:

The Greeks loved beautiful art. When the Romans con-quered the Greeks, they copied them.

Beautiful art was loved by the Greeks. The Romans copied the Greeks when they conquered them.

If we started with a longer list of propositions, of course, there would be a larger set of optional variations with which we could represent the text base in real sentences. Kintsch does not pro-vide rules for how we can go between the underlying text base and the actual English sentences they represent. These issues raise the matters of *parsing* (going from the surface sentences to the underlying meaning) and *grammar* (going from the meaning to the surface sentences), respectively. Instead, Kintsch's pur-pose is to show that his propositional system is capable of repre-senting the meaning of observed language.

The propositions in a text base are not equally important to the overall meaning of the text. For example, the fact that the art was beautiful, in the foregoing segment, is not as important as that the Greeks loved art. These relationships among proposi-tions are represented by Kintsch's assumptions on the *macro-structure of a text*. He says that if we know which proposition is the key one for a particular text base, we can order the other propositions in importance by applying the *repetition rule*.

First, how do we decide which proposition is central? One guide is that in a properly written paragraph, the first sentence is usually written to convey the main point. The repetition rule then assigns to the next level of importance propositions that mention the arguments from the main, or central, proposition. For ex-ample, if (LOVE, GREEKS, ART) is the key proposition, then

The *Greek Art* Paragraph

The Greeks loved beautiful art. When the Romans conquered the Greeks, they copied them, and, thus, learned to create beautiful art. (21 words)

```
1  (LOVE, GREEKS, ART)
2    (BEAUTIFUL, ART)
3  (CONQUER, ROMANS, GREEKS)
4  (COPY, ROMANS, GREEKS)
5    (WHEN, 3, 4)
6    (LEARN, ROMANS, 8)
7    (CONSEQUENCE, 3, 6)
8    (CREATE, ROMANS, 2)
```

Arguments	Argument Count	
	Repetitions	Totals
GREEKS	2	3
ART	1	2
ROMANS	3	4
Propositions appearing as arguments		6
		15

Figure 7.3 *A macrostructure assigning eight propositions to a hierarchy depending on their importance to the text.*

(CONQUER, ROMANS, GREEKS) would be assigned to the next level of importance, because it repeats one of the arguments from the former (i.e., GREEKS). To the next level down the hierarchy would be assigned propositions that repeat arguments of the second level but not of the first level. The proposition expressing that when the Romans conquered the Greeks they copied them is the only third-level proposition in our example here. The whole macrostructure that goes with the propositions we are considering here is shown in Figure 7.3 (taken from Kintsch, 1977). There is evidence that people's recall of propositions in a text is related to their roles in a macrostructure such as this one. Specifically, the "further out" a proposition is on this type of tree, the more poorly it is likely to be retained in memory.

READING COMPREHENSION AND PROPOSITIONAL REPRESENTATIONS. What is the relation between this propositional representation and reading? One aspect of this question is that two texts can stand for the same propositional text base but differ in grammatical complexity. This should affect the time to get from the sentences "down" to the propositional base. However, once this text base has been achieved, retrieval operations on it should not differ according to whether simple or complex texts were presented at the start. In other words, if a simple and a complex paragraph lead to the same propositions, and these propositions are what is remembered, questions based on those propositions should be handled identically later. These ideas were tested with materials like these:

Simple:

The Council of Elders in the land of Syndra meets whenever a stranger arrives. If the Council meets and if the stranger presents the proper gifts to the council, he is not molested by the natives. The explorer Portmanteau came to Syndra without any valuable gifts.

Complex:

The arrival of strangers in the land of Syndra, like the explorer Portmanteau, who did not bring valuable gifts, always resulted in a meeting of the council of elders, which insured that the stranger was not molested by the natives upon receipt of the proper gifts.

In one set of conditions, people studied these paragraphs for as long as they liked, and then were given questions probing for comprehension, such as "Was Portmanteau molested by the natives?" Two results are of interest. The first is that people took reliably longer to read the complex version than to read the simple version (25.8 seconds to 29.2 seconds). This is not a trivial result—notice that there are 46 words in each paragraph. The added grammatical complexity in the second version had a measurable effect on reading speed.

The second result was that time to answer questions based on the text was not different in the two conditions (4.9 seconds for the simple and 4.8 seconds for the complex, both based on correct responses). This means, in accordance with Kintsch's expectation, that the complexity of a text affects the ease with which it is translated into propositional format but, once that format has been reached, the original layout of the information becomes unimportant. A result like this does not *prove* Kintsch's theory, of course, but it is quite consistent with that theory.

In another study (Kintsch & Keenan, 1973), the comparison was between sentences whose surface complexity was not obviously different but whose underlying text bases had different numbers of propositions. Consider the following two passages:

> Romulus, the legendary founder of Rome, took the women of Sabine by force.

> Cleopatra's downfall lay in her foolish trust in the fickle political figures of the Roman world.

These materials are interesting for us not only because their text bases have different numbers of propositions but also because the two macrostructures—binding the propositions together—are differentially complex. These propositions and their interconnections are shown in Figure 7.4.

One major result of tests with a large set of materials like these was that reading time was highly dependent on the number of propositions in a text base. Even though the sentences were all within a few words of each other in length, there was considerable variation in how many propositions they represented. The reading-time results showed that each of these sentences took about 6 seconds to read *plus* almost a second for each proposition in the sentence. Thus a sentence with five propositions would take 6 seconds plus $5 \times 1 = 11$ seconds while a sentence with eight propositions would take $6 + 8 \times 1 = 14$ seconds. Of course, that assumes people really encode these extra propositions that are presented. The only sure way to show that the propositions were encoded is to ask for recall of the sentences afterward and see whether people were able to recall the information in each proposition. Kintsch and Keenan did this and found that performance was good but not perfect. If we count

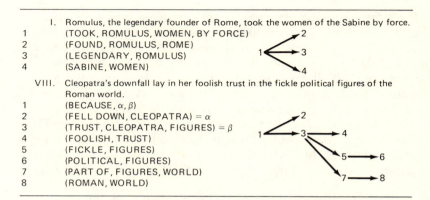

     I. Romulus, the legendary founder of Rome, took the women of the Sabine by force.
1   (TOOK, ROMULUS, WOMEN, BY FORCE)
2   (FOUND, ROMULUS, ROME)
3   (LEGENDARY, ROMULUS)
4   (SABINE, WOMEN)

    VIII. Cleopatra's downfall lay in her foolish trust in the fickle political figures of the Roman world.
1   (BECAUSE, α, β)
2   (FELL DOWN, CLEOPATRA) = α
3   (TRUST, CLEOPATRA, FIGURES) = β
4   (FOOLISH, TRUST)
5   (FICKLE, FIGURES)
6   (POLITICAL, FIGURES)
7   (PART OF, FIGURES, WORLD)
8   (ROMAN, WORLD)

Figure 7.4 *Two sample sentences from Set A (sentences I and VIII), together with the propositional analyses.*

only propositions actually recalled later, and look at reading times as a function of number of propositions, the result is that each new proposition adds about 1.5 seconds to a base reading time of 5.5 seconds.

The dependence of reading times for these materials on number of propositions is important for the concept of *readability*. This measure of the difficulty of a text has long been measured by some combination of sentence length and word frequency. The strong dependence of reading times on number of propositions in the Kintsch and Keenan study suggests that some measure of readability that includes propositional structure would be useful.

It would be a mistake to generalize that people can read forever at a clip of 1.5 seconds per proposition. Kintsch and Keenan also tested paragraphs from 43 to 58 words in length. They found that time per proposition was much slower, on the average, for these long paragraphs than for the sentences; for the paragraphs, the average time required for a proposition *that was recalled* was 4.3 seconds. (We can't estimate how many propositions were understood but then forgotten so this estimate almost surely undersells the efficiency of reading.) There was also evidence that reading gets "bogged down" during the encoding of long paragraphs.

INFERENCES DURING READING. As we all know, reading is not just a matter of transfer of information from the print to the reader's mind, there is also an active contribution from the reader's store of knowledge. We bring our own experience to bear on what is being read by filling gaps, by interpretation, and by extrapolating from what is given in the text. The reader's active contribution to reading is the primary concern of many workers in the field of Artificial Intelligence and Cognitive Science (see Schank & Abelson, 1977). We will review very briefly some work by Kintsch that is related to this problem. It concerns that process of filling in propositions that are necessary for a text base but not necessarily stated explicitly in the test.

Consider the following two texts that could be derived from the same underlying text base:

Explicit

A carelessly discarded burning cigarette started a fire. The fire destroyed many acres of virgin forest.

Implicit

A burning cigarette was carelessly discarded. The fire destroyed many acres of virgin forest.

Both of these two short texts include the two propositions ((DISCARD, CIGARETTE) = X) & (CAUSE, X, FIRE). The second of these is stated explicitly in the first version but not in the second. However, in order to achieve the text base that is intended by the author, it is absolutely necessary to include that proposition, whether it is stated explicitly or not.

There are two measures of interest with these materials. One is the reading time. It might be expected that deriving the crucial proposition through inference might take longer than having it "served on a silver platter" and that the implicit versions would therefore be read more slowly than the explicit versions. The other measure is the time required to answer true-false questions of the sort "THE DISCARDED CIGARETTE CAUSED THE FIRE." If the proposition underlying this statement has become part of the text base, then it should not matter whether it had been stated explicitly or implicitly.

The results of this study—which used a great many more kinds of materials than is even suggested by our example texts— were a surprise. There was no evidence, even with paragraphs of over 100 words, that the implicit versions took longer to read than the explicit versions. Furthermore, there was a significant difference in time to answer questions about the implied propositions: It took longer when these propositions were not stated explicitly than when they were stated explicitly. These results are consistent with the idea that subjects were *not filling in the inferences as they read the passages, but were* instead figuring out the correct answer when the questions were asked. It is as if they were saying to themselves. "Aha . . . it must have been that same discarded cigarette that caused the fire." This process of inference would be occurring at the time of testing and not at the time of comprehending the original paragraph.

However, there is another interpretation possible. It could be that subjects do, after all, tend to make crucial inferences during their original reading of texts and store these inferences in memory. We saw earlier that it is the number of target propositions in a text base that affects reading time, so perhaps it was unrealistic to have expected shorter times for the explicit than for the implicit versions. The question then becomes: What accounts for the faster question answering in the explicit than in the implicit group? One possibility is that people carry two forms of memory for the text—a propositional, abstract, memory structure that would be the same for the two groups and also a verbatim memory for the sentences actually presented. The explicit group would carry a verbatim memory for the test statement (THE DISCARDED CIGARETTE CAUSED THE FIRE) but the implicit group would have had no such corresponding verbatim memory. If the explicit group could have used the verbatim memory *or* the propositional memory, whichever worked faster, then they would have been at an advantage, which is the result obtained.

To test this proposal for why question-answering times were faster in the explicit than the implicit versions, Kintsch imposed a delay between the initial reading of the materials and the test. The idea was that if 15 minutes elapsed between reading and testing, it would be likely that the verbatim memory would decay but that the propositional memory would survive. (This is a common assumption in memory theory, with much evidence to support it.) The same experiment was therefore repeated with such a 15-minute delay and the results confirmed what had been expected—that there was no longer a difference in time to verify true-false statements based on the crucial proposition that was either present or missing in the text. Therefore, it is possible to conclude that, at least under the conditions of this experiment, people do indeed draw inferences that are implied in the text and necessary for a complete text representation. These inferences are made whether or not the proposition is stated explicitly in what the person reads. For a brief period following reading, there is also a verbatim memory for the actual sentences that were read, which may be used in cases where the question being asked taps an explicit statement from the text. However, in the long run, we must depend on a more abstract form of memory for the gist of the text.

Conclusions

In one sense, this is the beginning of the story. Kintsch's work on implicit and explicit statement of propositions in a text shows, in miniature, how the reader participates actively in the comprehension process. This filling in is grossly underestimated by the examples we have been looking at. The more common experience is probably that enormous knowledge structures are called up by what is written on the page, rather than some tiny but crucial detail. That is, the only kind of inference we have dealt with here is *interpolation; extrapolation* may be the more important inferential process.

But our purpose in this chapter has not been to erect an inclusive theory of comprehension. It has been, instead, to show how aspects of the comprehension process link up with aspects of reading behavior. We saw this occurring in the eye-fixation studies of Rayner and of Carpenter and Just. Kintsch's propositional theory has provided a different perspective. It proposes first a way that the sentences on a page could be represented meaningfully in memory—by propositions. Then, through the examination of reading times, and the speed and accuracy of answering questions based on texts, it offers reasonable demonstrations that such a system for storing meaning could work effectively in reading. The likely possibility that a similar mapping of sentences onto meaning units, propositions, occurs in auding should not detract from our need to discover how it operates in reading.

REFERENCES AND NOTES

A full discussion of the Sticht classification in Figure 7.1 would raise questions about intermediate levels of linguistic classification. In particular, one can be exposed to the written form of a foreign language and recognize individual *letters*, or one can hear the familiar spoken elements of his or her own language used in different combinations in a foreign language. In this sense the auditory and visual processes occurring prior to auding and reading are not really precategorical. However, for simplicity, we can define categorization on the basis of meaning units in this discussion.

We said in connection with Figure 7.2 that reading and auding capacity generally grow hand in hand after a child learns to read. This is true on the average for most literate adults but exceptions are interesting. Individuals can deviate "above the line" if their reading vocabularies become larger than their auding vocabularies. This can occur when one gains reading knowledge of a foreign language but little or no command of its phonetics or phonology. Even in one's native language, there are sometimes words one reads fluently but never uses in spoken form and, indeed, cannot correctly produce or understand. There was a time when I thought the word MISLED was the past participle of a nonexistent verb TO MISLE, meaning to throw off the track, and pronounced like THISTLE.

Two important discussions of the comprehension differences between written and spoken language have become available recently. One, by Adams (1980), challenges the conventional notion that reading is grafted on an essentially *mature* language system in the 6-year-old. A contribution by Rubin (1980) contains a highly original classification of the various differences that exist between the spoken and written language channels. There are, according to Rubin, not only differences in the "medium" but also in the "message."

Vast confusion in psychology, education, and in the public press has resulted from overlooking the common-sense distinctions that go with the auding-reading analysis. School systems, for example those in large cities, observe that their adolescents are only semiliterate by standardized reading tests. School systems then check and find that their first and second graders are behind in reading skills. Assuming that the latter causes the former, the schools pour more money into elementary reading skills. This has undoubtedly good consequences but the causal chain may be quite mistaken: It could be poor general language skills or comprehension difficulties that are causing the poor reading both at the early and at the later ages. Children that grow up without hearing a real sentence from either their parents or from their TV are likely to have trouble dealing with language, of any kind, written or spoken. As a society, we might make different decisions about how to cope with the urgent needs of our school-age children if we could be more analytical about where the problem lies.

A fully worked-out theory of reading has recently been published by Just and Carpenter (1980). This theory relies on the assumption that eye fixation times are very heavily determined by "high-level" linguistic factors. This approach is a bold departure from previous attitudes that eye fixations are a rather automatic and uninteresting information-gathering operation on which the higher processes operate. The garden-path demonstrations we looked at in this chapter certainly reinforce the newer

Just and Carpenter approach. However, the latter authors have not yet convincingly shown that there is very much reliable influence of higher-order linguistic factors when word length is partialed out.

The lively new field of cognitive science is intensely concerned with the structure of texts and the effects of this structure on comprehension. This field combines cognitive psychologists, computer scientists interested in artificial intelligence, and linguists, among others, and its workers will surely be frustrated by the coverage of text structure here. I have raised the Kintsch system mainly because it has been related experimentally to "true" reading and not because I think it has more ultimate promise than other approaches. Cognitive scientists will complain that Kintsch's theory depends on word concepts rather than some more abstract representational format (Schank, 1972), for example.

It is also true that Kintsch's theory has little to say about the enormous set of knowledge structures that readers bring with them to their task, the kinds of "world knowledge" that allow even gross stretches of stories and texts to be filled in by the reader without depending on the written text itself. This is the process of *extrapolation* in inference that I have been referring to. These matters are the subject of important discussions in Schank and Abelson's *Scripts, Plans, Goals, and Understanding (1977)*. An up-to-date summary of the script concept and of research done to test it is found in Abelson (1981). The underlying structure of stories is also currently an active research topic, and introductions to this area can be found in the various chapters in a new book by Spiro, Bruce, and Brewer called *Theoretical Issues in Reading Comprehension* (1980).

My favorite summary of this whole area is Part 1 of a book by Sanford and Garrod called *Understanding Written Language* (1981). In these 88 pages, Sanford and Garrod do, for the area of comprehension, what I have tried to do in this book for the reading process prior to comprehension. I strongly recommend the three chapters contained in these pages as a continuation of these five chapters (3 through 7) we have concluded here.

The topic of *readability* is too complex to discuss more fully in this book. The traditional Flesch count (Flesch, 1948; see also Coke, 1974) is a low-level measure that gives negative weight to long words and long sentences. Kintsch's analysis of "idea density," as revealed by propositional structure, is a promising idea that may someday affect the way we measure readability. Recall that in the Kintsch and Keenan (1973) experiment, the number of words varied only slightly and yet there were large differences in reading time associated with propositional length.

CHAPTER 8

Writing and Spelling

Beware: This chapter has nothing to do with penmanship and very little to do with becoming a "good speller." In Chapters 3 through 7, we built a story of what happens in the mind when print strikes the retina of the eye. This chronology has been carried as far as we could carry it in the context of our primary subject. Now we back off and approach the mental operations in reading from another perspective. The new approach complements, in a way, the chronology of Chapters 3 through 7: There, we were interested in the visual and cognitive processing that meets the print on the page. Now we examine print itself.

What is the nature of our writing and where did it come from? These questions lead us first into ancient history but—amazingly soon—these same questions bring us back into psychological issues of the deepest importance. The discussion begins with the question of how writing represents our language. That seems like a foolish question—obviously writing represents words and sentences and meanings. However, there is room for enormous variety in the level of the language at which writing is organized. In fact, there really *is* enormous variety among the languages of the world in respect to how their writing stands for language. And this variety will be our starting point, through a historical and cross-cultural perspective on writing systems.

WHEN AND WHERE WRITING STARTED

Experts say that human language may have had its origins around 1 million years ago. The earliest evidence of visual marks used to record human experience are the cave paintings, which date from only approximately 50,000 years ago. Writing and art really began together with this development. The two have obviously diverged since. The separation of art and writing was clear by around 10,000 years ago. These numbers are, of course, only good as order-of-magnitude estimates. Even if they are grossly mistaken, however, they still demonstrate that writing was invented only a tiny fraction of the way back into our history as a linguistic species.

It is quite probable that writing was invented many times in many different places. However, it "took" on just five occasions, always in societies with stable agriculture.

In Sumeria (modern Iran and Iraq), there was a system of cuneiform writing some time after 4000 B.C. This writing was produced by pressing wedge-shaped instruments into clay and it died out at around the time of Christ. In the Indus Valley, writing appeared around 2500 B.C. and lasted only a few hundred years before disappearing with little trace. (Modern Indian writing is not derived from this ancient source.) A third independent invention of writing occured in the Yucatan Peninsula of Central America, in what is now Mexico and Guatemala. It lasted from about A.D. 1 to 1500, when it was snuffed out abruptly by the Spanish invasion. These three kinds of writing did not survive as living systems, although we have records of what they looked like.

There were two additional inventions of writing and these two did remain alive until modern times. The Egyptian writing system, which appeared around 3500 B.C., led, through a direct but complicated evolutionary process, to our own alphabetic system. Second, the Chinese writing that appeared around 2000 B.C.

is similarly the direct ancestor of the modern Chinese system. Gelb (1963) can be consulted for illustrations of this, and for the fascinating details of these episodes from the dawn of literate civilization. (More references are cited in the References and Notes at the end of this chapter.)

THE VARIETY THAT IS POSSIBLE. Our theoretical interest in the history of writing comes from the fact that writing could represent any of a number of levels of language. The writing system could match up against the articulatory gestures we use to produce the spoken language, for example: A written symbol would stand for the lip closure that occurs in letters such as P and B, another for the nasal sounds M and N. To represent the letter M, one would need both the symbol for nasal production and the symobl for lip closure, because M is produced by closing the two lips and allowing sound to escape through the nasal passage. There is no writing system that really works like this. However, Taylor (1980, 1981) points out that the Korean "Hangul" writing system, which was introduced by a fifteenth-century king and an appointed committee of scholars, has elements of articulatory representation.

Another possibility is to represent the sounds of language directly in the written symbols. It may seem as if this is what we do in our alphabet but it is not. The P in PARTY is actually a different sound than the P in APART. So are the D's in RIDER and DRUMSTICK. On the other hand, the middle letter in the two words RIDER and WRITER are the same, phonetically, yet they are represented with different letters. There are also interesting cases like EXTREME and EXTREMITY, where the second vowel has a consistent spelling but quite a different pronunciation. Clearly then, English orthography does not represent sound in any simple fashion.

Our alphabetic writing is not just an imperfect or careless effort to represent sound, either. English orthography represents language at the level of *systematic phonemes*—the abstract spellings that illuminate meaning roots in words in addition to sound values. Representation at the level of systematic phonemes is one of the main themes of this and the following chapter. It will be explained carefully in due time. For the moment, however, we just observe that English writing is related to the sound of the word being represented, but with compromises. Sometimes the compromises seem to retain the history of the word's meaning, as in the words DEBT and DEBIT: The B is not faithful to the way DEBT is pronounced, but it does reveal its relationship, in meaning, to DEBIT.

Some writing systems represent the language at the level of syllables. A *syllabary* has written symbols that represent the sound of the language, but standing in a one-to-one relation to syllables, not to phonemes or elementary (phonetic) sound units. The Japanese Katakana and Hiragana syllabaries are examples in use today. The efficiency of a syllabary depends, of course, on the number of different syllables there are in the spoken language of a community. It is no accident that Japan should have hit on syllabic writing, for the Japanese language has a very regular CVCVCV . . . (consonant-vowel-consonant . . .) structure. English, on the other hand, has many more syllables than Japanese, due to the large number of permissible consonant clusters. (Consider the word STRENGTHS—one syllable but eight consonants!)

There could be a writing system with units standing for morphemes. Morphemes are elementary units of meaning. In such a system, a word like RECOVER would have two symbols, one for the prefix RE and another for the root COVER. The word KANGAROO would have a single symbol while the word UNREMITTING would have four. There seem to be no strict *morphographic* writing systems although elements of morphography occur as transitional states in the evolution of alphabetic systems, as we will see.

In *logographic* writing systems, the symbols stand in a one-to-one relation to words. The base LOG- refers to WORD, as we observed in analyzing the word *logogen* in an earlier chapter. Chinese writing is our best example of the logographic writing principle (although, of course, any writing system is a mixture of principles and almost never a pure form of just one type). Closer to home, our numerals (1,2, and so on) are logographic writing. The symbol stands for the word and the way the numerals look tells us nothing whatever about the way they are pronounced.

Finally, there could be writing systems that tap the language at even more abstract a level than the word. The written symbols could somehow match up with the ideas that stand behind the verbal expressions. One way to think of this is that words that share a thesaurus classification would be written in a similar way: FIGHT and BATTLE would look similar, as would MUSIC and SONG. There is no writing system like this.

One point of this survey has been, then, to show that writing could correspond to any of numerous level of the language and still "work" in some sense. It is interesting that the writing systems that have been used do not come from the full range of possibilities. The closest to the sound stream one gets (with the possible exception of Korean writing) is our own alphabetic system, and it is by no means phonetic (i.e., representing the sounds as they occur in real speech—remember DEBT and DEBIT). At the other end of the scale, writing systems do not get more abstract than the word level, or logography.

Evolution of Writing

When writing systems evolve, through the centuries and millenia, they do so in only one direction. They progress in the opposite direction to the one we just followed in our survey: Roughly, they go from representing meaning toward representing sound.

Remember that writing begins on the wall of caves, intertwined with artistic representation. The form of this earliest writing is *pictographic and ideographic*. Pictographs simply look like the objects they are designed to name—the word SUN as a small circle with rays radiating out in all directions. Ideographs are streamlined, and therefore more abstract, versions of pictographs. Early and late hieroglyphic writing styles in Egypt show this differentiation between pictography and ideography well. A great many of the logographic symbols in Chinese are ideographic and pictographic.

In some forms of *logography*, the relation between symbols and their corresponding words is no longer apparent, although that relationship can often be traced historically. One important step in evolution of writing is the way in which a logographic system can begin to capitalize on homophones (words that sound alike but mean different things). Consider a logography that had a symbol for the word SUN consisting of a small circle with radiating lines. The language might also have a word meaning male offspring, SON, pronounced identically. The evolutionary step we are talking about here would occur when scribes would start to use the circle-with-radii symbol for SON as well as for SUN. This would complete the destruction of a natural relation between symbols and the way things look; it would make the relation quite arbitrary. But the way things are written would, at the same time, become *less arbitrary* with respect to the sounds of the language. The principle is obvious: There is only an arbitrary relationship between the sounds of words and the meanings they represent. If two words are synonyms, there is no implication that they will sound similar. If two words are homonyms, there is no implication that they will be similar in meaning. A writing system that chooses one of these levels to portray in visual forms must be arbitrary with respect to the other level.

Another landmark in the evolution of writing was to take the sound values of symbols standing for words and to use them as syllable signs. To continue our example with the SUN symbol, we might combine it with another word symbol—standing for DAY—and make a two-symbol sign for SUNDAE. The meanings of the two symbols would be totally arbitrary with respect to an ice cream sundae but not arbitrary with respect to the sound of that word. This step would lead us into a *syllabary*, or syllabographic writing.

From syllabaries, writing systems evolve toward alphabetic representation. It may be a little grandiose to generalize this way, however, because that step (syllabary to alphabet) happened only once, really, in the Near East in the last millenium B.C. It was from this development that our own writing came.

(It is true that the modern Chinese are introducing phonetic principles of writing these days but we can hardly count this as an independent evolutionary development. It is, to linguistic evolution, like genetic engineering is to biological evolution.)

Our English orthography seems to be changing in a way that will better represent the sounds of our language and perhaps more poorly represent underlying morphology (roots of meaning). The reforms of the *Chicago Tribune* some years ago, such as TELEGRAF, FOTOGRAF, and THRU, may not have caught on (yet), but subtler changes, like AWAY for AWEIGH in ANCHORS AWEIGH, serve the same function. The main point is that when change occurs, it always has occurred in the direction that carries writing away from the representation of meanings and toward the representation of sounds. We now give some examples of this change.

EXAMPLES OF DIVERSITY AND CHANGE IN WRITING

The two main points so far have been that writing systems have surprising diversity in how they match up with the spoken language and that the flow of change is always in the direction of tracking sound and away from meaning. We now turn to some illustrations of these points in ancient writing systems.

THE SUMERIAN SYSTEM. Figure 8.1 shows how the Sumerian cuneiform writing evolved from pictographic symbols. This writing system (the one on the right of Figure 8.1) was a syllabary by around 3000 B.C. It included 600 signs for words and about 150 signs that stood for syllables. As neighboring societies adopted and borrowed this cuneiform writing system, they purified it as a syllabary. This makes good sense, because a different language community would not be expected to retain word-symbol associations for words they didn't use or understand.

Some scholars believe that the Ras Shamra syllabary, shown in Figure 8.2, was such a derivation from Sumerian cuneiform writing. In this system, each of the 30 signs stood for a different consonant sound, with the understanding that any vowel could follow. Thus, the symbol for the syllables GOO, GEE,and GAA would all have been the simple down arrow shown in the fifth position of Figure 8.2. (Modern Hebrew is a writing system that uses this convention.) For this reason, the Ras Shamra system has been called an alphabet, but its independence from the Semitic alphabets has been questioned and the point is controversial. If the Ras Shamra signs were used as an alphabet, we have

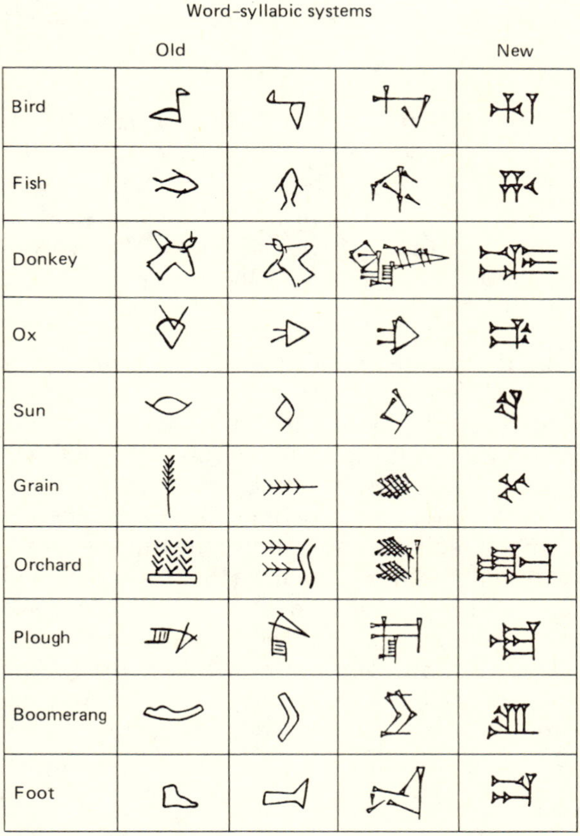

Word–syllabic systems

	Old			New
Bird				
Fish				
Donkey				
Ox				
Sun				
Grain				
Orchard				
Plough				
Boomerang				
Foot				

Figure 8.1. Pictorial origins of ten cuneiform signs. (Reprinted from A Study of Writing, second edition, by I. J. Gelb by permission of the University of Chicago Press. All rights reserved. Protected by the International Copyright Union. Published 1952.)

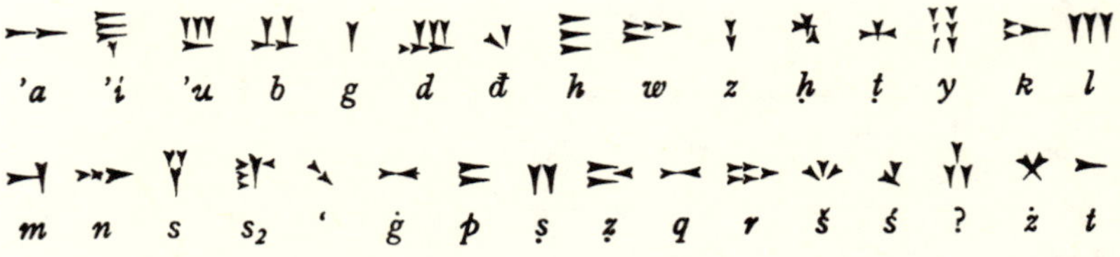

Figure 8.2. The Ras Shamra alphabet. (Reprinted from A Study of Writing, second edition, by I. J. Gelb by permission of the University of Chicago Press. All rights reserved. Protected by the International Copyright Union. Published 1952.)

in figures 8.1 and 8.2 the whole evolutionary story, from pictographic signs to a phonographic alphabet.

The use of the word *evolution* in this chapter is no shallow metaphor: The Darwinian associations in this word—that the fittest survive a process of natural selection and go on to produce the next generation—is fully intended. Nowhere is this truer than with cuneiform writing, which died out around the time of Caesar mainly because it was so much work! To make the marks, you had to use a wedge-shaped stylus pressed into clay. Although the pace of life was slow then compared to ours (surely there were no court stenographers), still, even to draw up a contract for selling some grain or cattle would have been a ponderously slow affair. Writing systems that permitted strokes to be scraped on some porous surface would have seemed irresistible in their efficiency. And, as we will see, such systems are the ones that have survived.

EGYPTIAN WRITING. A major event in intellectual history was the discovery in 1822 of the Rosetta Stone by the Frenchman Champollion. This tablet contained sufficient information to allow decipherment of Egyptian hieroglyphics. Among other things, it showed Greek equivalents for many hieroglyphic symbols. Figure 8.3 shows several of these symbols and their evolution across thousands of years of ancient history. (Notice how slowly some of these changes occurred.) It is evident that the signs are gradually losing their pictorial value, for one thing. The writing is specialized, furthermore, into the hieratic (religious) and demotic (civil) scripts in the later phases.

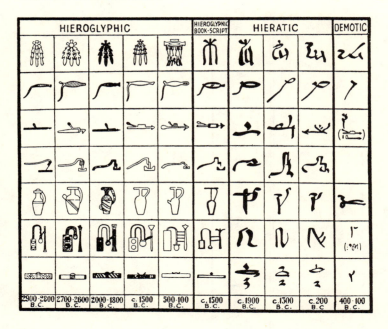

Figure 8.3. *Formal development of some of the signs in the hiero-glyphic, hieratic, and demotic. (Reprinted from A Study of Writing, second edition, by I. J. Gelb by permission of the University of Chicago Press. All rights reserved. Protected by the International Copyright Union. Published 1952.)*

Figure 8.4 shows the syllabary into which Egyptian writing evolved. These signs, like those of the Ras Shamra syllabary, specified the consonant value and it was understood that any vowel would be possible (as if we wrote GEESE and GOOSE the same). This syllabary became widely used in the Near East as a phonographic way of writing. People combined the *idea* of recording the sounds of language in signs with their own spoken language; the Egyptian syllabary was accepted and handy for this purpose. It mattered little that the vowel values were not represented: Our own orthography has quite a few examples of ambiguities in pronunciation that have to be resolved by context. The

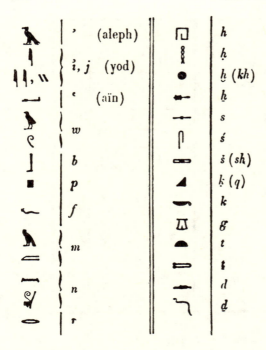

Figure 8.4. *Egyptian uniconsonantal syllabary. (Reprinted from A Study of Writing, second edition, by I. J. Gelb by permission of the University of Chicago Press. All rights reserved. Protected by the International Copyright Union. Published 1952.)*

word HOUSE is pronounced differently, for example, in the following two sentences:

> I hope we shall be able to house the refugees.
> I hope the refugees will be able to find a house.

The point is that we ourselves get along quite well with ambiguity in our spelling about how vowels are to be pronounced.

A large number of alphabet systems appeared in the Sinai Peninsula around 1000 B.C. Some of them are shown in Figure 8.5 along with their correspondence to Greek and Latin alphabets from later on.

West Semitic											Greek		Latin
Ahīrām	Ruweiseh	Azarbaʿal	Yehīmilk	Abībaʿal	Elībaʿal	Šapatbaʿal	Mešaʿ	Zincirli	Cyprus	Sardinia	Old	Late	Latin
K	K	✶	K,✶	K	✶	✶	✶	✶	✶	✶	⊅, A	A	A
৭	৭	◁	৭,৭	৭	৭	৭	৭	৭	৭	৭	⊿, ৪	B	B
⌐			∧	∧	⌐	∧∧	⌐	⌐	⌐	⌐	⌐, ∧	Γ	Γ (L ε replacing z)
◿	◁		◿		△	△	◁	◮	△,△	△	△	△	D
⅄			⅄			∃	∃	⅄	∃	∃,৸	E	E
Y		Y	Y		Y	Y	Y	৸	৸	৸	⅂, Y, V	(Y at end)	F (u v v, y at end)
I		I	I		I	I	エ	I	I		I	Z	(Z at end)
⋈	8	8	⋈,8		8	8	⋈	⋈		8	8	H	H
⊕					⊖	⊗	⊕			⊖	⊗, ⊕	⊙	
৭	z	z	ʓ		z	৲	⋋	৲	৲	৲	⟨, ⟨	I	I
✦	✦	✦	✦	✦	✦	✦	✶	メ	メ	৸	⟩, ৸	K	K
⌇		⌇	⌇	⌇	⌇	⌇	⌇	⌇	⌇	⌇	⌐, ⌇	Λ	L
ৡ		ৡ	ৡ	ৡ	ৡ	৴	৸	৴	ৡ	৸	⌐⌐	M	M
৸	৴	৴	৴		৴	৴	৸	৸	৸	৸	৸	N	N
⊤		⊤				⊤	⊤				⊥	⊞	(X at end)
o	o	o	o	o	o	o	o	o	◌	o	o	O	O
⌐		7:৴)			⌐	⟩	⌐	⌐	⌐	⌐	⌐, ⌐	π	P
	h		ᴕ	h			⊦	ᴦ		h	⋈, ⋈	(M)	
			φ			৭	φ	φ	φ		φ, ৭	(৭)	Q
◁			◁	◁	৭	◁	◁	◁	◁	◁	◁, P	P	R
w		w	w		w	w	w	w	w	w	⟨, ⟨, ⟨	Σ	S
+,X		+	x		✦	+	X	✦	✦	X	T	T	T
											Υ,Φ,Χ,Ψ,Ω	U.V.X,Y,Z

Figure 8.5. *Comparative chart of Greek and West Semitic writings.* (Reprinted from *A Study of Writing, second edition,* by I. J. Gelb by permission of the University of Chicago Press. All rights reserved. Protected by the International Copyright Union. Published 1952.)

THE INVENTION OF VOWELS. The Semitic alphabets shown in Figure 8.5 had no vowels represented. The events by which signs for vowels came into usage can now be reconstructed and it completes our historical survey. The Phoenicians brought their current alphabet with them to Greece around 1000 B.C. They, and the other Semitic peoples, made many distinctions among glottal and laryngeal sounds that the Greeks did not make. (The glottal stop occurs when we say the word ONLY at the beginning of a sentence, or in the Brooklyn dialect pronunciation of BOTTLE [ba'l]. The French r uses a laryngeal fricative, as does modern Arabic.) The Semitic languages had different symbols for these various glottal and laryngeal consonants. For example, the letter O stood for the glottal stop ['o]. Alternatively it stood, of course, for ['i, 'e, 'a,] and so on, because the vowels were unspecified.

The Greeks didn't use and couldn't hear the differences among these different glottal and laryngeal sounds. They all sounded the same to the Greeks, just as [r] and [l] sound the same to modern Japanese, who do not use that distinction. So the Greeks had the insight of using these "extra" letters to represent the vowel sounds. And one by one the symbols for these foreign and unintelligible consonant phonetic segments were converted to represent vowel sounds. The present-day A, E, I, and O, at least, can be traced to the Semitic glottals and laryngeal sounds that the Greeks found so useless.

COMMENT. This has been a highly ethnocentric survey of writing. It has also been a little smug in suggesting that the evolutionary process comes to rest in the "ideal" system of today's alphabetic, morphophonemic English writing. On the first matter, ethnocentricity, we must reluctantly conclude that a full survey of Oriental writing is just too complicated to perform here. So is a summary of the rest of what happened to Near Eastern writing systems after the time of Caesar, in the Coptic, Gothic, Armenian, Georgian, and various Slavic writing systems, some of which were still undergoing change in the nineteenth century. On the second point, the smugness, we should recognize two things: First, the invention of printing is bound to slow down the process of evolution in letter forms themselves. So while changes must still be occurring it is harder than ever to see them in progress. Even without the agency of printing, however, it is unlikely that any society is able to see a slow evolutionary process at work. On the other hand, the evolution of handwriting seems to continue at a brisk pace. There must be about as much diversity and as rapid change in script, these days, as there was in spelling during the time of Shakespeare.

We must now distinguish between the writing system and the orthography. The writing system, as it is used here, refers both to the shapes of the marks used to represent language and also to the level at which this representation takes place (pictographic, syllabic, alphabetic, and so on). The orthography, on the other hand, refers to spelling conventions within our alphabetic system. We have already alluded to orthographic change above (AWEIGH, AWAY). Printing has an unquestioned freezing effect on the orthography but the process of change is still evident. Consider AEROPLANE, COLOUR, and KOOL-AID, for example.

ENGLISH ORTHOGRAPHY AND THE QUESTION OF OPTIMALITY

In this section, we return to the previously made claim that English orthography is morphophonemic—that orthography uses symbols related to the sound of the language (phonemes) but honors meaning units (morphemes) as well. A specific version of this idea is found in the work of Chomsky and Halle (1968), who were interested in how verbal knowledge is stored in the mind as well as in orthography. They said that our knowledge of words in our language (the mental lexicon) is represented by highly abstract strings of units called *systematic phonemes*. This morphophonemic level of representation corresponds, according to Chomsky and Halle, roughly to the spellings found in English orthography. If true, this pair of circumstances would be a very lucky thing for the reader of English—the marks on the page would then correspond to the organizing system the reader already has for storing language in the mind. This is what Chomsky and Halle meant by the *optimality* of English orthography.

Let us skip immediately to some examples to show what is meant by the morphophonemic level of representation in the mental lexicon. Take the three words HEAL, HEALTH, and HEALTHFUL. According to Chomsky and Halle's theory, these three words are all located in the lexicon under the same entry, whose spelling is something like /hēl/. In other words, the family of words related to each other from the same root are all stored under the same abstract spelling. This is true even though the vowels of those three words are not pronounced the same way. Thus, lexical storage at the morphophonemic level is not at all the same as lexical storage just based on the sounds of words, which we would call the *phonetic* level. In that latter kind of system, one would have to look in different regions for words such as HEAL and HEALTH, with different sounds. It is in this sense that the lexical representation is abstract.

Another widely cited example is the pair EXTREME-EX-TREMITY. These two words differ in the pronunciation of their second vowel and, if the lexicon were organized strictly by the sounds of items, they would be located differently in the lexicon. However, given an abstract phonological (or morphophonemic) system, they share the same lexical address. The same is true for BOMB and BOMBARD. The third letter in the word DEBT seems at first to be a cruel trick of our spelling system. Why not spell it DET to rhyme with GET? However, the correct form shows its family resemblance to other words with related meanings, like DEBENTURE and DEBIT, as we observed above. In these examples, the spelling of the printed word seems to follow the root meaning rather than the surface pronunciation.

Thus, to summarize, the organization of the lexicon is abstract yet still morphophonemic: The abstractness comes from the fact that families of linguistically related items are stored together, whether or not they get pronounced similarly in overt speech. The storage organization is, however, morphophonemic and related to speech, because even the abstract spellings preserve much of the spoken form. For example, the abstract morphophonemic representation of KANGAROO must be much longer than that for DOE. It is a safe assumption that each of these two words is monomorphemic (contains only one morpheme).

One example of the advantage of an optimal othography comes from words displaying the *vowel shift rule*. According to this phonological rule, a vowel sound that is tense is relaxed when a suffix is added to the end of the word in which it appears. Thus, EXTREME and EXTREMITY are related by a shift from tense to lax on the second e when the suffix *ity* is added. (You can almost feel the relaxation process by alternating pronouncing these two words; the "EE" sound feels tense and the "EH" sound feels more relaxed.)

According to Chomsky and Halle, there is an internal lexical spelling of the word EXTREME that corresponds roughly to the regular dictionary spelling of that word. What happens now when we consider the word EXTREMITY? According to what we may call the "perverse orthography hypothesis" this latter word really should be spelled something like EXTREHMITY, or perhaps the root word should have been spelled EXTREEM. In any case, there should be different orthographic representations for the second vowel sound in the two words. According to the "optimal orthography hypothesis" on the other hand, we have the best of all possible worlds with this situation. First, the consistent spelling of the root EXTREM-, whether or not there are different endings attached at the end, helps us to see the underlying similarities within this word family. At the same time, the argument goes, there is no doubt how to pronounce the word EXTREMITY: This is because we all know the phonological rule that calls for relaxing a tense vowel when a suffix is added at the end. So, in other words, the relation between the written word and the sound is given by the general phonological rules whereas the visual aspect of the word gives us clues as to what it means. Furthermore, it could be added, the flexible relation between spelling and sound makes it so that different dialects of our language community can all use the same orthography. It makes no difference that PIN and PEN are said differently in one dialect and not in others—the orthography is not designed to track the exact sounds in either one.

ENGLISH ORTHOGRAPHY IS NOT ALWAYS OPTIMAL. The word NATION would cause less grief in the third grade if it were spelled NASHION or NASHUN. However, its relation to the words NA-

TIVE and NATIVITY are probably more readily apparent to mature readers with the present arrangement. The same is true of ROTATE and ROTATION. Klima (1972) has observed that there are other words that do not follow this morphophonemic convention. For example the word DELUSION is based on the root DELUDE and not DELUSE. It really should be spelled DELUDION, if English were to follow the morphology consistently. Thus, the lawfulness of English orthography is not absolute. This raises the question of whether literate users of English can capitalize on the alleged optimality of English spelling.

EVIDENCE ON THE OPTIMALITY OF ENGLISH ORTHOGRAPHY

For this whole argument to be persuasive, it has to be assumed that people really do know such phonological rules as the one that governs the EXTREME/EXTREMITY alternation. Steinberg (1973) has proposed a methodology for testing the proposition that people have internalized this rule.

STEINBERG'S EXPERIMENT. Steinberg began by testing people to make sure they knew how to pronounce words like BASE and MAZE, both of which have no suffix and use the stressed or tense vowel sound. The next step was to give people two suffixes, perhaps -ITY and -IC and ask which would be appropriate in a context that was presented verbally. Such a context might have been the following:

> The library used to be a terrible maze. People were always getting lost but now it is better. The shelves are reorganized around reading areas and the whole place is much less _____.

The idea was that subject should fill in the word MAZE, suffixed with either -ITY or -IC to complete the text. The subject thought it was a test of grammatical skill, whereas in fact Steinberg was interested in how the subject pronounced either word.

The finding was that people said the "correct" MAZIC—to rhyme with MAGIC—only 10% of the time. The more usual response was a rhyme with PHASIC. This result, on the surface, challenges the Chomsky and Halle "optimal orthography hypothesis." If people really had internalized the vowel shift rule, they should have applied it in deriving the pronounciation of MAZIC or MAZITY; the suffix should have reduced the original vowel to relaxed form, as in the pair HUMANE/HUMANITY.

The idea behind the experiment is much more important than the 10% figure, however. There are technical reasons why this particular experimental situation might well have badly underestimated how readily people apply the Vowel Shift Rule to new word (see the References and Notes at the end of the chapter). The main point is rather that some of these ideas concerning the nature of English orthography are indeed open to experimental investigation. Hopefully, in view of the importance attached to a morphophonemic orthography in this chapter and the next, more investigators will apply their talents in this direction.

SUMMARY

The main points in this chapter are as follows:

1. We can't just say that writing expresses the language visually. There is great variety in the aspect of language that writing conveys, from levels that are close to the sound to levels that are close to the meaning.

2. As languages change and evolve, they tend to move toward representing the sounds of language and being arbitrary with regard to the level of meaning.

3. The English alphabet and orthography represent language at the morphophonemic level, morphemic in the sense that related words look similar even if they are pronounced differently and phonemic in the sense that letters stand roughly for speech units.

4. It may be that this is an excellent system to have, provided our internal lexicons are organized by systematic phonemes and provided we have internalized the phonological rules.

REFERENCES AND NOTES

There are several good accounts of the history of writing that have been written from the point of view of an interest in reading. A book-length survey is Gelb's *A Study of Writing* (University of Chicago Press, 1963). Three excellent shorter accounts have been written by psychologists: Huey's classic *The Psychology and Pedagogy of Reading (1908/1968)* includes a sophisticated and highly readable discussion of writing systems. Gleitman and Rozin (1977) have two chapters back to back in the book by Reber and Scarborough, *Towards a Psychology of Reading*, that cover much of the same ground and integrate it with information processing theory and reading instruction. Finally, Taylor's (1981) chapter on writing systems and reading in MacKinnon and Waller (*Reading Research: Advances in Theory and Practice*) is another valuable source.

If one wanted to make a writing system based on underlying meanings, one could begin with a comprehension system like Schank's Conceptual Dependencies (Schank, 1972). In this scheme, which was invented for the development of intelligent computer progams, word meanings are decomposed into a small number of Primitive Acts and other relationships. For example, KILL is decomposed into constituents standing for an "act that causes a drastic reduction in the 'health index' of another person." KICK might reduce to "physical translation of position of a lower limb that results in an impact against some other object." The words appearing in the decompositions here might be further reducible to still more fundamental relationships. One of Schank's major results is that one can build a serious understanding system with a very small number of primitive concepts. One can imagine writing where symbols stand for these primitives.

On the matter of change in script, take a look at fourth-grade primers 20 or 30 years apart and you will see big differences. There are letters my father makes differently than I do—for example, the letter r in the middle of words and a t at the end. I found recently that I had almost forgotten how I had been first taught to make several uppercase script letters, including Q, S, and F. A look at archives such as a family Bible shows even more conspicuous differences.

A now-classic paper on how alphabetic orthographies might represent sound and meaning structure is the one by Klima (1972). His paper is especially good in showing that English orthography is a compromise that only approximates a pure morphophonemic system.

One problem with the Steinberg experiment is that having the suffixes separated from the root words may have led to their being pronounced separately. A better technique might be to hit the subject with the compound MAZITY right from the start. Another difficulty is that in gathering oral responses, the experimenter might have set the subject up to want to communicate meaning efficiently. To do so, the subject might have stressed the root MAZE in pronouncing MAZITY so that the other person (the experimenter) could recognize the root. This could be avoided by the use of nonsense words, perhaps NAZITY, where there is no implicit demand for communication.

I have actually performed an experiment incorporating these and other modifications of the Steinberg design and have obtained rates of up to 70% vowel shifting, rather than his 10%. Thus the empirical question remains open.

There is another issue that deals with the nature of the orthography and its relation to the spoken language—whether beginning readers should be introduced to reading from textbooks whose orthography is adjusted to match their dialects. This arises most frequently in connection with the situation existing in many inner-city schools where the teacher and students speak quite different versions of English. Is it an unfair handicap to a black child when he or she finds a familiar word spelled more or less the way the teacher pronounces it but not the way the child does? See Chapter 10 for more on this.

CHAPTER 9

The Role of Speech in Reading

In many ways, the relationship between speech and reading is the single biggest theoretical issue in the psychology of reading. Is there some internal form of speech going on as we read silently? Of course, we all take varying degrees of pride in not moving our lips visibly, when we read silently, and we may even make fun of our neighbor on the subway who does. But let us back up for a moment and keep an open mind: The central theme in this chapter is the possibility that all of us, in silent reading, may make reference at some level to speech, at least some of the time.

In earlier days, people would not have questioned that talking is inherently linked to reading because silent reading, as such, was not common. In his *Confessions*, St. Augustine (Oates, 1948) remarks on the practice of the monk Ambrose to read without obvious speech at the same time:

> But while reading, his eyes glanced over the pages, and his heart searched out the sense, but his voice and tongue were silent.

Others since then (e.g., Lewis, 1936, p. 64) have seen in this early report of silent reading a profound insight into the ancient mind.

Augustine himself was a little more pragmatic, suggesting that Ambrose was worried that onlookers would ask him tough questions for clarification of what they heard him reading aloud or, even more pragmatically, that he might have wanted to save his voice! The fact remains that silent reading in Augustine's time was an accomplishment worthy of mention.

The Practical Importance of This Issue

The issue of speech in reading should interest us even if we care nothing for classical scholarship or nothing for the information-processing analysis of reading that has been built up to this point in the book. There are three basic questions that really require us to take a stand on the issue of how speech is used in reading:

1. *How do we teach reading?* Most people are aware that there are at least two main opinions on how to approach the 6-year-old with reading. One, the *phonics method* emphasizes learning the sounds made by letters first, then learning to blend these sounds so that the written symbols make contact with their meanings through the spoken language. The other method, sometimes called the *whole-word method*, emphasizes learning a direct connection between the written word, as a pattern, and the meaning for which it stands. This latter approach bypasses speech, partly on the claim that speech is unnecessary for mature reading. We have more to say about instruction in reading in Chapter 10. For now, the point is that one's attitude about the proper teaching method relies partly on what one thinks the fluent adult reader is doing: If the fluent reader is necessarily making reference to speech at some internal level, then the faster we can get children to do it that way, the better. If the mature reader is bypassing speech on his or her way to the intended message, then perhaps children should be started accordingly.

2. *How do we teach the beginning deaf reader?* Whatever our answer to question 1, the child who has been deaf from birth poses a special problem. If reading is fundamentally grounded in speech, and there is no way to escape it, then perhaps deaf children should first be drilled in the spoken language before being introduced to printed language. (Training in lipreading and vocal

articulation are laborious but possible in deaf children.) If, on the other hand, the print-to-meaning conversion can bypass speech, then the deaf child should be guided in that direction.

The practical answer to question 2 depends somewhat on the prevalent writing system: The Chinese ideographic system does not have the potential for representing the spoken language that an alphabetic system like ours does (as we saw in the previous chapter). Indeed, the Chinese writing system works equally well for dialects of the spoken language that are so far apart they are mutually incomprehensible. This observation brings up question 3.

3. *How do we deal with dialect mismatch?* One of many difficulties faced by inner-city schools is that the spoken language of teachers sometimes contrasts sharply with that of the students (the so-called Standard versus Black English dialects in the Northeast). The teacher is trying to convey spelling-to-sound rules for the spelling unit *th*, for example, and yet the child pronounces the word *mouth* as "mouf." What should the teacher do—adopt the pronunciation rules of the students, abandon the effort to teach conversion rules, or settle for an inconsistency? This issue, too, comes up in Chapter 10. For now, it reflects again the crucial importance of how reading maps onto the spoken language.

Not that this question, and the other two, will be answered point-blank by a breakthrough on the speech-reading issue. Instead of such a breakthrough, it is realistic to hope for some partial answers on the scientific question, which may possibly illuminate the practical questions just identified. Our approach will be to deal thoroughly with a few basic experiments that illustrate the power of currently available methods and that show the directions in which answers now seem to be pointing.

Why Even Propose A Speech Process in Reading?

Where did the suggestion come from that inner speech has anything to so with silent reading in the first place? There are several sources: First, the story about Saint Ambrose and his ability to go directly from the print to "the heart" without moving his lips shows that there used to be an unquestioned link between talking and reading.

Second, there has always been a desire, in psychology, to find bodily processes that correspond to internal mental events. There is not time to build this background here, but Watson's behaviorism included the argument that thinking itself was basically internal speech and the debate about visual images often turned (and still does) on the relation of imagery to actual vision. The concealed nature of thought during silent reading and the obvious role of words in reading made it natural to wonder whether inner speech might be involved.

The third source of the idea can be found in Chapter 4. There we saw that the most complete models for how information is extracted from displays of unrelated letters used a speech process. Following representation in a visual icon, information is rescued by a process of silent naming. This recoding by speech is relatively slow and is revealed by memory confusions among similar sounding letters (Conrad's effect). As we said in the close of that chapter, the main thrust of much of the rest of this book has been whether the Sperling-type model of processing can be applied to "real" reading situations. In other words, is there a continuity between the extraction of information about unrelated letters flashed on a screen, as opposed to what happens when those letters form coherent words in a meaningful string? If there is this sort of continuity, then we should expect to find evidence for the speech-related naming process in any kind of reading. (But surely the naming process in reading would not be applied to individual letters; instead, the unit processes by innner speech would be the word or some syllablelike portion of the word.)

Finally, there have been various kinds of more direct evidence on whether reading curtails inner speech over the years. People's intuitions are not worth much in these matters, but some observers have always claimed to hear their own voices internally during reading. (Others claim with equal force that they don't.) Many studies have been done recording electrical impulses on skin that lies directly over speech muscles (electromyography or EMG). The idea is that if there is internal speech, EMG recordings might reveal tiny amounts of muscular activity in the corresponding muscles. A survey of many such studies (Edfeldt, 1960) concludes that there is speech activity during reading. The following experiment by Hardyck and Petrinovich (1970) is a good, clean example of this approach.

THE HARDYCK AND PETRINOVICH (1970) STUDY. In this experiment, the question was whether biofeedback techniques might be used to teach people *not* to use speech-related activity during silent reading. If so, then would reading suffer? If reading were harder when people had to suppress their speech activity, then it would suggest that speech is a natural accompaniment to reading.

The subjects in this experiment were selected from remedial reading classes for undergraduates at the University of California, Berkeley. Some were trained, while reading, to avoid producing these tiny electrical impulses (recorded by EMG). A bell sounded when EMG activity occurred and subjects learned to keep the bell silent. Other subjects had the same biofeedback training, but applied to EMG impulses in their forearms, not the chin-lip area. A control group received no special training. EMG recordings were taken from all subjects' forearms, larynxes (Adam's apples), and lips during both periods of relaxation and periods of reading. The reading material was difficult in one condition and easy in the other condition.

The results showed that neither of the training conditions had any effect on the lip or forearm recording sites. However, the group that received training in suppression of speech activity showed significantly less larynx EMG activity during reading than the other groups. Thus, they *had* learned to keep their speech activity "electrically quiet." The most interesting result was that the consequence of this EMG suppression on reading depended on what it was they were trying to read. A comprehension test on the easy reading matter showed the experimental group (suppress speech EMG) was no worse than the control groups. However, for the difficult material, this experimental group showed poorer comprehension scores than the control groups. The interpretation is that speech does indeed have a role in silent reading (because removing speech, as it were, hurts reading comprehension) but only when the material becomes more difficult. We mention this result again after survey-ing some more analytical investigations of speech mediation in reading.

THE SYLLABLE AND OTHER SUBLEXICAL UNITS

If it could be shown that the syllable is an important unit in fluent reading, it would be relevant to deciding what kind of speech process is going on, if any, because the syllable is usually defined as a pronunciation unit. The background for this ap-proach comes from the theory of word perception, covered in Chapter 5. Recall that Cattell showed first that a short word was perceived better than a single letter and that a word was per-ceived better than a nonword of equivalent length. Reicher and others have expanded on this result much more recently. One question is whether the wordness effect (word perceived better than nonword) is lexical—that is, whether the word is handled better because it is a true word or whether it is better because it obeys the rules of English orthography. The items SPINE and TGFXO differ in both respects whereas SPINE and PLINE differ only in lexicality. (PLINE isn't, but could very well be, an En-glish word.) We showed in Chapter 5 that, according to some experiments, lexicality is *not* always the important factor. A legal nonword like PLINE was not consistently inferior to a true word (Baron & Thurston, 1973). This fact suggsts the importance of some sublexical unit in reading, some intermediate unit of per-ception shorter than the word itself. If we went directly from the shape of the word to its meaning, how could we so efficiently perceive a new shape that has no meaning, like PLINE?

What Kind of Sublexical Unit Is Used?

Eleanor Gibson and her associates (Gibson & Levin, 1975) have suggested that *spelling patterns* are the important sublexical units. Spelling patterns are familiar English letter combinations like CK, SH, STR, AKE, and so on. The claim is that if a unit can be decomposed into these familiar visual patterns, it will be perceived efficiently, but not necessarily through any reference to speech. Both normal and deaf children, for example, perform better on legal nonwords that contain regular spelling patterns, like GLURCK, than on nonwords that do not, like GRKLCU. Although this would seem to be evidence that some visual unit unrelated to pronunciation is important in reading, we do not know the training histories of the deaf subjects in this study; they may have had enough experience with speech to employ a strategy that used pronunciation for reading.

Smith and Spoehr (1974) have proposed instead that readers employ a syllablelike unit for getting from print to meaning. Their proposal describes how printed words are subdivided automatically into these syllable units, before access to the sound and from there to the meaning. Their proposal amounts to a sounding-out process that goes on by syllable rather than by letter. Smith and Spoehr's big experimental demonstration was that the nonword BLOST was perceived better than the nonword BLST (using Reicher's experimental technique). This result is telling: BLOST has one more letter than BLST and therefore more uncertainty about spelling patterns. But despite its greater complexity BLOST is handled more easily. What BLOST has going for it, of course, is that it easily forms a syllable. Now we examine other evidence on the perceptual role of the syllable in reading.

The Syllable Effect in Word Perception

Eriksen, Pollack, and Montague (1970) measured how long it took people to begin pronouncing words that appeared suddenly on the screen. Their main interest was in whether the word was long or short in terms of syllables, as in the comparison of MAIN and MAINTENANCE. They found that people were 20 to 25 milliseconds slower in beginning to name the longer words, provided that people were uncertain of what was going to be presented on each trial. If the subjects were warned ahead on which word would appear next, however, there was no difference.

But MAINTENANCE is wider *visually* than MAIN; perhaps that had something to do with its slower processing. Therefore, the authors replicated their experiment using two-digit numbers whose names varied in syllable length. For example, 14 and 20 have two syllables each whereas 87 and 79 have four each. Using the numbers equates visual complexity for the syllabically short and long items. The result was basically the same—each time the name of the two-digit number increased by one syllable, the reaction time increased by about 11 milliseconds.

Other experiments on the syllable effect are mixed, especially when regular words are used instead of numbers. One problem is that extra syllables could extend naming reaction time in two different ways: First, the possibility of interest is that it is necessary to vocalize items internally in order to perceive what they are. Second, however, the syllabically longer items could be slow because it takes longer to organize them *as responses* than the short items. This second mechanism is less interesting to us, in this context, than the first. For this reason, we now discuss experimental methods that adopt a different approach.

THE LEXICAL DECISION TASK

It can be argued that pronunciation time is not a fair measure of reading because one might be able to pronounce some item without gaining access to its true identity as a word. When HORSE-WHIP occurs in the course of real reading, it has to make a connection with *lexical memory,* the place where words are stored in something like a dictionary format. Speaking the word, even speaking it rapidly, does not necessarily entail this connection. For example, we can pronounce FLACKSTROM easily enough, but this misses something essential in reading because this item has "nowhere to go" in lexical memory.

The same sort of criticism applies to other tasks that have been used by experimental psychologists to evaluate the role of speech in silent reading, such as proofreading, letter cancellation, and deciding whether two simultaneous letter strings are the same or different. We consider now the *lexical decision task,* which is less prone to these complaints. In the lexical decision task, a string of letters is presented on a screen and the subject has to decide, as rapidly as possible, whether the string is a word or not. The response to HORSEWHIP is "yes" and to FLACK-STROM is "no." To keep the subject's job straightforward, extremely low-frequency words like GLEDGE are simply not used. Using lexical decision times as a measure of processing difficulty, rather than pronunciation time or same/different time, assumes that the subject must at least locate the item in question in his or her store of words. The subject does not have to respond to the meaning of the term, it is true, but once the lexical address of the word is located, its meaning is available for retrieval.

Evidence for Speech Coding in Lexical Access

A provocative article by Rubenstein, Lewis, and Rubenstein (1971) first suggested the power of lexical decisions to reveal an underlying speech code in reading: The results of several of their individual experiments are given in Table 9.1 which shows lexical decision times and error percentages. Consider first the upper section, from Experiment 1 of Rubenstein et al., where only non-words (correct answer = "no") are of interest. For these non-words, performance was fast and accurate when they were orthographically illegal and unpronounceable (LIKJ), intermediate when they were orthographically illegal but essentially pronounceable (GRATF), and slow, with many errors, when they were legal and pronounceable (STRIG).

This pattern is consistent with (but does not prove, of course) the idea that people sound out a letter string and then search through a morphophonemically organized lexicon. (Recall that the first part of the this word *morphophonemic* shows the importance of morphemes—meaning units—in our writing system; the second part of the word shows the importance of systematic phonemes—the abstract sound units. The term *phonological* is sometimes interchangeable with the term *morphophonemic*.) The idea is that the printed word is translated into some form of speech and then a lexicon, which is organized by phonological segments, is consulted to see if such an item exists. In the conditions we have discussed so far from the experiment of Rubenstein et al., the search would be fruitless. However, if a pronun-

Table 9.1 Lexical Decision Times (Errors) from Rubenstein et al. (1971)

Experiment and condition	Measure	
	Reaction time	Error %
1: Illegal and nonpronounceable (LIKJ, SAGM)	859	1
1: Illegal and pronounceable (GRATF, LAMG)	874	3
1: Legal and pronounceable (STRIG, BARP)	966	6
2: Nonhomophone (SHART)	1013	3
2: Homophone (TRATE)	1060	15
3: Nonhomophone (MOTH)	894	9
3: Homophone (YOKE)	918	15

ciation cannot even be derived for a letter string (LIKJ) then it is easy to report that it could not be a word, without even having to begin searching. It is not surprising that GRATF falls somewhere between; a pronunciation can be cranked out, but only with effort, and this effort would tend to tip the subject off that the correct answer is "no."

Consider now the second group of observations in Table 9.1, again from performance on nonword trials. (Of course, sprinkled in with these nonword trials were many trials where the correct answer was "yes"; we are disregarding those now.) Here the items are all legal and prounounceable. Here, interest is in comparing a control item (SHART) with items that are *homophones* with regular English words (TEW, TRATE). Homophones have the same sound as words, but may be spelled differently. The main finding for these items is that the homophones lead to less accurate and slower performance than the control items. This suggests that once a pronunciation is derived for the letter strings, a matching morphophonemic representation is *found* in the lexicon, making it hard to reject the item. We have to assume that once a matching morphophonemic representation is found, additional processing has to occur to prevent the subject from responding "yes" incorrectly. Specifically, the subject must check to see if the spelling on the screen matches the spelling associated with this stored lexical representation just found. In other words, when the subject finds /treit/ in the mental lexicon, having started from the nonword TRATE on the screen, he or she compares the two spellings before making a final decision, otherwise errors would jump to 100% for homophone nonwords. However, this spelling check takes time, and hence the poor performance shown for the homophone items in the middle section of Table 9.1.

The third batch of data in Table 9.1 is from the third experiment in this series. Now we are interested in performance on positive trials, where the correct answer is "yes." The comparison of interest is between control words like MOTH and word pairs where one word is a homophone of the other word (YOKE-YOLK, SALE-SAIL). The finding is that such items (like YOLK) are difficult—accuracy goes down and reaction time goes up in comparison with appropriate control words. This finding is more subtle but more powerful than the others in the table: These data are hard to accommodate with any theory that says people go directly from the print to the meaning (remember St. Augustine's heart!). The situation is portrayed in Figure 9.1, which shows the "direct" case in the upper panel. There is no basis for predicting a difference between YOKE and MOTH here. Shown in the lower panel of Figure 9.1 is the case where morphophonemic access precedes lexical access. In this instance, it is reasonable that the homophone should behave differently from the nonhomophone.

Exactly *why* the homophone word should be at a disadvantage in lexical decisions is not the important issue. The main point is that Figure 9.1 shows why there could be some effect of homophony if there is access to speech and not according to the direct theory. (The disadvantage of homophones in lexical decision may come from the fact that there is more "spread" among

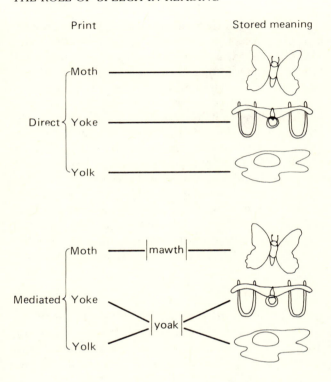

Figure 9.1 *The difference between direct access and speech-mediated access to meaning.*

their interconnections than with nonhomophones. See the greater complexity in the lower part of Figure 9.1 for MOTH than for YOKE. It is widely believed that this spread of connections slows down processing.)

Thus, the slowness of words like YOKE in lexical decision is consistent with a speech-based lexical access theory. But single experiments are seldom quite that conclusive in psychology and it was not long before the YOKE-MOTH comparison came under closer scrutiny. Meyer, Schwaneveldt, and Ruddy (1974) objected that the Rubenstein et al. evidence was not really conclusive on the matter of speech coding in lexical access. Meyer et al. maintained that homophones tend to *look more alike* than non-homophones whether the pairs are composed of two words or a word and a nonword (YOLK-YOKE or TRATE-TRAIT). If the lexicon—the store of words in dictionary-type form—were organized according to the spelling of words rather than according to their sounds, then items that looked like other words would be slowed down relative to those that did not. Meyer et al. performed an ingenious experiment to choose between these possibilities. Their results tended to support the earlier conclusion— that speech does mediate lexical decision. However, the lexical decision technique is remote from the ordinary reading process and so we prefer not to focus too much on it. As a matter of fact, the next research to be covered shows that the lexical decision procedure gives different answers depending on exactly how the experiment is conducted.

Flexibility in Access to the Lexicon

The evidence from the previous section points toward a role for speech in gaining access to the lexicon, and hence in gaining access to meaning. In this section, we suggest that people have more than one way of going about reading. It is unfortunate that many experts in this field have posed the central question of this chapter as an either/or proposition. There is a more important question: *Under what circumstances* are various strategies used?

REMARK. A purely visual access route to meaning, without speech mediation, is highly likely on logical grounds, even though the Rubenstein et al. research on lexical decision supported the lower panel of Figure 9.1, rather than the upper panel. An old law of psychology is that repeated contiguity (happening at the same time) of two events produces an association between them, so that when one occurs alone, people tend to think of the other. After years of reading, a person may have had hundreds of times when the word COW occurred in print and, because the reader was paying attention to meaning, he or she thought of the animal at about the same time. It doesn't matter that the word may have been sounded out, initially, or that access to it still occurs through the mediation of speech. The important point is that repeatedly thinking of cows and seeing the word together would almost necessarily produce a direct association between meaning and print.

Thus, the question is not so much whether there ever can be direct access to meaning from print. It is, instead, how words could possibly *not* arouse their referents (the concepts they represent) directly and automatically. But the law of contiguity doesn't tell us how much repetition is necessary to produce an automatic association of a word and its concept. Therefore, all we can say is that both systems shown in Figure 9.1 are plausible on logical grounds, a priori. It is up to experimental research to show that both access systems—mediated and unmediated—are used, and when. (This approach is what distinguishes an experimental psychologist from a philosopher or a linguist.)

FLEXIBILITY IN LEXICAL DECISION. Davelaar, Coltheart, Besner, and Jonasson (1978) showed the dependence of the homophone effect, in lexical decisions, on the kinds of items being tested in the experiment. The homophone effect is the slower time to respond "yes" to YOKE than to MOTH. The result was used to support the view that speech mediates lexical access (see Figure 9.1).

Now what if this reflects a phonological (speech-based) *strategy*, at least partially under the subject's control? It would have been an intelligent strategy in the Rubenstein et al. experiment, where nonwords were items like SLINT. For such items, a lexical address cannot be found in a morphophonemically organized lexicon. Davelaar et al. had the insight that this strategy would be a poor one when the nonwords included many items like BRANE. Such items are not words but *are* homophones of true words and they would be "found" by a lexical search, if that search were based on speech. Lexical access through inner speech would, when BRANE-type nonwords are used, require the time-consuming and error-prone complication of a spelling check (for example b-r-a-n-e versus b-r-a-i-n). The spelling check would not be necessary with words like SLINT as the "no" items. If—and this is the main point—the decision to use speech in lexical access were under the person's control, then we might expect not to find YOKE slower than MOTH when nonwords include homophones to real words. In that case, when the homophones include BRANE, the subject would be better off not using speech at all, if there is the option of another route, such as a visual route to the meaning. But if the subject uses a visual route, then it should not matter that YOKE has a homophone, so the difference between MOTH and YOKE should disappear.

Davelaar et al., being careful investigators, included one comparison (MOTH versus YOKE) under the Rubenstein et al. conditions, with nonwords like SLINT. The result was the same: YOKE was reliably slower than MOTH (628 versus606 milliseconds) and more error prone (9 versus 3%). However, when the experiment was changed only by including nonwords that were homophonic with real words, the difference vanished (600 versus 596 milliseconds and 0 versus 3% errors). The important conclusion is that there is an optional, not compulsory, speech process involved in lexical access and that the subjects can bypass it when the task demands make it a poor strategy.

FLEXIBILITY IN TACHISTOSCOPIC RECOGNITION. Hawkins, Reicher, Rogers, and Peterson (1976) performed an experiment that makes very much the same point using Reicher's forced-choice method for testing word recognition. In this technique, a test word is flashed briefly, say COIN, and then two choices—both words—are presented for the test, say JOIN and COIN (see Chapter 5). The special feature of the Hawkins et al. experiment was including pairs like SENT and CENT as choices, following brief presentation of the word SENT. The appropriate control stimulus is a choice between SOLD and COLD, following presentation of SOLD. The SENT/CENT comparison asks the subject to choose between two homophones. If the subject has encoded the original item in terms of speech, he or she is in a lot of trouble! If, however, the subject has encoded the original item visually, then the SENT/CENT choice should be no harder than the SOLD/COLD choice—in both instances, it would then be a matter of choosing between the same two letters.

The variable that Hawkins et al. manipulated was the proportion of homophone items in the experimental session. Imagine if *nearly all* trials were of the CENT/SENT type: Then, if subjects had any control at all over their processing operations, they would surely abandon speech coding of the stimuli and try to use the visual code instead. If, on the other hand, there were very few homophone items, there would be little penalty on speech coding and we might expect to see more of it in the results. The measure of whether speech coding is going on is the difference between the homophone pairs and the controls. If SENT/CENT trials are harder than SOLD/COLD trials, then subjects must have been using a speech code. If there is no difference, we can conclude they were using some other form of coding, perhaps visual.

The results showed that subjects were able to select a strategy that depended on the experimental design. When there were only very infrequent homophone pairs, the SENT/CENT trials were much harder than the control trials (58.3 to 72.5% correct). When fully two-thirds of the trials included homophone pairs, however, the difference disappeared (66.5 to 67.8%), suggesting that under these latter conditions, subjects abandoned speech coding. [This latter result confirmed an earlier finding of Baron and Thurston (1973) who introduced this comparison and the lucid reasoning behind it.]

Thus, with both lexical decision (Davelaar et al.) and tachistoscopic recognition (Hawkins et al.), there is solid evidence that people can adjust their dependence on speech to suit the specifics of the job they have to do. Neither of these two experimental tasks demands access to meaning, of course. We must infer that the same flexibility characteristic of these tasks is found at higher levels, as well. Kleiman's research (1975) is useful in extending this conclusion to semantic decisions, however, and we turn to it now.

SPEECH FOR LEXICAL ACCESS OR FOR SHORT-TERM MEMORY?

Now we discuss a distinction that is important for the rest of the chapter and later on, as well. For this distinction, we need to pay careful attention to two different words, *phonetic* and *phonological.*

People outside of psychology are often impatient, and even contemptuous about "jargon" terms they find us using. Sometimes, social scientists do indeed seem to go out of their way to use obscure words for no good reason (remember *saccade*). On other occasions, the unfamiliar terms work hard in maintaining sharp distinctions between related concepts. This is true with *phonetic* and *phonological*. The phonetic level of speech is quite close to the sound stream. As we said above, the letter *p* is a different phonetic segment in the two words POKE and SPOKE. Similarly, the phonetic segments that make plurals out of the words HOGS and RATS are different. The phonological level, on the other hand, corresponds to the abstract, systematic phonemes described in Chapter 8. At the phonological level, DEBT is spelled with a *b* and EXTREME and EXTREMITY have the same spelling in their second vowel position even though the phonetic segment is different in the two cases. Phonological coding is found at the morphophonemic level of abstraction.

One role of speech in reading might be to mediate access of individual printed words to their lexical addresses. This is the role suggested by the Rubenstein et al. and Meyer et al. experiments. Another role of speech in reading might be a speech-based, short-term memory code. This short-term memory process could occur well after the printed words have individually come in contact with their lexical addresses. A phonetic code for short-term memory would not even necessarily *occur* when it is a question of only a single word. Instead, this form of speech coding would be used to maintain a series of several items in memory. Why would we want to have a way of holding the last few words in a phonetic short-term memory during reading? One reason is that sentences often have large distances between related words. (As in "Throw the horse over the fence some hay.") It is good to be able to go back to reinterpret some earlier parts of a sentence, in light of later evidence that has come in. Without a verbatim short-term memory, this would be difficult. The phonetic mode would be a suitable memory format because of its special capacity for temporal order information, as discussed in

Chapter 4. This distinction will make more sense after we look at an experiment by Kleiman (1975).

The Kleiman Experiment

Kleiman (1975) observed that the main difference between these two hypotheses is in whether the reference to speech occurred before lexical access in reading or afterward. His method for producing evidence on this matter was to distract the speech system by having people "shadow" digits played through earphones. (In shadowing, a stream of items is heard and the subject must repeat the items with his or her own voice as fast as possible. With a fast continuous stream, it is a task that demands considerable attention.)

During the time they were shadowing, subjects were given visually presented words on which they had to make a timed yes-or-no decision. The question was how much the shadowing disrupted the time required for the decision, as compared with control conditions in which there was no shadowing required. Kleiman reasoned that the damage done by simultaneous shadowing ought to depend on the type of decision being made about the word. If the decision were based on how the word *looked*, then little disturbance would be expected. However, if the decision were being made about the *sound* of the word, then it might well be very difficult to make that decision while speaking rapidly at the same time. In fact, the logic of the experiment depended on a larger shadowing effect with sound judgments than with visual judgments for the word. Luckily, this finding did occur.

Now what would happen if a decision on the *meaning* of the word were required? If access to the lexicon—and to the meaning representation reached through the lexicon—depended on inner speech, then the meaning decision should be disrupted as much as the sound task by the vocal shadowing task. If, on the other hand, access to meaning could occur independently of the speech system, then the meaning task should resemble the visual task. In this latter case, we would conclude that the speech hookup in reading may occur after lexical access, perhaps for the purposes of a speech code in short-term memory.

Table 9.2   Major Results of Kleiman (1975) Experiment 1.

			Reaction time	Result (% error)
Task	Example of "Yes"	Example of "No"	Without shadowing	With shadowing (increase)
Phonemic	TICKLE PICKLE	LEMON DEMON	1137 (8.3)	+372 (+7.7)
Graphemic	HEARD BEARD	GRACE PRICE	970 (4.5)	+125 (+0.4)
Semantic	MOURNE GRIEVE	DEPART COUPLE	1118 (4.2)	+120 (+3.8)

In Kleiman's first experiment, pairs of words were presented on a screen during either a period of digit shadowing or a period when the subject was free from distraction. In one condition, the subject was to make a rhyming judgment (TICKLE-PICKLE = yes, LEMON-DEMON = no). In another, the decision was on graphemic similarity (HEARD-BEARD = yes, GRACE-PRICE = no). (A *grapheme* is a linguistic unit that stands for abstract letters— A and a are both instances of the grapheme of the first letter of the alphabet.) In the critical condition, the decision was on meaning (MOURNE-GRIEVE = yes, BRAVERY-QUANTITY = no). Table 9.2 shows the main results. In the left column, we see that the graphemic task was somewhat faster than either of the two others. However, the real interest is in comparing the amount by which subjects were slowed down when shadowing was added to their burden. In this respect the semantic task was clearly similar to the graphemic task in showing a smaller decrement than the rhyme task, where simultaneous shadowing extracted a heavy price in terms of both reaction time and errors.

Why did shadowing have any effect at all on the graphemic task? We must assume that any simultaneous distraction would have some interfering effect on performance. This is not particularly interesting; after all, making a person pet a dog while receiving occasional lexical decision trials would probably slow the person down too. The crucial result is that the semantic task "goes with" the visual (graphemic) task. This means that in order to perform judgments of similarity in meaning, it is not necessary to engage in the degree of inner vocalization that is necessary for the rhyme task. Indeed, the results show that the meaning judgment seems to engage the speech system no more than the visual-similarity judgment.

Kleiman presented sentences in another experiment. Again there were graphemic, rhyme, and semantic judgments made by the subjects with and without distraction from shadowing at the same time. The result was essentially identical to that shown in Table 9.2. This second experiment also contained a condition where subjects had to make judgments of *sentence acceptability*. (NOISY PARTIES DISTURB SLEEPING NEIGHBORS = yes, PIZZAS HAVE BEEN EATING JERRY = no.) Kleiman included this sentence accepability task to test the idea that speech coding is used for short-term retention when a string of items longer than the word must be maintained. Notice that the acceptability judgment does require such short-term memory; one must at least remember the subject until the object and verb have come in, if one wants to verify that they go together. Kleiman found that the sentence acceptability task was very badly disrupted by shadowing digits, even more so than the rhyme task.

Kleiman took this pattern of findings as evidence that the meanings of individual words can be obtained without reference to inner speech but that inner speech becomes necessary when the task demands holding a string of items in short-term memory. This hypothesis makes sense of the finding by Hardyck and Petrinovich that EMG suppression hurt comprehension of difficult, but not easy, passages. One way in which the difficult material may be distinguished from the easier material would very likely be longer sentences, with more distributed syntactic forms—just the sort of thing that would require more support from short-term memory.

So, Kleiman concluded that inner speech comes into use for purposes of short-term memory, not lexical access. Of course, everything depends on what one means by inner speech. More on that later; however, for the moment we can conclude that whatever level of processing is engaged by the shadowing task is not necessary for lexical access but is necessary for some subsequent processing that is brought out by sentence materials.

A Developmental Study by Barron and Baron

We continue now with another experiment that sheds light on this question of whether inner speech is needed for lexical access. Barron and Baron (1977) began from a very common and a very sensible assumption, that the role of speech in lexical access changes as children gain more experience in reading. At the first stages of reading, children may need to sound out words in order to match them with the only lexical system they have at the time—a lexical system organized in morphophonemic terms. However, the reasoning goes, as children develop fluency, direct connections emerge between the printed words and their meanings—in effect, a visually organized lexicon.

In line with this proposal, Barron and Baron reasoned that access to meaning might include access to sound in early readers but not in more fluent readers. The stimuli were short lists of paired drawings and words. In the meaning task, subjects had to say as rapidly as possible whether the two items in a pair "went together' as do the word SHIRT and a drawing of a pair of pants. In the rhyme task, the subjects had to decide whether the two items, one a picture and the other a word, had a similar sound, as do the word CORN and a picture of a horn. In one condition this was the only thing the subject had to do but in another, there was an articulatory suppression task—repeating the word DOUBLE over and over again—during the decisions about the word-picture pairs. The subjects were children in grades 1, 2, 3, 4, or 6.

The first result of interest is in the time required for the sound and meaning tasks as a function of age, disregarding, for the moment, the distraction activity. These results are shown in Table 9.3 where each entry is the average time required for processing five picture-word pairs. As one would expect, children got faster overall, with age. However, the important result is that the relative speed of the two tasks did not change over development. The ratio of times for the two remained quite constant.

Table 9.3 Barron and Baron Study (1977)

Grade	Task		Ratio:S/M
	Sound	Meaning	
1	17.3	14.9	1.15
2	11.4	9.9	1.15
3	10.3	8.8	1.17
4	8.0	6.8	1.17
6	7.0	6.1	1.15

What other result would one have expected, from this study? If the reference to speech were necessary to derive meaning at the early ages, but not at the later ages, it would show up in the results as a relatively larger improvement in the meaning times than in the sound times. Hence the ratio in Table 9.3 would have increased with age.

Table 9.4 shows the result of the articulatory distraction manipulation (DOUBLE-DOUBLE-DOUBLE . . .) on the two tasks. Quite clearly, and as expected, the distraction had an interfering effect on the sound task. (It would not be worth looking at the rest of the results had this not been the case.) However, there was no interference effect that was reliable on the meaning task. Furthermore, neither of these patterns of results changed at all with age. One might have expected that the interference task would disrupt meaning judgments at early stages of reading, when the use of inner speech is likely to prevail, but not at later stages of reading, where the mediator would presumably have dropped out. But the results clearly violate this reasonable expectation: The evidence for direct access to meaning—that is, no interference from concurrent speech—was equally strong at all ages tested.

There are then two lessons for us in the Barron and Baron study. First, aside from the age variable, here again is evidence, like that of Kleiman, favoring access to meaning without the intervention of speech. At least access to meaning seems to occur without referring to that *level of speech* that is used in shadowing or repeating the word DOUBLE. That is, the speech system probably operates at a wide range of levels of abstraction; we

Table 9.4 Barron and Baron Interference Study (1977)

	Task and condition					
	Sound (d)			Meaning (d)		
Grade	Interference	Control		Interference	Control	
1	16.3	7.5	+8.8	9.0	9.3	−0.3
2	13.3	8.3	+5.0	6.7	6.0	+0.7
4	11.5	6.5	+5.0	5.7	3.5	+2.5
6	10.0	8.5	+1.5	4.3	4.3	0
8	9.0	5.5	+3.5	3.0	3.7	−0.7

know that access to meaning at least does not require the particular portion of the speech system that is kept busy with digit shadowing or mindless chanting. This qualification is important; we suggested before and will discuss more fully the point that there might be more than one level of internal speech mediating reading behavior.

The second message from the Barron and Baron study is that even early readers seem to do without speech mediation. Of course, it was important that children in this experiment were reading words they had already learned; the result might be different if children were presented with words they knew in spoken form but not in written form, requiring "sounding out."

CONCLUDING DISCUSSION

What generalizations can be drawn now, looking back on the evidence pertinent to how speech is involved with reading? In the first place, we demonstrated with the Hardyck and Petrinovich study that there is *some* relation between inner speech and reading behavior, at least for more difficult passages. This evidence would be consistent with either of the two hypotheses distinguished by Kleiman, however: Biofeedback training to suppress EMG potentials during reading could have slowed down lexical access, in difficult passages, or it could have interfered with a short-term memory system dependent on speech.

More diagnostic procedures, such as the lexical decision task, give cleaner answers because they stress different components of the overall reading situation. For example, there is no need for a process of short-term retention in the lexical decision task. One solid conclusion (Davelaar et al., 1978; Hawkins et al., 1976) is that people have two strategies available for word processing tasks—one using speech and the other bypassing it. When these two strategies come into play can be affected by the experimental design. If the items are designed to penalize a reliance on speech coding, people simply make lexical decisions relying on some other code. Although this conclusion about flexible coding makes the question of whether there is some internal form of speech occuring as we read silently seem oversimplified, flexibility does not mean the system is fickle. It should be reassuring, rather than confusing, that the answers given by our experiments tell a perfectly sensible story, that people read in a way that suits their purposes and the situation at hand.

In later parts of the chapter, we discussed a wider variety of decision tasks that measure different levels of word perception—visual, rhyme, and semantic. Here (in the studies of Kleiman and of Barron and Baron), the conclusion seems to be emerging that access to the meaning of a single word does not necessarily require prior access to its sound, at least for familiar words. But we saw that there is still another important function for speech mediation in reading: Understanding sentences makes it necessary to hold several words in short-term memory at the same time. It is possible that people use a speech code for short-term memory. We already knew there was a special relationship between short-term memory for temporal order and phonetic coding; this came out of the studies by Conrad and others discussed in Chapter 4. Here, we have proposed that the close tie between short-term memory and speech is important in silent reading.

What Happened to the Original Speech-Recoding Hypothesis?

Why is it that some evidence favors a role for speech in reading and other evidence discourages that hypothesis? Between the evidence for flexibility in lexical access and the evidence for meaning judgments under conditions of articulatory distraction, we certainly have had to scale down the original hypothesis— that internal speech is required by silent reading. It would be just as mistaken, however, to reject any role of speech mediation in reading, as it would be to cling to the original hypothesis. In this concluding discussion, we suggest that one key to the issue is to be found in the distinction between phonology and phonetics. Lexical access might very well occur through the phonological level and a phonetically coded short-term memory might be used for analysis of extended linguistic forms.

PHONOLOGY FOR LEXICAL ACCESS. When the child first tackles reading, he or she is already a fluent speaker of the language, with a vocabulary of about 10,000 words. A great advantage of our alphabetic writing system is that one *could* use the spelling-to-sound rules for deciphering new words: When the child sees an unfamiliar word on the page, he or she can "sound it out" and match it up with its familiar spoken form. Most everyone agrees that this sounding-out strategy is valid for early reading when some kind of phonic (sound-based) method has been used to teach reading. The sequence of processing is from the printed form to the spoken form, and only then, on to the meaning. The question is whether the same sequence, which uses phonological level, also occurs in mature, fluent reading.

A PHONETIC CODE FOR SHORT-TERM MEMORY. Consider reading aloud: There is a well-known gap between the word on which the eyes are resting, at any moment, and the word that is being pronounced. This gap is called the *eye-voice span* and it shows that the eye is typically about four words ahead of the voice. To measure the eye-voice span yourself, get someone to read aloud from a sheet of paper in front of you. Then, suddenly and without warning, snatch the paper away and see how many words more can be reported accurately. On the average, it will be about four words under normal conditions. If the reading material were a list of unrelated words, instead of text, the span drops to about two words. It is also reduced to around two words in young children who have just learned to read are tested.

Now what about the possibility that a similar span exists in silent reading—a sort of eye-inner-voice span? (There is as yet no hard evidence for this conjecture, by the way.) Such a trailing process of inner speech would be very handy for short-term memory and analysis of syntax, as we will see shortly. For the moment, however, the subvocal eye-voice span is being distinguished from the phonological, sounding-out process suggested above.

One basis for distinguishing these two kinds of speech mediation in reading is their timing. We usually gain access to the meaning of a word within a fraction of a second. However, the four-word, eye-voice span means that some considerable delay—perhaps as much as two seconds—would occur between the time a word was looked at and the time it was overtly or silently pronounced. Therefore, the mechanism that produces the eye-voice span could not be the route for gaining access to the meaning of a word; the speech response in the eye-voice span occurs too late. Another way of looking at it is this: How could we possibly look at a familiar word and *postpone* access to its meaning for two seconds? Try it on a friend. Suddenly expose to the friend the word ELEPHANT and see how successful the friend is in not thinking of its meaning for two seconds, while you count "one one-thousand, two one-thousand, go."

A second basis for distinguishing phonological access from the lagging phonetic short-term memory responsible for the eye-voice span is found in some research on Chinese writing. Since Chinese logographs bear no relation to the sound of the spoken language, unlike our alphabetic system, what we have been calling phonology could not possibly be used to gain access to meanings of words. There is just no sounding out that can be done in Chinese. However, Tzeng, Hung, and Wang (1977) have shown that readers of Chinese characters make the same memory cofusions among words that Conrad identified in Western subjects. That is, Chinese ideographs become confused in memory, following visual presentation, if they have similar pronunciations. This result would follow from a universal tendency to pronounce words internally in passing them into a phonetic short-term retention system, just as we repeat a telephone number internally while crossing the room to a telephone.

In a way, it was never very reasonable to expect a single type of speech mediation serving both lexical access and also serving short-term memory. For one thing, as we said above, the timing is wrong—access to meaning can be shown to occur well before a phonetic short-term code is used (in the eye-voice span).

SPEECH MEDIATION AND THE ORTHOGRAPHY. If we concede that access to the lexicon and, from there, on to meaning, does not occur through the sort of inner speech that is disrupted by articulatory interference, however, what becomes of the good arguments for having the lexicon organized in terms of speech? These arguments were made in the previous chapter, on writing systems. Recall that there were great advantages to grafting the written language system onto the processing machinery the child already knows how to use for spoken language. One advantage is the ability to analyze new printed words. Another is the efficiency of not having to construct an entire new set of correspondences between the organization of the mind and physical features, making two whole lexicons.

With the kind of morphophonemically organized lexicon introduced in the previous chapter, we can have our cake and eat it too, theoretically. The trick is to line up the morphophonemically organized lexicon with an abstract, phonological level of speech mediation and to line up overt articulation with the phonetic short-term memory. It is not surprising, then, that articulatory distraction has no effect on access to meaning: The phonological level that may be used for lexical and semantic access is far more abstract than the systems controlling the overt aspects of talking. In other words, the speech production machinery is too far "out" into the muscular control systems to get in the way of a lexical search organized phonologically. Thus, the Kleiman and Barron and Baron results pose no real problems. One can still, if one wishes, believe that reference to speech, *at the morphophonemic level*, is important for lexical access.

So, we do not have to give up the strong points of a lexical organization that capitalizes on morphophononemic coding. That is, we do not have to give up the "optimality" that was explained in the last chapter. If the lexical access process goes on through a phonological code, then it is no longer troublesome that Kleiman and others have shown lexical access not to be disrupted by keeping the articulatory muscles occupied.

This reasoning puts reading and auding on an equal footing: In both cases, there is the need to match the physical signal against a phonologically organized lexicon. By this view, speech perception is not at all direct, as some have argued. There is a complicated process through which the acoustic waveform has to be brought into a form that can use the morphophonemically organized lexicon. A phonologically organized lexicon could thus serve equally well for the perception of spoken and written language.

FLEXIBILITY AGAIN. Having distinguished between a phonological process of lexical access and a phonetic short-term memory, we need to ask again how much flexibility people can use in modifying these processes. The key observation. here, is that homophones are no harder to process than nonhomophones if the experimental session is "loaded" with homophones (which presumably discourages the subject from using speech coding). The most straightforward interpretation is that when people no longer find homophones harder than nonhomophones, they have switched to a purely visual strategy of lexical access. That is the conclusion most experts have reached.

However, it would be possible to maintain that the switch in processing strategy is from a more phonetic to a more phonological mediation strategy. This would satisfy those who wish to hold on, at all costs, to a universal speech-mediation position for lexical access in reading. Whether or not further research supports this last-ditch speech hypothesis, however, the distinction between phonetic and phonological mediation is extremely important in refining the question posed by this chapter.

REFERENCES AND NOTES

The theoretical question of speech and reading has been such a flourishing business that several reviews of the literature have appeared. The intention of this chapter was by no means to survey the field. For that purpose, Edfeldt (1960) reviewed studies of speech indicators in silent reading. Garrity (1978) reviewed EMG studies of reading-related tasks. Actually, the article by Kleiman (1975) contains an excellent literature review from a theoretical perspective. Finally, a major literature review has appeared in *Psychological Bulletin* (McCusker, Hillinger, & Bias, 1981), which I recommend for those interested in following this topic.

The matter of syllable effects is highly confusing at present. There are several studies on either side of the issue (Do extra syllables slow down processing?) for each experimental technique. With my colleague, Patrick Nye, at Haskins Laboratories, I have conducted such studies and consistently failed to find syllable effects for word stimuli (although we had some success with numbers). I was tempted to include some of this work here because there is a lesson it contains: Our failures to find increased processing with syllable length always occurred when we measured visual fixation times on a particular printed item. If the main speech-related coding process were *phonetic*, however, and lagged behind the eyes, one would not expect to have had any luck with visual processing times. This episode and reasoning made Nye and me especially receptive to the distinction between phonological processing for lexical access and phonetic processing for short-term memory. A good linguistic perspective on this distinction is found in Mattingly (1980).

I emphasize that the resolution of how speech enters into reading, offered in this chapter, is really very tentative. It fits the facts, but there is little evidence for it. In particular, there is no evidence I know of saying that phonological coding, specifically at the *morphophonemic level,* is occurring when evidence for speech is found in lexical access tasks. The second proposed mechanism—phonetic short-term memory for understanding syntax—is also only a speculation that fits the facts. It would need to be shown that the short-term memory confusions based on speech coding (Conrad, 1964) reflected the phonetic, rather than phonological, level.

Finally, I have resisted continuing at length about the role of short-term memory in sentence comprehension. However, the picture is not quite as neat as one would wish. Levy (1978) has done experiments on the effects of vocal suppression (saying one-two-three- . . . repeatedly) on sentence comprehension. She finds that there is indeed a price connected with having this articulatory distractor going on while reading (or hearing) sentences. This would be expected from Kleiman's work on the grounds that sentence comprehension requires a phonetic short-term memory. Levy has shown, however, that when the sentence comprehension test does not depend on *verbatim memory* for the sentence, but rather on paraphrase, the distractor effect disappears. That is, when the test of sentence comprehension had the subject select sentences that either did or didn't mean the same as the sentence presented, it was not damaging to have read the sentences during articulatory distraction. The subjects do seem to lose the exact words, when articulatory distraction is required, but it does not impair their access to meaning. A similar result was obtained by Baddeley and Hitch (cited in Baddeley, 1979). These are new results, and they remain to be integrated with other knowledge in this area, but they are provocative in suggesting that the phonetic short-term memory system may not, after all, be strictly necessary, at least not all the time.

CHAPTER 10

Learning How To Read

Education libraries are ready to collapse under the weight of books on teaching reading. Universities have whole departments devoted to the training of front-line reading teachers. We might begin to wonder whether this concern is not obsessive. But if education, and indeed civilization, could be boiled down into one crucial step, it would be the achievement of literacy. No wonder, then, that so much attention should have been aimed at how best to bring it off.

Our goals in this chapter are modest in light of this massive social effort at literacy: We sketch the broad outlines of what teaching methods have been used in the past and are currently favored. We suggest lines of research that pertain to settling some old arguments on teaching methods. And finally, we explore some recent evidence on how good readers and poor readers differ. In Chapter 11, we continue with the theme of poor readers and examine the concept of *dyslexia*.

HISTORICAL

Modern science has proven conclusively that it was impossible to learn to read with the instruction methods used prior to some

time in the nineteenth (or possibly the twentieth) century. Whatever arguments experts may have, now, about the preferred
teaching method, they agree that the ancient, traditional, *ABC
Method* was a disaster in educational terms. We will see why
presently. For the moment, note well that people learned to read
anyway from ancient times down until almost the present, under
this system. Perhaps not as easily as they would have learned
with one of the modern programs, granted, but the fact remains
that most motivated children, exposed to written language, do
learn to read. It is the highest vanity for us to suppose this learning is caused directly by what we do, as instructors. Learning to
read is mainly caused by what the learner does and our role is to
make it a bit easier, at best.

The ABC Method

This time-honored approach to reading begins by teaching children the letter names. Wealthy Greeks in the ancient world hired
24 slaves to coach their children, each slave to represent one of
their letters, a "hot" teaching approach worthy of our contemporary Sesame Street. In eighteenth-century America, gingerbread
cookies were baked in the shapes of letters, in the same spirit.
The way into a child's mind was apparently believed to be
through his or her stomach. Once the letter names were mastered
one way or another, simple syllables were learned, some of them
words and some not. The child would spell the syllable and then
pronounce it: WAF—"Double-you-ay-eff—waff." Later, more and
more words were mixed in, usually with the same spelling requirement prior to pronunciation. The subject matter was uniformly religious, in Christian times, until there was some loosen-
ing after the Reformation. Pictures were introduced in the 1600s
and early 1700s. Some highlights of North American reading
instruction under the ABC system are given as follows.

THE HORN BOOK. Not so much a book as a panel of wood
shaped like a small canoe paddle with a broad blade, a single
sheet of print was pasted to the wood and then covered for pro-

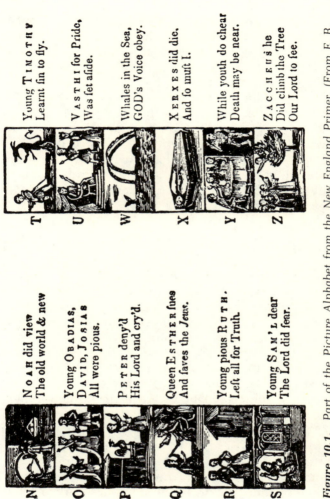

NOAH did view
The old world & new

Young OBADIAS,
DAVID, JOSIAS
All were pious.

PETER deny'd
His Lord and cry'd.

Queen ESTHER fues
And faves the Jews.

Young pious RUTH.
Left all for Truth.

Young SAM'L dear
The Lord did fear.

Young TIMOTHY
Learnt fin to fly.

VASTHI for Pride,
Was fet afide.

Whales in the Sea,
GOD's Voice obey.

XERXES did die.
And fo muft I.

While youth do chear
Death may be near.

ZACCHEUS he
Did climb the Tree
Our Lord to fee.

Figure 10.1. Part of the *Picture Alphabet* from the *New England Primer. (From E. B. Huey, The Psychology and Pedagogy of Reading,* MIT Press, 1968.)

tection by a transparent sheet of horn (like thick, clear plastic). The message printed looked just like a sewing "sampler"—the alphabet, perhaps some words, and then the Lord's Prayer. Horn books were used from about 1450 on.

THE NEW ENGLAND PRIMER. Figure 10.1 shows a segment from the New England Primer (1729), popular in somewhat later times, when real books and engravings were technically possible. This picture alphabet was intended to provide vivid associations to the individual letters. All bases were covered: The associations included pictures, rhythmic meter, alliteration, and an uplifting message. The New England Primer is believed to be the original source of the "Now I lay me down to sleep . . ." prayer.

WEBSTER'S SPELLING BOOKS. Noah Webster published his first spelling book in 1783. It and subsequent editions were intended for beginning readers of all ages. The contents included a list of approximately 9000 words, arranged by length, along with elements of a primer and first reader. There were also rhymes, fables, and moral instructions considered wholesome for children. Webster's spelling books were still selling over a million copies annually in the early 1870s. (His first dictionary, prepared for literate adults in the newly independent United States, came out in two volumes, in 1828, and contained about 70,000 words and their definitions.)

McGUFFEY'S READERS. McGuffey's graded series of six books first appeared in 1837. These books dominated the field for about 40 years and, in isolated rural areas of the country, have been discovered in use surprisingly far into the twentieth century. They contained more pictures than had earlier reading materials, along with the traditional emphasis on syllables, repetition of words, and patriotic, morally uplifting prose. The upper-level books also contained selections of literary, geographical, and social science material, however, and the McGuffey readers are believed to have had a significant impact on American society in the nineteenth century.

Theory and Innovation in Reading Pedagogy

Under the ABC method, most people (who tried) learned how to read, as we commented above. But then, as now, everyone did not have an equally easy time of it. Therefore, efforts began appearing, early on, to devise teaching methods that would make it easier. These proposed reforms had little impact on practices of their time, but they anticipated to a startling degree some of the issues now still being argued among specialists.

THE WHOLE-WORD METHOD. As early as 1657, Comenius published *Visible World*, of which a page is reproduced in Figure 10.2. Although the setting is archaic, the strategy is quite modern—teaching words directly by associating them with their meaning without intervention of the alphabetic principle. The words themselves are introduced in a meaningful context with pictorial reference to the named objects. (Note that Latin and English were taught side by side.) We have made reference to the philosophy behind this method in Chapter 9: Why should the child bother with the constituent letters when he or she can instead learn to go from the printed shape of the word to its meaning? In Figure 10.3 we see a modern descendant of this word method, a typical "basal reader" designed to weave in the words to be learned with a narrative that would make sense to the child. The whole-word approach was defended on rational grounds as early as 1828 in the Worcester primer:

> It is not very important, perhaps, that a child should know the letters before it begins to read. It may learn first to read words by seeing them, hearing them pronounced, and having their meanings illustrated; and afterward it may learn to analyse them or name the letters of which they are composed.

There is much of interest in this quotation, once one recovers from the adult-chauvinistic use of "it" to refer to children. Particularly, the author recognizes that analytic skills are a desirable objective—the child needs to know the alphabet, and the principle on which it is based, in order to figure out new words never

The Barbers Shop. LXXV.   *Tonſtrina.*

The Barber, 1.	*Tonſor,* 1.
in the Barbers-ſhop, 2.	in *Tonſtrina,* 2.
cutteth off the Hair	tondet *Crines*
and the Beard	& *Barbam*
with a pair of Sizzars, 3.	*Forcipe,* 3.
or ſhaveth with a Razor,	vel radit *Novaculâ,*
which he taketh out of his	quam è *Theca,* 4. depromit.
Caſe, 4.	
And he waſheth one	Et lavat
over a Baſon, 5.	ſuper *Pelvim,* 5.
with Suds running	*Lixivio* defluente
out of a Laver, 6.	è *Gutturnio,* 6.
and alſo with Sppe, 7.	ut & *Sapone,* 7.
and wipeth him	& tergit
with a Towel, 8.	*Linteo,* 8.
combeth him with a Comb, 9.	pectit *Pectine,* 9.
and curleth him	criſpat
with a Criſping Iron, 10.	*Calamiſtro,* 10.
Sometimes he cutteth a Vein	Interdum Venam ſecat
with a Pen-knife, 11.	*Scalpello,* 11.
where the Blood ſpirteth out, 12.	ubi Sanguis propullulat, 12.

Figure 10.2. A page from Orbis Pictus (visible world) by Comenius (1657). (From E. B. Huey, The Psychology and Pedagogy of Reading, MIT Press, 1968.)

Something Pretty

Mother said, "Look, look.
See this."

"Oh, oh," said Sally.
"It is pretty."

"Yes, yes," said Jane.
"Mother looks pretty."

21

Figure 10.3. *A page from a typical word-method primer. "Something Pretty" by Gertrude Warner from* The New Fun with Dick and Jane. © *Copyright 1956 Scott, Foresman and Company. Reprinted by permission.)*

seen before. However, the assumption is that once a child is already reading, he or she will then induce the letter sounds. That is, the child will eventually notice that words beginning with the letter *b* tend to have similar sounds, and so forth.

In the twentieth century, there was believed to be actual experimental justification for the whole-word method: In the 1930s, Gestalt psychology was a major influence in the study of perception. Its theorists believed that perception—of anything—was best considered in terms of the overall shape (Gestalt means configuration in German) rather than in terms of individual details. In Chapter 3 we referred to this type of theory as a *template* system. Applied to reading, these ideas clearly implied that it is the overall shape of the word that counts and not the individual alphabetic characters of which it is composed. It follows that children should be taught, right from the start, in a way that is consistent with how they will be reading later, when they achieve fluency.

THE SENTENCE-METHOD. Experiments in Binghamton, New York, in the 1870s were interpreted to support what we might call a "whole-sentence" method of reading instruction. This might seem a *reductio ad absurdem* of the word method, but it was apparently taken seriously by some. Basically, one would expose a sentence to the child visually, at the same time reading it aloud distinctly. Then another sentence both visually and aloud, and so on. As the child noticed the relation between the print and the speech was not random, he or she would gradually be expected to see the correct correspondences, and then to generalize them to fresh samples.

One could defend the sentence method on the grounds that a sentence is a complete idea and, therefore, beginning with any lesser unit forces the child to make unnatural segmentations. Of course, extensions of this logic are staggering—it is really the *paragraph*, it might be claimed, that contains whole ideas, not the individual sentence, therefore. . . .

THE PHONICS METHOD. The idea behind the methods grouped together as phonics methods is to teach the individual letters by the sounds they make—not by their conventional names—and then to induce children to blend these sounds together in new letter combinations. This general approach was advocated as early as the 1700s in the French Jansenist and Port Royal schools. We will be talking on and off about the phonics method for the rest of the chapter and so a detailed outline of it is not necessary here. The important point is that an emphasis on phonics teaches an *analytical* approach to words, one that is designed to exploit the alphabetic principle. The phonics method is sometimes equated with what is called "sound emphasis" but there is more to it than that: You could emphasize sound but treat words as logographic symbols—whole shapes—and not make use of the alphabetic principle. Somehow, the elementary school term *sounding out* captures the essense of the phonics method, being able to get to the identity of the word by taking it a sound at a time and blending them together.

In the word *phonics* we have yet another word, like phonological, phonetic, morphophonemic, and others, derived from the Greek word for sound. We are simply stuck with this term, phonics, it is so permanently fixed in educational and popular usage. It refers only to this one particular approach to the teaching of early reading and not to any specific level of linguistic abstraction (the way some of the other terms do).

ORTHOGRAPHIC REFORM. Of course, the problem with learning the sounds made by the letters is that, in many languages including English, individual letters just *don't have* consistent sounds. In some cases, such as those discussed in a previous chapter, the inconsistency in letter-sound associations is for profound historical reasons (DEBT) that can preserve morphophonemic consistency (EXTREME-EXTREMITY). But there are many other cases, where we can't invoke these arguments of "optimality" and regularity at the abstract levels: Some of these other cases derive rather from the history of English as a mixture of French and German words dating from the Norman invasion of England in 1066. Take the C in CAT, CHILD, and CELLAR, for example. What can we instruct the child to do with this letter? One popular approach to this problem has been spelling reform. Here again, new developments such as the Initial Teaching Alphabet of Sir James Pitman, have antecedents in earlier innovations. Figure 10.4 shows a reform published in the Funk and Wagnalls *Standard First Reader* called the Scientific Alphabet, and Pitman's ITA next to it.

We would hardly propose to raise our children being able to read *only* one of these reformed alphabets! That is why they are deliberately intended only to ease the child into the concept of reading and the early stages of skill. Then, either a cold-turkey or gradual phasing out of the unusual symbols is arranged. There seems to be little controversy about whether the reformed alphabets are easier to start with or not. We would have to junk a lot of the psychology of learning if this were not true. The debate over reformed alphabets is on whether the time and effort required to wean children from the novel symbols makes up for the easier time they have at the beginning. A book by Pitman and St. John (1969) summarizes some of the research on the Initial Teaching Alphabet from what is understandably a less than disinterested perspective.

A different reform strategy is adjusting spelling, usage, and syntax to fit nonstandard English dialects of beginning readers, particularly children speaking black English. Proposals have been offered for preparation of reading materials that are specifically written in black English (e.g., see Stewart, 1969).

The reasoning is straightforward: We observe that inner-city school children, from lower socioeconomic status families, are often disadvantaged in early reading, relative to middle-class suburban children. Second, we note that the inner-city children also speak a different dialect of English, one that is nonstandard with respect to the English spoken by those in charge of educating them. It is perfectly natural to reach the conclusion that the second circumstance is the cause of the first. However, it is a fallacy that when two things happen together, one of them necessarily causes the other.

In the case of black dialect and reading, we have some evidence that is relevant. Labov (1970) studied the dropping of suffixes in black dialect and its relation to reading comprehension. He did find that specific confusions can occur as a result of

Wʊns, Rip Van Win'-kl went ʊp
   a-mʊng' the hilz, hwãr hî sē
   cwîr lit'-l men plê'-ing bēl.
The gêv Rip sʊm -thing tū drink,
   hwich put him tū slîp.
Hî slept twen'-ti yîrz, and hwen hî wōk ʊp
   hî wɵz an ōld man with grê hāɪ and bîrd.
Hî went hōm.   Nō wʊn niū him at fẹrst.
Hî wɵz tōld hwɵt had hap'-nd
   hwɑil hî wɵz a-slîp' a-mʊng' the hilz.

Figure 10.4. *The Scientific Alphabet (above, From E. B. Huey, The Psychology and Pedagogy of Reading,* MIT Press, 1968) and Initial Teaching Alphabet (right). Both were invented to provide children with direct and lawful relation between letters and sounds in order to make phonics instruction work better.

different speech patterns that occur in standard and black English. However, the main result was that the tendency to make these confusions was not correlated with overall reading comprehension skill. Simons (1979) has reviewed other studies that force exactly the same conclusion—that the phonological differences in dialect do not predict general reading progress. Thus, we cannot hold the dialect-based confusions responsible for poor progress in reading among these children.

Even if the dialect difference were somehow contributing to relatively poor reading scores in the inner-city schools, the evidence is weak that adopting materials designed for black English would help. Simons (1979) has recently reviewed a large number of studies comparing performance on standard English materials with performance on texts specially designed for black dialect. The results show either no differences, for children who speak the black dialect themselves, or an *advantage* of the standard-English version.

The relative failure of orthographic reform in reading instruction leads us to a lesson that echoes what was said in the previ-

THE INITIAL TEACHING ALPHABET

Number	Character	Name	Example	Traditional spelling
1	æ	ae	ræt	rate
2	b	bee	big	big
3	c	kee	cat	cat
4	d	dee	dog	dog
5	ɛɛ	ee	meet	meet
6	f	ef	fill	fill
7	g	gae	gun	gun
8	h	hae	hat	hat
9	ie	ie	tie	tie
10	j	jae	jelly	jelly
11	k	kae	kit	kit
12	l	el	lamp	lamp
13	m	em	man	man
14	n	en	net	net
15	œ	oe	tœ	toe
16	p	pee	pig	pig
17	r	rae	run	run
18	s	ess	sad	sad
19	t	tee	tap	tap
20	ue	ue	due	due
21	v	vee	van	van
22	w	wae	will	will
23	y	i-ae	yell	yell
24	z	zed or zee	fizz	fizz
25	ʃ	zess	houses	houses
26	wh	whae	when	when
27	ᚳh	chae	chick	chick
28	th	ith	thaut	thought
29	th	thee	the	the
30	ſh	ish	ship	ship
31	ʒ	zhee	mezuer	measure
32	ŋ	ing	siŋ	sing
33	a	ah	far	far
34	au	au	autum	autumn
35	a	at	appl	apple
36	e	et	egg	egg
37	i	it	dip	dip
38	o	ot	hot	hot
39	u	ut	ugly	ugly
40	ω	oot	book	book
41	ꞷ	oo	mωn	moon
42	ou	ow	bou	bough
43	oi	oi	toi	toy

(From J. A. Downing, *The Initial Teaching Alphabet*. Scott Foresman and Company, 1965. Reproduced by permission.)

ous chapter: In one form or another, the reforms proposed all carry the writing system back further toward a direct translation of sound stream into print. That direction of change seems not to pay off. It is perhaps for good reason that our writing system has settled at a morphophonemic level. It is abstract enough to embrace different ways we, as individuals, pronounce related words (EXTREME-EXTREMITY). It is abstract enough, as well, to embrace different ways that members of our language community pronounce the very same word (MOUTH-MOUF). At the same time, is is related to phonology and therefore allows the sounding out of new words for the beginning reader.

THE LINGUISTIC METHOD. By the time of World War II, American education was sold on the whole-word method of teaching reading. As we saw, it fit with psychological research in the Gestalt tradition. Furthermore, its emphasis on meaning rather than rote drill was attractive in the climate of "progressive" and "creative" education. In 1955, Rudolf Flesch published a book called *Why Johnny Can't Read*, which had an enormous impact on the public and became a best seller. The book charged that the abandonment of phonics in favor of the whole-word approach was seriously threatening national literacy.

The kinds of arguments Flesch used were related to our discussion of the advantages of phonological mediation in Chapter 9. Phonics gives a way of figuring out new words and connecting print, generally, with the spoken language already partially mastered. The whole-word system, typified in standard basal readers, was sacrificing these benefits in order to give children a cheap way of recognizing the shapes of familiar words right off the bat. Did Flesch lead the public reaction that ensued away from pure whole-word teaching and back to a more eclectic blend of look-say and phonics? It is possible. However, it is also possible that Flesch's book was a symptom of that reaction rather than its cause. The fact is, most methods today include elements of both approaches but the balance between phonics and whole-word materials has considerable variation.

Actually, the linguist Bloomfield voiced objections to the prevailing basal (look-say, whole-word) approach in 1942. And although Flesch used Bloomfield's arguments, he (Bloomfield) had no use for conventional phonics either. However, instead of re- forming the alphabet, to get around the inconsistency problem, Bloomfield proposed introducing a *restricted set of words* in the early phases of reading instruction. These carefully selected words would protect the child from spelling inconsistencies and also would be chosen so as to maximize the chances to learn phonic principles. Figure 10.5 shows a page from a elementary reader based on Bloomfield's linguistic method. Notice that there are no spelling-to-sound inconsistencies and that the words are arranged in a way that emphasizes phonic rules.

The strategy with these materials is to teach "as if" by the whole-word method. However, the special materials make a big difference: The child is almost forced to make phonetic general- izations—that is, to discover what sounds the letters stand for by observing that, for example, RAP and GAP differ in their first segment. This may seem like only a minor adjustment of the whole-word method but it is in fact major. The linguistic method chooses words on the basis of their sounds, not their meanings. Refer back again to Figure 10.3 and notice that this page, from a basal (look-say) reader, includes four words with the letter O— LOOK, COME, GO, TO—all pronounced differently. They were selected because they are among the most common words in the child's vocabulary and the primary objective of whole-word teaching is to attach meaningfully to the child's existing lan- guage. But each of these words from a single page has a different pronunciation of the letter *O!* The linguistic reader sacrifices the familiarity of the high-frequency words for the consistency of specially selected words like GAP and RAP, even if they are not in the child's active vocabulary.

SOME RESEARCH RESULTS

It is quite reasonable to expect that investigators would have tried to find out which of the methods reviewed in the last sec- tion work best. Indeed, there has been a vast research effort on this set of questions for a long time. We cannot review, or even

37

A rap. A gap.

Dad had a map.
Pat had a bat.
Tad had a tan cap.
Nan had a tan hat.

Nan had a fat cat.
A fat cat ran at a bad rat.

Can Dad nap?
Dad can nap.
Can Pat fan Dad?
Pat can.

Figure 10.5.   *A page from a primer based on the Linguistic Method. The use of rhyming words emphasizes phonic rules without misleading the child about the consistency of English orthography. (From L. Bloomfield & C. L. Barnhart, Let's Read, Part 1. Clarence L. Barnhart, 1963. With permission of Clarence L. Barnhart, Inc.)*

summarize this entire effort here, but we will take time for a selective survey of results that give some insights.

Does It Help To Learn the Letter Names?

One approach to understanding the process of reading acquisition is to examine presumed components of this or that method and see how they work. This is not always possible—often one must compare whole teaching programs, intact. However, some research questions are amenable to less than a wholesale approach, for example, the question of whether knowing the letter names helps reading acquisition: It is a fact that children who "know their letter names" before formal reading instruction starts are later found to be higher in reading achievement than those who do not. The correlation is about + .60. This is not only a large relationship; knowledge of the letter names is known to be the single best predictor, by far, of reading progress for children entering kindergarten and first grade. That is, if you wanted to predict which children would do well in initial reading instruction, and you were allowed to use only a single piece of knowledge to make your prediction, knowledge of letter names would be your best choice. But, of course, a relationship between two variables does not tell us that one causes the other. It could be that some third factor *both* promotes preschoolers' learning of the letter names and, independently, their success in school later. Perhaps parents who encourage their children to learn the letters also help them later with all school subjects.

Experimental evidence by Onmacht (1969) suggests training in the letter names is not useful. In this study, intact classes were taught either (1) the letter names alone, (2) the letter names and their typical sounds when pronounced, or (3) nothing at all. The results showed that only the group taught sounds (phonic training, essentially) was better than the no-training control.

On the basis of common sense, we would expect differences among the letters in this: Sometimes the letter name is a handy clue for how it is spoken and other times the name is actually misleading. Letters like *P* have names that match well their usual phonetic value. But there are only 16 like this, according to one count. Other letters—G and C—have names that contain their common sound, but it is another pronounciation of them that is taught first in school. Still others still have no relationship—for example, W. The early success of the ABC teaching method may thus have been more in spite of the insistence on knowing names of letters than because of it.

Another possibility is that the ABC method had the good side effect of directing children's attention to the level of letters in written text. Even though the names of many letters are misleading as to how they are pronounced, a focus of any kind on letters and their sounds might pay off when it is an alphabetic writing system in question.

Experimental Comparisons of the Methods

Naturally, the most valid and ambitious kind of research on reading instruction is the experimental comparison. An entire school system can commit itself to a year or two in which all its first-grade classrooms participate. Classes and their instructors are, at best, randomly assigned to one of two or more curricula. Publishers of reading programs have considerable variety in approach and so one can simply select different "packages" for as many treatments as one wants to compare.

The programs available cover a wide range of theoretical persuasions. However, the relatively pure options include Scott-Foresman's basal series (whole-word without explicit phonics), Lippincott's systematic phonics approach, and the so-called *intrinsic phonics* methods, including the Bloomfield-Fries "linguistic" method. (Intrinsic phonics means there is no drill on letter sounds but the materials are arranged to emphasize phonic rules, as in Figure 10.5.)

In 1967, Chall reviewed the hundreds of studies including comparisons of reading instruction programs then available and concluded that there is only one real issue at stake—whether or not it is important to introduce an emphasis on the phonic code early in the game. Her summary of the results of the research was that, by the fourth grade, having had an early emphasis on the code was beneficial to children. What was the scale on which these beneficial effects were measured? As we would expect, the advantage of systematic phonics was particularly evident in spelling, reading new words, and reading aloud. There was some slight evidence that an early meaning emphasis (basal, whole-word approach) led to better comprehension, but this evidence was not as reliable as the evidence that phonics improved other aspects of reading. Indeed, there would *have* to be at least some advantage in comprehension for the whole-word method very early in training; the whole point of that method is to use the easiest possible words in order to get children reading for comprehension right from the start. Chall found that children's interest and involvement in reading was not affected by the teaching method.

In other findings, Chall noted that systematic phonics, explicit drill on letter sounds, may well work better than the "intrinsic" phonics of the linguistic method. Another result was, not surprisingly, that a modified alphabet such as the ITA leads to faster progress initially than other approaches. Finally, the benefits of systematic phonics drill were greater with lower-class children than with upper- and middle-class children. Chall suggested that this last result may come from the high odds that "brighter" children would figure out the phonics-type code *anyway*, without specific training.

Williams (1979) has recently reviewed some of the literature since 1967 and concludes that, if anything, the evidence is now stronger favoring a phonics-drill approach in early reading instruction. This conclusion has met with firm resistance in some educational circles and we might well wonder why. Williams suggests that this resistance is partly due to conventional beliefs that education should be "meaningful" and that rote drill is "bad." These beliefs are quite a bit more consistent with the whole-word than with the phonics approach.

One thing is sure: The experimental effects that can be assigned to teaching methods are miserably small compared to those that can be assigned to what the individual child brings with him into the classroom. Whether it is IQ, motivation, basic language skills, or some combination of these, most investigations have found that the student is the major factor in the outcome and the method produces only a minor adjustment. This conclusion is evident in a large study by Newman (1972) on the sixth-grade performance of 230 children who had been behind in reading in first grade, and subjected to different types of remedial instruction. Newman concludes that general IQ is the major factor by far in the follow-up performance, more important than teaching method or reading readiness scores in first grade.

We began this chapter with the caution that, somehow, most children learn to read at about the same stage of development, however they are taught. These sources of evidence we have just been discussing are entirely consistent with that observation. However, as a society, we don't want to settle for getting "most children" to read—all normal children should learn. Compare auding with reading, as we have done before several times: Apart from special problems like deafness, it is fair to say that all normally intelligent children really do learn to aud. Why is reading not equally effortless and universal?

WHEN INSTRUCTION FAILS

In the remainder of the chapter, we are concerned with reading failure. Our reasons for being interested in reading failure should be made clear right from the start: The goal is to learn about the *process of reading* from this material, not to come up with specific clinical remedies. Remediation of reading is, of course, an urgent human and national priority and it would be impudent to claim that it is not. However, the limited objectives of this book are to characterize and understand the normal reading process. It so happens that many "pure" experimental psychologists are convinced that, ultimately, the way to deal with abnormal functioning is first to understand normal fuctioning. For example, it could be argued that normal growth has to be understood before the abnormal growth that occurs in cancer can be understood. Others have argued that it works the other way as well—that abnormalities provide crucial information for theories of normal function. Certainly color blindness was important in guiding us toward an adequate theory of normal color vision. As so often happens, there is probably truth on both sides. But without doubt, the study of delayed reading acquisition belongs on our agenda.

There will be a bias to the coverage in this treatment, and we might as well announce it here: Much evidence suggests that reading failures in children (and perhaps in adults) are caused by a lack of awareness of the spoken language. That is, children who are ready to learn to read can become conscious of, or gain access to, the structural properties of the language they speak. Again, in terms of a simple example, one can hardly imagine a child's being able to match up written letters with elements of the spoken language if they can't analyze their speech into phonological units.

Not all workers agree with this attitude. Some argue, rather, that it is a failure in the comprehension process that holds back new readers. We return to this issue later.

Children's Phonological Awareness

Here, we present two specific demonstrations that children are insensitive to the structure of their own spoken language prior to being ready for reading or prior to instruction in reading.

ARE PREREADERS INSENSITIVE TO RHYME? Everybody knows that little children like nursery rhymes and that they can recite such verses well before they go near a first-grade classroom. The assumption is that the rhyming scheme is somehow important for them but the facts seem to deny this: Calfee, Chapman, and Venezky (1972) tested a group of 5½ year-olds on their understanding of rhyme. In one part of the test, they were given two words and asked "Do these words sound the same at the end?" The rate of correct responding was 49%, essentially the same as we would expect from guessing (50%). This was *after* a preliminary session in which they were given feedback and corrected. Another part of the test focused on production—Could the children give a word that rhymes with a presented word? The overall rate of success in production was only 39%. The interesting feature of this last result was that the distribution of scores around this average was bimodal. That is, few of the scores were actually near 39%; some were much better and some were much worse, so that the average fell in between. There was a very high correlation between scores on the rhyme-production test and initial progress in reading. Like all correlations, this one does not prove that rhyme awareness causes good progress in reading but at least it shows that there is an association.

THE MOW-MOTORCYCLE TEST. Rozin, Bressman, and Taft (1974) demonstrated an even more striking association between reading progress and awareness of the structure of spoken words. They held up two cards, side by side, one containing the word MOW and the other MOTORCYCLE. They pronounced the two words carefully, telling the children that one of the cards had one of the two words and the other had the other printed on it. Which was which? If children understood that MOTORCYCLE had a longer pronunciation, with more phonetic segments, than MOW, they would easily choose the correct card, even without being able to read. Many other stimuli were used, some words and others not (UB-UBIQUITOUS, ERG-ERGONOMIC) in order to rule out specific familiarity with the written or oral versions of the items.

The finding was that prereaders were little better than chance at this task. There were differences between urban and suburban children but, generally, there was a transition between guessing at prekindergarten age and doing fairly well after the first grade. This corresponds, of course, to the period over which reading is introduced and typically mastered at a low level. Rozin et al. found that even elaborate training procedures and systematic explanation failed to produce gains in children who could not perform the task.

Studies of Good and Poor Readers

One popular approach to reading failure is to perform experiments using separate groups of good and poor readers as subjects. Provided one can rule out such group differences as IQ, one can look for patterns of differences in performance that may underlie progress in reading acquisition.

This matter of separating IQ differences from differences in reading, as such, is a sticky one. The main point is that if one child is behind his or her classmates in reading *and also behind in absolutely everything else* (arithmetic, understanding spoken directions, perhaps even tying shoelaces) it is of less theoretical interest to us than if the problem is specifically with reading. The plain fact is that all children are not equally smart (or motivated) and differences in reading ability that go along with IQ (or motivation) are not as interesting as specific problems with reading.

PHONETIC SEGMENTATION. Isabel Liberman and Donald Shankweiler, with their colleagues (Liberman, Shankweiler, Liberman, & Fowler, 1977) have examined the performance of good and poor readers on a phonetic segmentation task, in which children are asked to tap in response to the number of units in a word. In one version of the task, they were asked to tap either once or three times depending on whether the word was one syllable in length or three (PIG versus ELEPHANT).

A second group of children were instructed to tap in response to the number of *phonetic segments* in single-syllable words (OH and EYE have one, OAT and PIE have two, and BOAT and SPY have three). The measure was whether they could tap the correct number of times. The children tested were either 4, 5, or 6 years old—a range that spans the prereading to reading-readiness years. For the three age groups, success in the syllable task went from 46, to 48, to 90%, respectively. Corresponding scores in the phonetic-segment task were only 0, 17, and 70% correct. In other words the task where children must detect letterlike units was substantially harder and the youngest group got essentially nowhere with it. However, their respectable performance on the syllable task shows that there was nothing wrong with their counting ability or with their understanding of the instructions. This result fits nicely with the MOW-MOTORCYCLE evidence.

Adult Illiteracy

Quite a similar message is now available concerning reading failure among adults: Morais, Cary, Alegria, and Bertelson (1979)

wondered whether access to phonetic segments—the skill lacking in poor beginning readers—arises spontaneously at a certain
age (around 6) or depends on specific training in reading. They
chose to investigate adult illiterates for the following reason: We
know that dramatic changes in phonological awareness occur
around five or six; see again the Liberman et al. data. The question is whether these changes occur only because the child
reaches a certain level of cognitive development that is locked
into time sequence, like walking, or whether these changes also
depend on specific training in reading. It would hardly be ethical
to perform the "proper" experiment because it would entail
withholding reading instruction for one randomly selected group
for a year or two!

Morais and his colleagues selected illiterate adults from a
poor, agricultural district in Portugal to use as subjects. Most of
these 30 individuals had had no instruction whatever in reading, and the rest had learned only letter names (often from their
children) or, at most, had had a few months of training in
school. A matched group of 30 subjects had been in a govern-
ment-sponsored literacy project after adolescence (22 passed
and 8 failed). In other respects the groups were comparable.

The particular task used by Morais et al. involved addition
and deletion of phonetic segments from words and nonwords. In
the deletion task, subjects were told to remove the first sound in
a word, giving FARM—ARM or SHIRP—IRP. In the addition
task, they had to do the reverse, adding a particular segment say
[p], to make a new item, as in ANT-PANT.

The results are shown in Table 10.1, which gives percent
success for the two groups on the four different versions of the
task. The illiterates were sharply inferior to the control group in
all respects. In fact, it was reported that 50% of the illiterate
subjects failed every single test, whereas none of the literate subjects did.

It was not the failure of illiterates to understand the instructions that was to blame, in all probability. In a supplementary
experiment, Morais et al. found that when asked to reverse phonetic segments within a word (PACK—CAP), the same illiterates
scored only 9% (range = 0 to 20) whereas when they were asked

Table 10.1   Results of Morais et al. (1979)

	Task	
Group	Addition	Deletion
Illiterate		
W→W*	46%	26%
NW→NW	19%	19%
Literate		
W→W	91%	87%
NW→NW	71%	73%

*W = word NW = nonword.

to reverse syllables (PACKRAT—RATPACK) they were much better, with a mean of 48% (range = 13 to 93).

Thus, the authors conclude, the ability to deal consciously with phonetic segments is not gained automatically, simply by virtue of being "old enough." Instead, it depends also, apparently, on learning to read an alphabetic orthography, whenever that learning occurs, given it is after the age of 5 or 6. This last conclusion comes from the results of the control group, who had become literate well into adulthood but did quite well on the experimental tasks.

Speech Mediation in Good and Poor Readers

In Chapter 9, we were careful to evaluate the case for some role of inner speech in reading. The bottom line of that accounting was that a phonological strategy in lexical access was at least a possibility, although not compulsory. There is now considerable evidence that good and poor readers differ conspicuously in reference to this mediation of inner speech. We suggest, in what follows, that poor readers do not exploit the phonetic code for short-term memory to the extent that good readers do. Not using a phonetic code in short-term memory is not the same as lacking *awareness of the spoken language*, on which we have until just now been concentrating. Inability to count phonemes in a single-syllable word is not the same as failing to show evidence that speech is used as a mediating code in short-term memory. However, both of these seem to be true of poor readers and, in the final analysis, there may be a profound theoretical relation between them. But let us inspect the evidence first.

SPEECH CODING IN IMMEDIATE MEMORY. Liberman et al. gave immediate memory tests to groups of good and poor readers in second grade. The children were to repeat back lists of letters in order immediately after they were presented. As in Conrad's work in the early 1960s, the letters within a list were either similar in pronunciation (BCTPZGD) or dissimilar (HFQWRML). Overall, the poor readers did worse than the good readers and the similar lists were harder than the dissimilar lists. However, the main result was a large interaction: The good readers were badly hurt by the similarity of the letters within a list whereas the poor readers were only slightly impaired. This is consistent with the interpretation that the good readers naturally used speech as a mediator for memory while the poor readers did so less.

Unfortunately, it is also consistent with another interpretation: Perhaps the degree of similarity effect (how much one is hurt by rhyming letters) depends on how much one rehearses the letters alone. The good readers, being smarter or more highly motivated than the poor readers, may well rehearse more energetically. It follows that they would be damaged more by similarity.

These ideas were put to test by Mark, Shankweiler, Liberman and Fowler (1977). Their technique was based on the use of *incidental learning* in which the person is not aware he or she will ever be tested on the stimuli that are exposed—and thus there is unlikely to be much or any deliberate rehearsal. Second graders from good and poor reading groups were given a 28-word "reading test" in which they had to pronounce each item as it appeared. Later, they were given an unexpected recognition test in which they had to say OLD or NEW in response to the same 28 words mixed in with an equal number of words they had not seen before. These latter words, the foils, were either similar in sound to the correct words or not. If the subject had learned

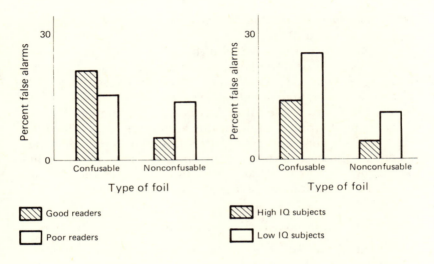

Figure 10.6. *Results of the Mark et al. (1977) experiments.*

KNOW, GOOD, and DOOR, among others, the confusable foils would have been GO, COULD, and MORE. In the nonconfusable condition, there was no relation between the items learned and the recognition foils.

The result is shown in the left panel of Figure 10.6 for the two reading groups and the two kinds of materials. The performance measure is the tendency of subjects to commit a "false alarm" to the two kinds of foil. If someone had remembered the original 28-word list mainly by reference to speech, then some of the similar foils might very well fool this subject into making a false alarm. However, if speech had not been the main memory format for the original encoding of the words, then there should be no difference between the two kinds. (Of course, all subjects pronounced the words using speech; we are speaking here of what code they used later, in remembering the list.) The result was clear cut. For the good readers, it made a big difference whether the foils were confusable in terms of speech with the correct items; false alarm errors were higher in the former case than in the latter. However, for the poor readers, there was no disadvantage for the confusable foils.

Evidence in the right panel of figure 10.6 suggests that IQ is not the variable operating to differentiate good and poor readers here. True, the high-IQ subjects in this study made fewer false alarms; however, high- and low-IQ subjects were equally affected by the similarity of the foils. This is a good example of how to disentangle IQ from reading in this kind of research. The difference between good and poor readers is all the more interesting if a split on the basis of IQ does not show the same pattern. Thus, again, there seems to be some special relation between the specific skill of reading and of a speech-based code.

Top-down and Bottom-up Factors in Good and Poor Readers

In Chapter 6, we became familiar with the opposition between top-down and bottom-up processing in perception. As we read a sentence, our expectations for what is not yet in view can sometimes permit a top-down solution (SET THE TABLE WITH KNIVES AND . . .); similarly, a word out of context or in inappropriate rattlesnake context must be processed bottom-up. It is a matter of warm controversy these days where the problem lies with children making poor progress in reading. The fact is, poor readers can often grind out the individual words in reading but show no comprehension whatever later; this suggests to many that comprehension is the obstacle that needs to be faced with poor readers. The other view is that because the decoding skills of poor readers are inadequate, they must devote their entire attention to deciphering the words, leaving no capacity for figuring out the meaning. This would suggest that drill in decoding is the answer. (Recall our discussion of the work of LaBerge and Samuels in Chapter 6.)

There is research relevant to the issue of how good and poor readers balance meaning against decoding; it suggests that inadequate decoding skills are to blame in the poor readers: Byrne and Shea (1978) tested Australian second graders in a continuous recognition memory task. The children saw one word after another and, eventually, each word occurred twice in the series.

As each word appeared, the person had to decide whether this was the first or the second occurrence (responses of NEW and OLD, respectively).

From time to time in the series, trick foils were inserted, similar to words that had appeared before, and interest was in the tendency to commit false alarms (OLD) on these items. The point of the experiment was that these similar foils were either similar in sound or similar in meaning to the prior list items. Assume the prior items were HOME and CARPET: HOUSE and RUG would be the semantically similar foils and COMB and MARKET would be the phonetically similar foils. If subjects encoded the items by meaning, they would be attracted to HOUSE and RUG; if they encoded the sounds, they would be attracted to COMB and MARKET.

The results are in terms of false alarms, saying OLD to a foil. The control foils were neither semantically nor phonetically similar to the correct items. Table 10.2 shows the results. For the poor readers, there was a large tendency to be fooled by the semantic foils and none to be fooled by the phonetic foils. For the good readers, both the semantic and phonetic foils led to false alarms. There are two results here. First, the good readers are again shown to use the phonetic code more than the poor readers, as in the Liberman et al. experiments. Now, however, there is the second observation that poor readers "choose errors" based on the semantic code *more than the good readers.*

The fact that poor readers seem to be using "too much" meaningful processing does not imply that they are *better at* top-down processing than good readers. It is just that they may be so deficient in bottom-up processing they have no other recourse. In plain language, they can't read the word very well so they have to guess, based on whatever other cues there are in the context. Poor readers may well be poorer at extracting this meaningful context than good readers but still making greater use of it.

A study by Perfetti, Goldman, and Hogaboam (1979) makes a similar point, and goes beyond the Byrne and Shea study. These authors studied the speed with which children of good and poor reading groups could begin to name words that were flashed on

Table 10.2   Results of Byrne and Shea (Entries are false positives)

Group		Condition Semantic	Phonetic
Poor Readers	Experimental items	3.07	.67
	Control items	.67	.60
	Difference	2.40	.07
Good readers	Experimental items	2.07	2.80
	Control items	.73	1.40
	Difference	1.34	1.40

the screen. These target words were either presented alone, or in the context of a list of unrelated words, or finally, in the context of a coherent narrative. In the two context conditions, the context was presented out loud and from time to time, the subject was interrupted to take a visual naming reaction-time test. In the coherent context condition, the narrative presented aloud "led up" meaningfully to the word presented for visual reaction time.

The question was whether the good readers or the poor readers would benefit more from the presence of context. If poor readers are deficient in top-down processing, they might be expected not to show much of an advantage of the context, at least less advantage than the good readers. Mean reaction time was 728 milliseconds for good readers in the isolated-word condition. These subjects were slightly slower when the word was presented in the context of a list of unrelated words (786 milliseconds) and much faster when the same word appeared in the context of a meaningful story (665 milliseconds). If we use the list context condition as the proper control, there was a facilitation of 121 milliseconds produced by the meaningful context. The poor readers were slower overall, with scores of 1023, 1069, and 751 milliseconds, respectively, for the isolated, list-context, and meaningful context conditions. These poor readers thus had a facilitation of 318 msec produced by the meaningful context. The conclusion is again that the poor readers are making more use of top-down processing than the good readers. In another version of their experiment, Perfetti et al. presented either the list context or the story context visually rather than auditorially. Here the facilitation was only 41 milliseconds for the good readers and was 200 milliseconds for the poor readers.

Thus, despite widespread beliefs to the contrary, poor readers seem to make more use of meaningful, top-down processing than good readers. Perhaps this should be no surprise, since they are deficient in bottom-up processing. Again we repeat, the greater use of top-down processing by poor readers than by good readers does not imply that poor readers are better at perceiving and using top-down strategies.

It is very important that in the Perfetti et al. experiment, children were classified as good or poor readers according to a measure of *paragraph comprehension*. In other research, such as that of the Liberman-Shankweiler group, the classification measure included mainly the child's fluency in reading nonwords presented one at a time. It might not be surprising to find decoding skills associated with this test. But to find a nearly pure comprehension measure giving the same results is strong evidence that major reading problems owe to bottom-up and not to top-down processing.

Now to be sure, there are probably comprehension difficulties associated with poor reading performance. However, these comprehension problems are almost undoubtedly evident in the understanding of spoken language as well as written language and therefore they have nothing to do specifically with reading.

SOME RESEARCH WITH TRAINING IMPLICATIONS

In this concluding section, we consider one of several proposals relevant to the teaching of reading that come from outside the traditional education discipline. We outline briefly the work of Gleitman and Rozin (1973, see also Rozin & Gleitman, 1977) at the University of Pennsylvania. This is a good project for closing the chapter because it brings together several themes from other sections of this book.

A Psycholinguistically and Linguistically Motivated Proposal

Gleitman and Rozin justify their proposal for an initial *syllable-based* reading program on one linguistic observation and one psycholinguistic observation. The linguistic observation is simply that, as we saw in Chapter 8, writing systems attach to various levels of the spoken language. Thus, Chinese logographs are designed to track meaning units, albeit with some phonetic hints added. Our alphabetic system, of course, is roughly lined up with the level of *systematic phonemes* as we noted in Chapters 8 and 9. Other writing systems take the syllable as the unit to be represented in the orthography.

The psycholinguistic result of special interest to Gleitman and Rozin is that the systematic phoneme is a particularly difficult one to bring into awareness—for anyone, but especially for children. On the other hand, they argue, the syllable is quite an easy unit to bring into awareness. Therefore, the initial stages of reading instruction should use a syllable-based orthography. This is because learning an alphabetic orthography requires a conscious matching up of letters with the phonological segments they more or less stand for. Now we need to unpack this argument more slowly as follows.

THE DIFFICULTY OF THE SYSTEMATIC PHONEME. The beginning reader really has to learn two things—that printed symbols represent units in the speech stream and that the particular unit represented is the systematic phoneme. The first of these lessons poses no particular problem. For example, Rozin, Poritzky, and Sotsky (1971) have shown that inner-city children with severe reading problems can easily learn to read English sentences with words represented as Chinese ideographs. The second lesson, that the phonological level is the one to attach to letter units, is the major difficulty. We have seen, earlier in this chapter, how difficult it is for prereaders to count speech segments. We have seen that even the awareness required for rhyming is badly lacking in such children. Gleitman and Rozin also report that bright, highly motivated but nonreading children cannot seem to learn to speak pig Latin. This is a "secret language" that requires awareness of phonetic segments. To speak pig Latin, you need to be able to peel off the first segment in a word (like the Morais et al. subjects had to do in Portugal) and add it at the end. The MOW/MOTORCYCLE phenomenon reveals the same problem.

Why should the phonological segment be so difficult to isolate consciously? One reason is that by the nature of speech, it is not possible to pronounce many segments alone; instead, they exist in an overlapping relation—called coarticulation—with their neighboring segments. Try to speak the segment [p] by itself. You will probably have pronounced a syllable spelled approximately PUH. This PUH is not an isolated phoneme, it is a two-segment syllable. Furthermore, the p sounds in the words POOL, PRAISE, and SPIN are really quite different acoustically because of the different sounds with which p has to overlap in these three words. For many, but not all, segments in the language, it is simply impossible to isolate them in speech production because of the coarticulation phenomenon. It is small wonder, then, that a child cannot deal consciously with a unit that he or she cannot "hear" in isolation.

Of course, we do not mean children do not perceive phonological distinctions in natural speech perception: The distinction between word pairs such as TIN and PIN depends on that. Instead, it is the inability to step back and be aware of these segments that we are interested in here.

THE SYLLABLE AS AN EASILY ISOLABLE UNIT. In contrast to the phonological segment, the syllable is almost completely free from coarticulation effects. Whereas the units within the syllable BAG are highly coarticulated, highly overlapped, this syllable is relatively the same whether in the word BAGGAGE, HANDBAG, or MONEYBAGS. We saw above that both illiterate children and adults, who have severe trouble with the phonological segment, are not bothered by having to count and manipulate syllables.

In view of the alleged ease of handling syllable units, it should be easy to learn to read languages where the orthography represents syllables, that is, languages with a syllabary writing system. And it is: The Cherokee chief Sequoia invented a syllabary for his language in the 1830s to enable his people to become literate. It is reported that literacy soon jumped to about 90% among the Cherokees and that by the 1880s, Western Cherokee literacy in English was higher than the average for all of Texas and Arkansas. Similar success stories have been reported for other syllabary systems including the Japanese and Faroe Islands writing systems. The presumption is that the syllabary makes it easy to comprehend the first of our two lessons—that the writing tracks the sound stream. Then, the problem of an alphabetic orthography can be dealt with later, and separately. If the Cherokees are any example, the alphabetic principle is easier after learning about how writing can attach to sound. Remember, the Cherokee syllabary transferred to English writing; the Cherokees stood out from among Texas and Arkansas whites in English literacy. This progression—first the syllabary and then the alphabet—is what Gleitman and Rozin propose trying with first graders.

APPLYING THE SYLLABARY IN INSTRUCTIONAL SETTINGS. How does one use this knowledge? After all, we are stuck with a nonsyllabic system in English. Moreover, English would not be well suited to a syllabary, even if we were willing to invent a new writing system. (This is because the frequent consonant clusters in English would produce too many syllables to represent efficiently, unlike the situation in Japanese where the structure tends to be alternating consonants and vowels.) Gleitman and Rozin propose a compromise: In the earliest stages of reading instruction, they prescribe a five-part writing system.

> . . . we try to unravel the components of decoding, presenting them in an order from easy to hard, from earlier to later historical appearance . . .
> 1. We teach the child that meaning can be represented visually, by various semasiographic [pictorial] devices.
> 2. We assign to each word its logographic representation [unique symbol].
> 3. We teach phoneticization notions: that spoken words are segmentable in terms of sounds and that written symbols can represent these sounds (hence, in par-

ticular, that words that sound alike can be written with the same character).

4. We give each utterable sound, each syllable, a unique writing and show that these syllables recombine and blend to form new words.

5. We try to teach the learner that each syllable can be dissected into integral parts, that approximately correspond to alphabetic symbols. (Rozin & Gleitman, 1977, pp. 113–114)

The rebus suggestion with syllable-sized units is the most novel part of the program suggested by Gleitman and Rozin. The child learns that when the symbols, perhaps pictographs, for SAND (a bucket of sand) and WITCH (mounted on a broomstick) appear together side by side, the correct interpretation is the food, SANDWICH. The materials designed by Gleitman and Rozin are shown in Figure 10.7. Notice that the regular English orthography is always printed underneath the special rebus characters introduced in the program. The theory is that once a child is thriving on the rebus syllabary, the special characters can be "faded out" to make way for the conventional characters.

The transition from rebus to alphabetic system should be made easy in two ways, according to Gleitman and Rozin. First, the child has already mastered the principle of how writing represents spoken language in segments that can be blended together. Second, the rebus is not difficult to learn, so the child should have a background of success, rather than failure, in reading; this should prevent all kinds of emotional blocks and resistance to instruction that are commonly observed in early reading. Early results with the Gleitman and Rozin program in the Philadelphia area have been promising. The chapter by Rozin and Gleitman (1977) contains some blow-by-blow accounts of the successes and failures of the initial application of this method to a population of seriously behind-schedule readers.

An interesting feature of the Gleitman-Rozin program is that children are carried through a progression of writing systems that repeats the history of writing itself. Recall from Chapter 8 that all orthographies seem to have followed the same progres-

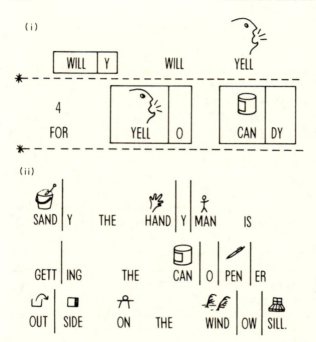

Figure 10.7. *Materials used by Gleitman and Rozin in their instruc-tional project in the Philadelphia schools. (From Gleitman, L., and Rozin, P. Teaching reading by use of a syllabary. Reading Research Quarterly, 1973, 8, 447–483. Reprinted with permission of L. Gleitman, P. Rozin, and the International Teading Association.)*

sion, from pictographs through ideographs, syllabaries, and fi-nally alphabets. It is tempting to attach considerable significance to this parallel: The direction in which writing systems evolve, in history, may be the best direction in which the individual reader should pass, in development.

REFERENCES AND NOTES

The early history of teaching reading is such a fascinating blend of social history, linguistics, and psychology, it is hard to resist spending more time on it here. Good summaries are found in Davis, *Teaching Reading in Early England* (1973), or in Huey, *The Psychology and Pedagogy of Reading* (1908/1968).

A reviewer of an earlier version of this chapter has quite correctly pointed out that I use the term *whole-word* in a way that could be misleading. One could theoretically endorse a "sound-emphasis" approach to reading instruction and yet still not believe in analytical, phonics training. For example, the term *look-say* emphasizes the pronunciation of the word (SAY) and not explicitly the meaning. Thus, the whole-word or look-say approach should technically be designated as a *logographic* strategy of instruction, rather than ideographic. One could still maintain that the route to meaning is through pronunciation and endorse the whole-word method. The fact is, however, the emphasis on going from print to meaning directly—meaning emphasis—has almost always gone hand in hand with the whole-word, look-say method. This is apparent in a very recent chapter by Beck (1981) reviewing instructional practices; thus, I have retained the terminology that best reflects common usage in the field.

A recent survey of the argument between advocates of the phonics and whole-word methods can be found in Williams (1979). In it, she cites the major national studies comparing methods including Chall's *Learning to Read: The Great Debate* (1967) and Project Literacy. Among other things, she comments on the immense resistance among professionals in reading to accept evidence that early phonics drill is beneficial. Chall's own updating of the great debate is also available (Chall, 1979). She asserts that not only would her conclusion favoring phonics be the same today as it was in 1967, but that published reading and TV sources (Sesame Street, for example) show that popular attitudes are coming around to her position.

Mattingly (1980) has written with care about the nature of linguistic awareness and how it may develop. It is interesting to follow his comments in light of the Morais et al. study on adult illiterates. Recall from that study that people who had learned reading *as adults* performed well on the phonetic segmentation tasks. The illiterates could not do these tasks, however. Being forced to perform unusual analyses of the language for the purposes of reading enables us to become aware of the structure of the language. At another level, many of us found that we were entirely unaware of grammatical rules (although we spoke correctly) *until* taking Latin or French in high school forced this awareness on us.

One interesting implication of the idea that poor readers are not adept at achieving a phonetic code (which they could use for short-term memory) is that the problem would occur in auding as well as in reading. Speech does not, after all, come served up in a phonetic format, it comes as sound waves that have to be classified into phonetic abstractions, just as patterns of light and dark on a page of print have to be classified. Ordinarily, poor readers have been observed to understand spoken language normally. Brady, Shankweiler, and Mann (1981) have recently gathered evidence that when nonsense words must be understood against a background of noise, the poor readers are at a disadvantage to the good readers. This cannot be as simple a problem as poor hearing because Brady, Shankweiler, and Mann found that when listening to difficult *nonlinguistic* sounds against a noise background, poor and good readers were not different, even though both groups were far from perfect.

In the effort to achieve clarity and consistency, I have probably minimized the excitement and controversy that exist in this field today. Wolford and Fowler (1982) have recently turned in a highly provocative result concerning memory confusions, for example. The point of departure is the Liberman et al. (1977) finding that good readers, but not poor readers, were damaged when phonetically similar lists were used in immediate memory (as compared to phonetically dissimilar lists). There was no evidence for visual similarity effects. However, visual similarity never makes a difference in immediate memory (see Chapter 4). Wolford and Fowler wondered whether the good readers might not be more handicapped by visual similarity, too, if only the task used were one in which visual confusions are routinely found for adults. They tested this hypothesis with a tachistoscopic task in which several letters were flashed briefly and found an unexpected and dramatic result: The good readers made more visual confusions than the poor readers in this second task but there were no differences in phonetic confusions. Their hypothesis is that good readers are just simply more likely to use partial information of any kind, in recall, than poor readers—either visual partial information or phonetic. This would reduce the special relation between reading ability and phonetic coding, if it were true. We will have to see how further experimentation and interpretation deal with this new hypothesis, in the months and years to come. For now, I include it as a good sample of the kinds of surprises and discoveries that lie at the cutting edge of the research effort.

For an authoritative three-volume collection of contributed chapters on reading instruction by leaders in several fields, see Resnick and Weaver's *Theory and Practice of Early Reading* (1979). Actually, the title of this work is not broad enough, for it contains up-to-date surveys by experts in virtually all of the research topics covered in this book.

CONFESSION. The approach reflects what I honestly consider to be the most productive approach given the evidence now in hand. However, the reader should know that other attitudes are indeed held by highly qualified experts. Particularly on the issue of whether poor readers are deficient in decoding or in comprehension there is a high range of views. For a readable presentation of the opposing perspective to the one presented here, see Smith (1971) or Goodman (1973); the latter reference is a specific critique of the Rozin and Gleitman program.

CHAPTER 11

The Problem of Dyslexia

Whatever the skill one wishes to measure—schoolwork, music, sports—individuals are bound to show a distribution of effectiveness, some better and some worse. It may be democratic to pretend that these differences aren't there but it is certainly not realistic. After all, our exterior traits, such as height and facial features, show large variation and there is every reason to expect the same from our interior (including mental) traits. In the previous chapter, we spent some time examining the performance differences between good and poor readers to see if we could capture fundamental processes in reading during their emergence. We may suppose that these differences between good and poor readers are the sorts of "normal" variation to be expected in any skill; everyone could not possibly be located precisely at the average for the population.

This approach is comparable to how a botanist might try to understand the organization of petals in blossoms by comparing buds at different stages of flowering. There is little concern that the later-developing buds will not open normally when they get around to it. The advantage of comparing different stages of development is to get a good look at examples from different points in time simultaneously.

Now we are faced with a different situation: Some poor readers may represent more than just routine variability. The common definition of the word *dyslexia* simply means poor performance in reading, so it is not helpful on this issue. However, some workers in the area like to reserve this term for a disorder that is distinctly more than just the consequence of "normal" variation. The full term is *Specific Developmental Dyslexia* and it means

> . . . failure to learn to read with normal proficiency despite conventional instruction, a culturally adequate home, proper motivation, intact senses, normal intelligence, and freedom from gross neurologic defect. (Eisenberg, 1978)

Whereas the "poor readers" of Chapter 10 are a population with many different likely causes of their backwardness, the target population for this chapter is much more carefully defined.

ARE THERE ANY TRUE DYSLEXICS? Experts are by no means agreed that there even *is* a group of poor readers to whom the definition we quoted applies. Some highly qualified authorities prefer to believe that all reading-disabled childern fit the Chapter 10 pattern, representing the expected normal variation in ability found in any trained skill. (However, advocates of this position would have to explain why there is a "bump" at the low end of the distribution of reading ability. Most normally distributed skills show a symmetric distribution.) By the chapter organization and evidence cited in this book, we are siding with those who separate "garden variety" poor reading from true developmental dyslexia. However, the reader should not get the impression that the issue is settled. Even a distinction that may have to be abandoned later can serve to present the issues clearly at first.

To make the case for a special dyslexic condition, we begin with a case study. The names and circumstances have been changed in the interests of privacy but the rest is true.

KAREN: AN ADULT DYSLEXIC

Karen P. was 24 years old when she approached a well-known remedial-reading school in southern New England. The problem was simple: She found her professional advancement was being held back by the fact that she could read only slowly, with unusual effort, and with very poor comprehension.

KAREN'S EDUCATION. Karen was raised in a small and wealthy New England community and went through the local public schools. It was clear from her record that she did very poorly in reading, but her other subjects were fine and there was no question of holding her back. Karen's predicament was not ignored in her early school years: She was tested repeatedly through those grades and went to summer school every year for special help. On the other hand, she was never identified as having a highly specific reading problem, as such. (As a result of this last circumstance, she grew up considering herself to be dumb. A growing realization that she was, in fact, smart, but handicapped by poor reading came only in her teens and was a major factor in her personality development.)

Furthermore, the reading problem became more concealed as she went through the primary grades in the following manner: Her quick mind compensated increasingly for her not having learned to read. That is, as the emphasis changes from decoding skills to comprehension skills in primary school, a bright child can compensate more and more for the former with the latter. Here is a scenario showing how this could work:

Karen sits in sixth grade listening to her classmates discuss a story they had just been told to read. The other children are trying to answer the teacher's question "Why did so-and-so do such-and-such in the story?" Karen had gotten next to nowhere trying to read the story herself. Now, however, listening to the groping comments of the other children, she figures out what must have happened. She gets an insight about the target question, raising her hand and impressing the teacher with her "reading" skill.

She was accepted into a major West Coast university after strenuous efforts by herself and some high school officials who believed strongly in her ability. On the basis of her grades and test scores, she would never have been admitted. College was an uphill struggle, at best, and she was forced by reason of financial hardship to drop out before the end of her second year.

Her style of work in college is revealing. She elected lecture courses whenever possible, hoping that the oral presentation of lectures would allow her to get along with minimal dependence on books. She would hire people to read to her from textbooks, when print was absolutely essential to the coursework. In fact the occasion for her leaving school exactly when she did was that her "reader" decided to leave school also and Karen faced having to find another on the spur of the moment. Until this happened, the strategy was working passably. She was so completely in command of the material in lecture courses, especially in science, she actually worked as a tutor for classmates having difficulty with the material. Ironically, she would invariably wind up with a lower grade for the course than those she tutored because the examinations were written.

KAREN'S JOB. It is worth pausing to mention Karen's work situation when she appeared for help. It shows two things: first, how far one can rise in professional life essentially without reading, and, second, that Karen is indeed, a productive, creative, motivated young woman.

Karen's job is designing, promoting, and marketing new products for direct-mail-order catalogues. She conceives of what new type of item would sell well, arranges for its production with appropriate contractors, and designs the promotion in the catalogue. It is a challenging and creative job. To cope with her reading disability, it is necessary for Karen to compensate with ingenuity.

She has gradually reduced to about one page, the formal written reporting for which she is responsible. She tries to do all her business in person or over the telephone. At meetings, her worst moments are when someone passes out a written memo of a page or so and asks for her reaction right on the spot. If she stops in to talk with an associate who is not in the office, the secretary will often suggest she leave a note. Karen's note is always the same—"give me a call."

A Closer Description of the Case

In this section, the purpose is to describe more carefully than above what Karen could and couldn't do. There are two forms of description—the psychometric, which measures her scores on standard tests of achievement and aptitude, and the preliminary efforts that have been made in the psychology laboratory (my own) to observe her performance on some of the most popular kinds of "reading experiment" that we have seen in this book.

KAREN'S READING BEHAVIOR. First, I will describe what happens when Karen is given a page of print and asked to read it. I presented her with a page from the manuscript of this book, chosen haphazardly from the middle of Chapter 9. Her oral reading sounded surprisingly good, from what I had been led to expect. The first few sentences were as fluent as anyone's. After that, her reading would fluctuate sometimes, trailing off in hesitations, and in stumbling over words, then recovering for a phrase or two. The main impression was reasonable fluency with poor confidence.

From the page I had given her to read aloud, Karen understood absolutely nothing, as far as I could discover. I then went on to read aloud, to her, a page from slightly further along in the same chapter. She startled me, then, by giving me a very intelligent summary of what I had been trying to say on that page. The material covered had been about phonological coding in lexical access and anyone could have been forgiven for not making much sense of that unfamiliar, technical material. I must say, it was at this point I appreciated that Karen presented an unusual situation in sharp detail.

PSYCHOMETRICS. With her history of reading failure, Karen has been tested again and again. The results of these tests confirm

what is most obvious from the start—that she can't read well—
and give reassurances that the problem is specific to reading. For
example, her scores on the WAIS scale of intelligence are not
only within the normal range, she is officially classed as "supe-
rior" in intelligence. And this is in spite of the fact that the
WAIS measure includes some forms of testing that put a pre-
mium on literacy skills!

Other standard tests show generally weak performance in
areas that demonstrate academic learning. Her short-term memory performance is only average, poor in comparison with what
one would expect from her IQ. Such memory tests, of course,
typically employ verbal materials and so the results fit well with
her persistent weak performance on anything that requires decoding, encoding, and manipulation of the language. Specifically, her "word attack skills" were at a sixth-grade level. Comprehension and expression, however, pushed at the upper limits
of the testing intrument (the Gilmore Oral Reading test). This
psychometric evaluation matches exactly what I discovered in
my office with the pages from Chapter 9. As would be expected,
spelling performance was poor, at seventh-grade level or lower.

As an aside, Karen observed to me that the illiterate tends to
be highly insecure about the *spoken language* by virtue of poor
spelling. There are many words she doesn't really know how to
pronounce with care because she doesn't know how they are
spelled. For example, the word in the title of this chapter—is it
really DYSLEXIC or is it DYSLECTIC? Is the word ATHLETE
correctly pronounced with two or with three syllables? Perhaps
for this reason, or perhaps not, Karen speaks rapidly and although her speech is animated and interesting, it is not notable
for either precise diction or fastidious grammar.

Specific mathematical skills (rather than more pure reasoning) were also low, at a middle ninth-grade level. Finally, there
was no known history of reading difficulty in the family and no
overt brain injury or the like.

PERFORMANCE IN THE LABORATORY. With the aid of a micropro-
cessor, a student and I took Karen through a set of experiments
that are popular among psychologists interested in reading. The

following is a report on what we found in this preliminary investigation. The report should not be read as a formal research report, for we had no specific control subjects (except ourselves) with whom to compare Karen. Instead, this information is presented as a provocation—a call for other workers to bring together the real-world concerns of school and clinic and the more abstract theoretical issues that have been of main interest in this book. This report is also a bit of a review: The experiments described are some of the main ones we covered in the earlier chapters of the book and they will be mentioned here in the same order they came up earlier.

We gathered some indication that the problem with her was not visual feature detection by itself: In one experiment, the subject has to watch a screen as occurrences of the letter *E* pop up at random locations. On half the trials, there is a single occurrence of the letter *F* in one of the random locations, along with the E's, and the task is to answer, afterward, whether or not there was an F. It is challenging because after the screen begins to fill up, there are too many E's, coming up too fast, to check each one; futhermore, the whole display disappears abruptly, before there is time to go back and scan it. In the easy condition, the F occurs fairly early and in the hard condition it occurs just before the whole thing disappears.

In this feature detection task, our result was easy to describe: Karen did better than either of us! This effectively rules out things like poor vision or wandering attention as simple explanations for her difficulty. (The lexical decision experiment, described below, allows a similar point.)

In another experiment, we presented Karen with letter feature detection in another task context—this time Neisser's "visual search" procedure (see Chapter 3). In this task, the subject sees an array of 10 or more rows of letters, each row with (in this case) five unrelated letters. The problem is to scan the list and to find a particular target letter; the measure is how long it takes to locate the target depending on how far down in the column of rows the target is located. As we learned in Chapter 3, the task is harder if one is searching for a letter in the context of similar nontargets (looking for X among letters such as Z, W, N, and Y)

THE PROBLEM OF DYSLEXIA

than is the nontargets are dissimilar (looking for X among C, Q, S, and G).

The results of this set of tests have to be divided into two parts. First, Karen found the visual search task highly disagreeable. The first time, she complained of a headache and the session had to be discontinued. She was willing to persist, on another occasion, and we were able to obtain useful data from her on two runs through the material. Even on these later occasions, however, she found the task unpleasant and complained of a "stinging" in her eyes.

Karen's objective performance on the Neisser visual search task was quite routine, despite her dislike for the activity. On two separate runs, the linear correlations between position of the target and search time were .855 and .734, showing that she was able to conduct an orderly search, row by row, of the display. Her overall processing times were 16 letters per second and 20 letters per second, which are consistent with the search speeds that have been reported in the literature (also see Chapter 3). These search speeds actually combine data from trials where the target and nontargets were physically similar and trials where they were dissimilar. Like everyone else, Karen was considerably faster in the latter case that in the former case.

We spent some time measuring Karen's performance in the Sperling experiment on brief presentation of unrelated letters (see Chapter 4). Although nothing surprising turned up—either in her performance or her reaction to the task—we have little confidence in this phase of the project. Getting truly reliable data on the partial- and whole-report conditions in Sperling's task depends on delicate adjustments of two sorts: The results depend on subjects' strategies such that they must be guided by the experimental conditions into relying on their icons, rather than adopting the policy of trying to outguess the experimenter. Second, the exact visual configuration of what the subject sees can drastically alter the obtained properties of iconic memory. For these reasons, we have chosen not to attach much weight to this portion of our testing project with Karen.

In a version of the Conrad experiment on phonological confusions in visual memory (Chapter 4), the results were mixed: First of all, Karen had a low memory span, finding a list of five letters a challenge, in contrast to most college students who can cope with lists of seven. Her overall scores on six-item lists were about .75—five letters correct. This being the case, however, she showed perfectly normal results with respect to the comparison of phonologically confusable and nonconfusable lists (CBTVZ versus GRMLF); the confusable items were much harder for her. Thus, if one is inclined to think of this "confusion effect" as showing the presence of phonetic processing in something related to reading, Karen's performance was quite normal.

In Healy's letter-cancellation task (Chapter 5), there was nothing unusual about Karen's performance. In that procedure, the subject must read through a paragraph of text crossing out all instances of the target letter T. For the exact passage reprinted in Figure 5.6, Karen's time was 40 seconds, slightly faster than the college students in Healy's experiment. Karen overlooked seven instances of the target letter, four of them on the word THE. In the scrambled-word version of the same passage, she tooked 33 seconds and made two errors of omission, both on the word THE. Thus, if we are willing to follow Healy's interpretation— that errors on the word THE show it is read as a unit—Karen has learned to process it as a unit in the same way as normal readers do.

Perhaps the biggest surprise was in a lexical decision experiment (Chapter 9) we did with Karen. This was a typical word/nonword experiment with reaction times measured. The word items were common words, some of them homophones of each other (MEDDLE and MEDAL). The purpose of the study was to observe repetition effects, at lags of either 2 or 12 intervening items, for words and their homophones. This experimental design is unimportant; the experiment had been prepared for other purposes than testing Karen. The surprise was that her performance was absolutely normal in all ways. Her reaction times were among the fastest ones of all the 18 students who completed the experiment, she made fewer errors, and her results were consistent with those of the group in terms of the comparisons of conditions.

This is a striking observation because the lexical decision task has been one of the most valued tools in studying information

processing and reading. It is slightly embarrassing to find a disabled reader doing normally in one of our favorite experiments.
What the task requires, of course, is only access to the lexicon in
order to decide on a yes or no response, not access to the meaning of the word. It may be that Karen has trouble with getting
from the lexical address of items to further information. Alternatively, it may be that she is unhandicapped with single words in
isolation and that multiple simultaneous words are what give her
trouble.

The next experiments in this project are obvious: We should
see whether making semantic decisions to single words in isolation is normal or impaired in Karen. But to fill in the rest of the
story is beyond the scope of this book.

The experiments with Karen do leave a slightly unsettling
message, however: So far in this testing, Karen is just too normal!
There is no doubt she is a badly disabled reader. The fact that
she does so competent a job on many of the most standard tasks
in the study of information processing in reading means that
these tasks must not challenge the particular aspect in which she
is lacking.

THE CHANGING CONCEPT OF DYSLEXIA

Even students in their first psychology course these days are
comfortable with the idea that different mental functions go on
in different parts of the brain. This concept of localization of
function that we take for granted is a relatively new idea. *Phre-
nology,* the "reading" of bumps on the skull as a method for
finding out about personality, sounds silly to us today but it was
actually a sophisticated phase in nineteenth-century intellectual
history and was taken seriously by thoughtful people. The first
reports of dyslexia, later in that century, should be seen against
this background of localization of function.

It was known, by that time, that there was a special connection between the left side of the brain and speech or language
functioning. This principle was supported overwhelmingly by
evidence from brain injuries, strokes, and other damage that

could be assigned to the left hemisphere. When the brain was injured on the left side, there was almost always a corresponding loss of speech and when it was injured on the right side there seldom was a loss of speech. Around the turn of the century, other patients with brain damage began showing up with more subtle symptoms, particularly the loss of the ability to read (with or without other impairment of language). This was called "word blindness." It was perfectly natural to wonder whether children who had trouble learning to read might not have some kind of *congenital* (present at birth) problem with the same brain region whose injury caused word blindness in adults. This was happening around 1900, with reports, often from eye doctors, of children whose intelligence was quite normal but who had not learned to read.

The Scottish surgeon James Hinshelwood was responsible for the systematic description of "congenital word blindness." He worked at the Glasgow Eye Infirmary and began publishing papers on the disorder in 1905, with his major work being a book of the same title published in 1917. Hinshelwood reported three characteristics of dyslexia (although he did not call it that) that are still important ones: One was that the disorder occurred considerably more often in boys than in girls. We now know that the ratio is somewhere around 4:1 (Rutter, 1978, p. 16). Second, there is a tendency for the problem to run in families (see Owen, 1978, p. 261). Third, dyslexia is associated with underdeveloped cerebral dominance—the asymmetry in the brain that leads to handedness, localization of language in the left hemisphere for most people, and other more subtle left-right differences. This third generalization of Hinshelwood is still a matter of lively controversy, however; reviews of the literature can be found in Rourke (1978) and in Young and Ellis (1981).

In this country, it was Samuel Orton whose work and ideas dominated the field from the 1920s through the 1960s. Orton rejected the hypothesis of Hinshelwood and others that children showing dyslexic symptoms suffer from actual brain damage to specific centers responsible for visual memory. His alternative view was that dyslexic children are (for some reason) slow to develop brain asymmetry, dominance of one hemisphere over the other. The idea was that in children where language was slow to "settle down" in one hemisphere, such language functions as reading would naturally be delayed. More specifically, Orton thought that one needed a strongly dominant hemisphere in order to prevent a particular letter form from stimulating its mirror-image opposite. If the left side of the brain were doing the main work of reading, Orton thought, then when it sees the letter *d*, it will suppress the right side of the brain from perceiving *b*.

It follows that a telling symptom of dyslexia should be errors confusing pairs like *b,d* and *p,q*. Indeed, children do read "bear" for *dear* and children who are poor at reading do this more often than those who are good at reading. However, most of the evidence available today says that the left-right reversals are just a consequence of dyslexia and not in any way a part of the cause for it. This conclusion is documented in recent writings of Rutter (1978, p. 7) and of Vellutino (1978, p. 86). Indeed, Vellutino has found that dyslexic children have much less trouble *copying* letters and other symbols than they have naming these same items. Under some conditions, he found that they are as good at copying as normal children. Therefore, the problem could not be due to anything like "seeing things backwards." Although popular culture has more or less adopted Orton's hypothesis, letter and word reversals seem thus to play only a small role; a full review of the literature on this point is found in Vellutino (1978).

MODERN ATTITUDES. Explanations in psychology are subject to what may be swings of a pendulum between two extreme attitudes—that behavior is to be explained mainly by hereditary, congenital forces or by learned, environmental forces. The swings are in very slow motion, furthermore. Led by men such as Freud and Watson early in the twentieth century, psychology turned away from genetic explanation toward radical environmentalism. Whereas people previously stressed that intelligence "ran in families," Watson's behaviorism argued that it was the quality of the environment that was more important. Similar assumptions dominated such questions as the origins of language and mental illness. Against this backdrop, it is easy to see that congenital, constitutional, or other explanations of dyslexia based on inborn mechanisms would be unpopular. To some extent, the controversy in the field today stems from this basic conflict: Approaches to dyslexia from the medical direction tend to emphasize these inborn factors whereas approaches from the direction of psychology and education tend to minimize them.

A good summary of current thinking is found in Gibson and Levin, *The Psychology of Reading* (1975): Gibson and Levin identify four causes of dyslexia, the first two "intrinsic" (genetic) and the second two "extrinsic" (environmental). The first of the two extrinsic causes is *communicative emotional deprivation*, a condition of poor language learning especially due to absent or subnormal mother-child interaction. The second extrinsic cause is *cultural or educational deprivation,* which is what Project Head Start was designed to remedy—a lack of linguistic stimulation in the home; absence of books; poor motivation for school; lack of rapport with teachers who, for little boys, are mostly women, and often of a different race to boot; and the like. These first two factors seem very similar, of course. They may be distinguished in that the first is based primarily on a transaction in early infancy between mother and child while the second is related to general sources of stimulation and motivation in the older child.

If we take seriously the Sticht distinction between reading and auding (see Chapter 7), these first two factors must refer to processes more general than reading, for they identify problems that should show up with the spoken language as well as with the written language. However, children by age 6 have generally worked out a fluent mode of spoken expression that sounds reasonably competent. It is when they are called on to learn a new mode of language behavior—literacy—that weaknesses in their overall language would show up conspicuously.

Of the two intrinsic causes of dyslexia identified by Gibson and Levin, the first is *minimal brain dysfunction*, which is indicated by a subtle pattern of symptoms that seem associated with central nervous system disorders but where no major damage to that system can be found. The currently popular term "hyperactivity" overlaps somewhat with minimal brain dysfunction.

Although there are no necessary conditions for diagnosis of

minimal brain dysfunction, some of the sufficient conditions include abnormalities of the electroencephalogram (brain-wave test), poor motor coordination, abnormal reflexes, and, significantly, mixed brain dominance (left handed for some things and right for others, or inconsistent patterns of preference). On the question of cerebral dominance, Satz and Sparrow (1970; see also Satz, 1977) have conducted research showing a systematic association between delayed reading and a large number of measures of laterality. Their hypothesis is that some children are subject to a lag in the "settling down" process we referred to earlier of language functions in the dominant hemisphere. The research shows that the order in which different kinds of left-right preference show up is similar in children of different reading ability but the process is slower with delayed readers than with normal ones. This type of evidence is congenial to the general spirit of Orton's proposals. (But the evidence is not unanimous on this association between reading disability and hemispheric asymmetry, as can be seen in a review by Young and Ellis, 1981.)

Minimal brain dysfunction is the most depressing diagnosis, for parents and educators, and Gibson and Levin are inclined to belittle it relative to the other causes. The fourth proposed cause of dyslexia is called by them *genetic makeup*, which is a lag in "inherited language ability." By pointing up this significant hereditary connection, Gibson and Levin are marking what may be a backswing of the pendulum alluded to above: Explanations of human behavior in fields as diverse as intelligence, language, and schizophrenia are beginning nowadays to return to some recognition of genetic factors, after the decades of radical environmentalism.

The best source of evidence for deciding there is a hereditary basis of any trait is the comparison of identical (monozygotic) and fraternal (dizygotic) twins. Identical twins have just the same genes from their parents whereas fraternal twins have no more similar heredities than would two siblings of different ages. Since the environmental influences on twins are likely to be no more similar for identical than for fraternal twins, the amount by which identicals are more alike than fraternals can be attributed to genes alone. The data are impressive: In one study (Bokwin, 1973, cited in Gibson & Levin, 1975) on 338 pairs of twins, the degree of similarity was 81% for identical twins and only 29% for fraternal twins. In another study (reported in Hermann, 1959) on only 20 pairs, the corresponding values were 100% and 33%. There is not space to go into the technical details of the argument but this evidence is overwhelmingly strong for an important genetic factor in dyslexia.

It is also relevant that the prevalence of dyslexia is greater in little boys than in little girls by a ratio of around 4:1. There are other traits, such as baldness, that are transmitted genetically in a "sex-linked" manner. However, someone more disposed to an extrinsic, environmental source of dyslexia could argue that the greater tendency of boys than girls for the disorder could reflect social factors: Perhaps boys have trouble more often because their teachers tend to be women in the early grades, with whom they have less rapport.

The test for this last proposition would be to observe rates of dyslexia in countries where teachers are more often men than women and see whether there are more girl dyslexics there than boy dyslexics. Although there is some indication that this might be true in Germany, the problem of comparing cross-national rates of reading disability is a notoriously difficult one and so the final answer must wait. There is no corresponding extrinsic counterargument to the twin studies, however, and therefore a genetic attribution does not have to depend on showing there is no social artifact in the sex-ratio data.

The multiplicity of sources of dyslexia implied by Gibson and Levin's survey of four factors is revealed in a study carried out in Edinburgh by Ingram (1970), which we discuss next.

The Edinburgh Study

Ingram (1970) reported a study of 176 dyslexic 7-year-olds (and older) undertaken in the city of Edinburgh, Scotland. The result give us some perspective on the kinds of problems and insights that come with the effort to grapple with dyslexia in the field.

All 176 children were referred to the investigators because of their reading problems, referred by whatever criteria the school saw fit to employ. Of the 176 original children, 54 were judged by Ingram not really to be failing seriously enough to include. Of the remaining 122, 19 were dismissed from the study by reason of low IQ. (This shows, of course, the investigator's position on an issue that is controversial. Excluding these 19 children says that low IQ is, by itself, reason enough for difficulties in reading without bringing in the concept of dyslexia.)

That left 103 children. Of these, 9 were found to have either poor eyesight or poor motivation. Of the remaining 94, 8 dropped out of the study and 4 were judged to be too old to be comparable to the other subjects. That left, finally, 82 children with a large discrepancy between their reading scores and their measured IQ.

These 82 children were further divided by their areas of backwardness. Sixty-two children were called "specifics" on the grounds that reading and spelling were their only difficult subjects in school. The remaining 20 ("generals") had problems with arithmetic as well as with literacy (although they had normal IQs).

These 82 children were next taken through a battery of neurological tests to determine whether they might be "brain damaged." They were tested for reflexes and electroencephalogram (EEG) responses, and their parents were interviewed carefully about any abnormal birth histories (forceps delivery and so on), histories of clumsiness, delayed motor development, and any subsequent head injury.

The main results of the study were a series of comparisons between the "specifics" and the "generals." First of all, there was no reliable difference between the two groups in age or in social class. (However, in the United States, there are more "general" types to be found in socially disadvantaged homes than "specifics.") The IQs of the two groups were roughly comparable but the "specifics" did have a slight edge that was reliable.

One striking result was that there was a 4:1 ratio of boys to girls among the "specifics" and a 1:1 ratio among the "generals." This finding is consistent with the hypothesis that "true" dyslexia can be distinguished from poor reading, even in groups that are all roughly comparable in IQ. It also argues against the claim that the preponderance of boys over girls in dyslexic groups results from the poorer interaction of little boys with female teachers than of little girls with female teachers: This social-interaction hypothesis should apply equally to the "generals" as to the "specifics."

The families of the 82 children on both groups were scanned for a history of reading problems. This, too, turned up a significant difference: Among families of the "specifics" there were 40% showing problems among relatives and among the "generals" there were only 25%. Thus, the specific disorder runs in families more than the general disorder, another plus for the hereditary factor in dyslexia. Finally, there was a gross difference in the two groups on whether they showed neurological abnormalities (reflexes, EEG). There were such symptoms for 32% of the "specifics" and for 68% of the "generals," over a 2:1 difference. Detailed interpretation of this pattern is difficult; we don't know where the neurological signs came from. However, to the extent the neurological abnormalities can be attributed to things like birth trauma, head injuries and the like, this set of results shows a trade off between hereditary and environmental factors, with specific dyslexia associated more with the former than with the latter.

CONCLUDING COMMENTS

This chapter has provided only the first steps in thinking about dyslexia in a focused way. It provided no real answers to questions of diagnosis and remediation. Instead, the main question was whether we are even justified in using the term itself, over and above the more general phenomenon of backward reading.

Our answer was positive and it had two parts. One part was the case of Karen P. If she had been only a backward reader in childhood, we would have expected her to catch up before reaching her middle twenties. There is no argument that she is either poorly motivated or unable to work effectively in other areas. The existence of people like her, however few there are, must suggest more than "normal" variability in picking up any skill.

The second part of the argument has been the type of evidence contained in the Edinburgh study, that careful definition of reading problems shows a group apart (the "specifics") who differ in theoretically important ways from other populations with reading problems. The hereditary nature of this specific disability may seem discouraging for teachers and parents, but, in a way, it should also reassure them that they have not bungled the education of these children themselves. We just don't know whether compensatory education will prove effective with true dyslexics. If it does not, recognition of the true nature of the disorder will allow parents and teachers to unload the heavy mantle of guilt and seek instead to find *compensatory* ways of using the language apart from literacy. These means exist now— cassette recorders and dictating machines, even reading machines in the 1980s. It will oblige dyslexics to "go public" and to accept inconvenience but, in a minor way, so does everyone who needs eyeglasses.

REFERENCES AND NOTES

The argument over whether poor readers include a subgroup of specific developmental dyslexics has had emotional, and even political consequences. Professional educators tend to conclude that all backward reading represents just the lower "tail" of a normal distribution. Medical people, on the other hand, are inclined to retain the neurological approach to dyslexia (covered briefly in the second part of Chapter 11) and to consider it a specific brain symptom, perhaps genetic in origin.

For dyslexics and their parents, obviously, the educators' assumption is the more optimistic, for it suggests that more or better training will make up the gap between those doing average work and those doing more poorly. Recall the image of a group of flowers budding and blossoming at slightly different rates.

The neurological assumption is more frightening to dyslexics and their families and more discouraging to the educational effort. It suggests a chronic condition firmly rooted in a brain disorder and likely to be resistant to compensatory training. The political ramifications of this argument are seen in the fact that different government agencies are responsible for funding programs aimed at backward reading. These agencies (NIH and NIE, currently) depart from different assumptions about the education-medical argument and use different language to describe the target populations involved.

There is a further comment to be made, although it has no bearing on the purpose of this chapter. The educational-medical argument over backward reading is really a modern expression of the old "mind-body distinction" that crops up so persistently— that a brain disorder is somehow different from an educational disorder. (As if education does not have its consequences in the brain!)

I want to convey my special thanks to Karen P. for her willingness to participate in this chapter. Her resourceful tutor, who was a student in my reading course, Ms. Christina Nordholm, was another indispensable contributor, for it was Ms. Nordholm who introduced Karen to the different psychological experiments we tried on her. Ms. Nordholm also helped me prepare the description of Karen's psychometric history and educational background.

As previously stated, I don't know why Karen has had trouble learning to read. The crude efforts to carry her through various psychology experiments on information processing have helped, but mainly by exclusion. We know a number of areas in which Karen is at no disadvantage whatever. I included this information mainly to stimulate others to think in this direction and to be open to different sources of analytic information about dyslexics' problem than the clinic has traditionally provided.

Karen herself is in good company: Nelson Rockefeller was apparently in just as bad shape as far as reading went; he needed helpers and secretaries to read aloud from documents and books and to take his dictation. It seems not to have held him back in his career!

In writing about dyslexia, I have relied heavily on Benton and Pearl (1978). Their book contains sections devoted to the definition of dyslexia; various psychological and neurological factors in it; and the prevention, remediation, and diagnosis of dyslexia, each section organized as a review of the literature by one recognized authority followed by critiques of those reviews by three other experts. The concluding chapter, by Benton, is an integrative survey of the entire book, emphasizing ways in which thinking has been changing recently. Another recent and valuable source is Vellutino (*Dyslexia: Theory and Research*, 1979). I recommend both of these books enthusiastically to anyone who wants more details about this complex topic.

Bibliography

Abelson, R. P. Psychological status of the script concept. *American Psychologist*, 1981, *36*, 715–729.

Adams, M. J. Failures to comprehend and levels of processing in reading. In R. J. Spiro, B. C. Bruce, and W. F. Brewer (Eds.), *Theoretical issues in reading comprehension*. Hillsdale, N.J.: Lawrence Erlbaum, 1980.

Allport, A. Word recognition in reading. In P. A. Kolers, M. E. Wrolstad, and H. Bouma (Eds.), *Processing of visible language, I*. New York: Plenum, 1979.

Baddeley, A. D. Working memory and reading. In P. A. Kolers, M. E. Wrolstad, and H. Bouma (Eds.), *Processing of visible language: I*. New York: Plenum, 1979.

Baddeley, A. D., Thomson, N., and Buchanan, M. Word length and the structure of short-term memory. *Journal of Verbal Learning and Verbal Behavior*, 1975, *14*, 575–589.

Baron, J. Mechanisms for pronouncing printed words: Use and acquisition. In D. LaBerge and S. J. Samuels (Eds.), *Basic processes in reading*. Hillsdale, N.J.: Lawrence Erlbaum, 1977.

Baron, J., and Thurston, I. An analysis of the word superiority effect. *Cognitive Psychology*, 1973, *4*, 207–228.

Barron, R. W., and Baron, J. How children get meaning from printed words. *Child Development*, 1977, *48*, 587–594.

Beck, I. Reading problems and instructional practices. In G. E. MacKinnon and T. G. Waller (Eds.), *Reading research: Advances in theory and practice*. New York: Academic Press, 1981.

Becker, C. A. Semantic context effects in visual word recognition: An analysis of semantic strategies. *Memory & Cognition*, 1980, *8*, 493–512.

Benton, A. L. Some conclusions about dyslexia. In A. L. Benton and D. Pearl (Eds.), *Dyslexia: An appraisal of current knowledge*. New York: Oxford University Press, 1978.

Benton, A. L., and Pearl, D. (Eds.). *Dyslexia: An appraisal of current knowledge*. New York: Oxford University Press, 1978.

Brady, S. A., Shankweiler, D. P., and Mann, V. A. Speech perception and memory coding in relation to reading ability. *Journal of Experimental Child Psychology*, in press.

Brooks, L. Visual pattern in fluent word identification. In A. S. Reber and D. L. Scarborough (Eds.), *Toward a psychology of reading*. Hillsdale, N.J.: Lawrence Erlbaum, 1977.

Byrne, B., and Shea, P. Semantic and phonetic memory codes in beginning readers. *Memory & Cognition*, 1979, *7*, 333–338.

Calfee, R. C., Chapman, R. S., and Venezky, R. L. How a child needs to think in order to learn to read. In L. W. Gregg (Ed.), *Cognition in Learning and Memory*. New York: Wiley, 1972.

Carpenter, P. A., and Daneman, M. Lexical retrieval and error recovery in reading: A model based on eye fixations. *Journal of Verbal Learning and Verbal Behavior*, 1981, *20*, 137–160.

Carpenter, P. A., and Just, M. A. Reading comprehension as the eyes see it. In M. A. Just and P. A. Carpenter (Eds.), *Cognitive processes in comprehension*. Hillsdale, N.J.: Lawrence Erlbaum, 1977.

Carver, R. P. Effect of a "chunked" typography on reading with comprehension. *Journal of Applied Psychology*, 1970, *54*, 288–296.

Carver, R. P. *Sense and nonsense in speed reading*. Silver Springs, Md.: Revrac, 1971.

Cattell, J. McK. The time it takes to see and name objects. *Mind*, 1886, *11*, 277–292, 524–538.

Chall, J. S. *Learning to read: The great debate*. New York: McGraw-Hill, 1967.

Chall, J. S. The great debate: Ten years later, with a modest proposal for reading stages. In L. B. Resnick and P. L. Weaver (Eds.), *Theory and practice of early reading, 1.* Hillsdale, N.J.: Lawrence Erlbaum, 1979.

Chomsky, N., and Halle, M. *The sound pattern of English.* New York: Harper & Row, 1968.

Coke, E. U. The effects of readability on oral and silent reading rates. *Journal of Experimental Psychology,* 1974, 66, 406–409.

Coltheart, M., and Freeman, R. Case alternation impairs word recognition. *Bulletin of the Psychonomic Society,* 1974, 3, 102–104.

Conrad, R. Acoustic confusions in immediate memory. *British Journal of Psychology,* 1964, 55, 75–84.

Conrad, R. Speech and reading. In J. F. Kavanagh and I. Mattingly (Eds.), *Language by ear and by eye.* Cambridge, Mass.: MIT Press, 1972.

Conrad, R., and Hull, A. J. Information, acoustic confusions, and memory span. *British Journal of Psychology,* 1964, 55, 429–432.

Crowder, R. G. *Principles of learning and memory.* Hillsdale, N.J.: Lawrence Erlbaum, 1976.

Crowder, R. G. Audition and speech coding in short-term memory. In J. Requin (Ed.), *Attention and performance, VII.* Hillsdale, N.J.: Lawrence Erlbaum, 1978.

Davelaar, E., Coltheart, M., Besner, D., and Jonasson, J. T. Phonological recoding and lexical access. *Memory & Cognition,* 1978, 6, 391–402.

Davis, W. J. F. *Teaching reading in early England.* London: Pitman, 1973.

Edfeldt, A. W. *Silent speech and reading.* Chicago: University of Chicago Press, 1960.

Eisenberg, L. Definitions of dyslexia: The consequences for research and policy. In A. L. Benton and D. Pearl (Eds.), *Dyslexia: An appraisal of current knowledge.* New York: Oxford University Press, 1978.

Eriksen, C. W., Pollack, M. D., and Montague, W. E. Implicit speech: Mechanisms in perceptual coding? *Journal of Experimental Psychology,* 1970, 84, 502–507.

Estes, W. K. On the interaction of perception and memory in reading. In

D. LaBerge and S. J. Samuels (Eds.), *Basic processes in reading.* Hillsdale, N.J.: Lawrence Erlbaum, 1977.

Estes, W. K. Is human memory obsolete? *American Scientist,* 1980, *68,* 62–69.

Feinberg, R. A study of some aspects of peripheral visual acuity. *American Journal of Optometry and Archives of the American Annals of Optometry,* 1949, *26,* 49–56, 105–119.

Flesch, R. A new readability yardstick. *Journal of Applied Psychology,* 1948, *32,* 221–233.

Forster, K. I. Accessing the mental lexicon. In R. J. Wales and E. Walker (Eds.), *New approaches to language mechanisms.* Amsterdam: North-Holland, 1976.

Frase, L. T., and Schwartz, B. J. Typographical cues that facilitate comprehension. *Journal of Educational Psychology,* 1979, *71,* 197–206.

Frazier, L., and Rayner, K. Making and correcting errors during sentence comprehension: Eyemovements in the analysis of structurally ambiguous sentences. *Cognitive Psychology,* 1982, *14,* 178–210.

Garrity, L. I. Electromyography: A review of the current status of subvocal speech research. *Memory & Cognition,* 1977, *5,* 615–622.

Gelb, I. J. *A study of writing, second edition.* Chicago: University of Chicago Press, 1963.

Gibson, E. J. *Principles of perceptual learning and development.* New York: Appleton-Century-Crofts, 1969.

Gibson, E. J., and Levin, H. *Psychology of reading.* Cambridge, Mass.: MIT Press, 1975.

Gleitman, L., and Rozin, P. Teaching reading by use of a syllabary. *Reading Research Quarterly,* 1973, *8,* 447–483.

Gleitman, L. R., and Rozin, P. The structure and acquisition of reading I: Relations between orthographies and the structure of language. In A. S. Reber and D. L. Scarborough (Eds.), *Toward a psychology of reading: The proceedings of the CUNY conference.* Hillsdale, N.J.: Lawrence Erlbaum, 1977.

Goldiamond, I., and Hawkins, W. F. Vixierversuch: The logarithmic relationship between word frequency and recognition obtained in the absence of stimulus words. *Journal of Experimental Psychology,* 1958, *56,* 457–463.

Golinkoff, R. M., and Rosinski, R. R. Decoding, semantic processing, and language comprehension skill. *Child Development*, 1976, *47*, 252–258.

Goodman, K. S. The 13th way to make reading difficult: A reaction to Gleitman and Rozin. *Reading Research Quarterly*, 1973, *8*, 484–493.

Gough, P. One second of reading. In J. F. Kavanagh and I. G. Mattingly (Eds.), *Language by ear and by eye*. Cambridge, Mass.: MIT Press, 1972.

Gough, P., and Cosky, M. One second of reading again. In N. Castellan, D. Pisoni, and G. Potts (Eds.), *Cognitive Theory (Vol. 2)*, Hillsdale, N.J.: Lawrence Erlbaum, 1977.

Hardyck, C. D., and Petrinovich, I. F. Subvocal speech and comprehension level as a function of the difficulty level of the reading material. *Journal of Verbal Learning and Verbal Behavior*, 1970, *9*, 647–652.

Hawkins, H. L., Reicher, G. M., Rogers, M., and Peterson, L. Flexible coding in word recognition. *Journal of Experimental Psychology: Human Perception and Performance:* 1976, *2*, 380–385.

Healy, A. F. Coding of temporal-spatial patterns in short-term memory. *Journal of Verbal Learning and Verbal Behavior*, 1975, *14*, 481–495.

Healy, A. F. Detection errors on the word *the:* Evidence for reading units larger than letters. *Journal of Experimental Psychology*, 1976, *2*, 235–242.

Healy, A. F. Proofreading errors on the word *the:* New evidence on reading units. *Journal of Experimental Psychology: Human Perception and Performance*, 1980, *6*, 45–57.

Henderson, L. A word superiority effect without orthographic assistance. *Quarterly Journal of Experimental Psychology*, 1974, *20*, 301–311.

Henderson, L. Is there a lexicality component in the word-superiority effect? *Perception and Psychophysics*, 1980, *28*, 179–184.

Hermann, K. *Reading disability: A medical study of word-blindness and related handicaps*. Copenhagen: Munksgaard, 1959.

Hochberg, J. Components of literacy. In H. Levin and J. P. Williams (Eds.), *Basic studies in reading*. New York: Basic Books, 1970.

Hubel, D. H., and Wiesel, T. N. Receptive fields, binocular interaction, and functional architecture in the cat's visual cortex. *Journal of Physiology*, 1962, *160*, 106–154.

Huey, E. B. *The psychology and pedagogy of reading*. Cambridge, Mass.: MIT Press, 1968. (Originally published, 1908.)

Ingram, T. T. S. The nature of dyslexia. In F. A. Young and D. B. Lindsley (Eds.), *Early experience and visual information processing in perceptual and reading disorders*. Washington, D.C.: National Academy of Sciences, 1970.

Johnston, J. C., and McClelland, J. L. Perception of letters in words: Seek not and ye shall find. *Science*, 1974, *184*, 1192–1193.

Just, M. A., and Carpenter, P. A. A theory of reading: From eye fixations to comprehension. *Psychological Review*, 1980, *87*, 329–354.

Just, M. A., Carpenter, P. A., and Masson, M. E. J. What eye fixations tell us about speed reading and skimming. Carnegie-Mellon University: EYELAB Technical Report, March, 1982.

Kintsch, W. Reading comprehension as a function of text structure. In A. S. Reber and D. L. Scarborough (Eds.), *Toward a psychology of reading*. New York: Wiley, 1977.

Kintsch, W., and Keenan, J. Reading rate and retention as a function of the number of propositions in the text base of sentences. *Cognitive Psychology*, 1973, *5*, 257–274.

Kleiman, G. M. Speech recoding in reading. *Journal of Verbal Learning and Verbal Behavior*, 1975, *14*, 323–329.

Klima, E. S. How alphabets might reflect language. In J. G. Kavanagh and I. G. Mattingly (Eds.), *Language by ear and by eye: The relationship between speech and reading*. Cambridge, Mass.: MIT Press, 1972.

Kolers, P. A. Buswell's discoveries. In R. A. Monty and J. W. Senders (Eds.), *Eye movements and psychological processes*. Hillsdale, N.J.: Lawrence Erlbaum, 1976.

Labov, W. A. The reading of the -ed suffix. In H. Levin and J. P. Williams (Eds.), *Basic studies on reading*. New York: Basic Books, 1970.

LaBerge, D., and Samuels, J. Toward a theory of automatic information processing in reading. *Cognitive Psychology*, 1974, *6*, 293–323.

Lesgold, A. E., and Perfetti, C. A. *Interactive processes in reading*. Hillsdale, N.J.: Lawrence Erlbaum, 1981.

Levin, H. *The eye-voice span*. Cambridge, Mass.: MIT Press, 1979.

Levy, B. A. Speech analysis during sentence processing: Reading versus listening. *Visible language,* 1978, *12,* 81–101.

Lewis, C. S. *The allegory of love.* London: Oxford University Press, 1936.

Liberman, I. Y., Shankweiler, D., Liberman, A., and Fowler, C. Phonetic segmentation and reading in the beginning reader. In A. S. Reber and D. L. Scarborough (Eds.), *Toward a psychology of reading.* New York: Wiley, 1977.

Liddle, W. *An investigation of the Wood Reading Dynamics method.* Ann Arbor: University Microfilms, 1965, No. 60-5559.

Lindsay, P. H., and Norman, D. A. *Human information processing, second edition.* New York: Academic Press, 1977.

Marcel, T. The effective visual field and the use of context in fast and slow readers of two ages. *British Journal of Psychology,* 1974, *65,* 479–492.

Mark, L. S., Shankweiler, D., Liberman, I. Y., and Fowler, C. A. Phonetic recoding and reading difficulty in beginning readers. *Memory & Cognition,* 1977, *5,* 623–629.

Mattingly, I. G. Reading, linguistic awareness, and language acquisition. *Haskins Laboratories Status Report on Speech Research.* 1980, *SR-61,* 135–150.

McClelland, J. L. On the time relations of mental processes: An examination of systems of processes in cascade. *Psychological Review,* 1979, *86,* 287–330.

McConkie, G. W., and Rayner, K. The span of the effective stimulus during a fixation in reading. *Perception and Psychophysics,* 1975, *17,* 578–586.

McConkie, G. W., and Zola, D. Is visual information integrated across successive fixations? *Perception and Psychophysics,* 1979, *25,* 221–224.

McCusker, L. X., Bias, R. G., and Hillinger, N. H. Phonological recoding in reading. *Psychological Bulletin,* 1981, *89,* 217–245.

McLaughlin, G. H. Reading at "impossible" speeds. *Journal of Reading,* 1969, *12,* 449–454.

Meyer, D. E., Schvaneveldt, R. W., and Ruddy, M. Functions of graphemic and phonemic codes in visual word recognition. *Memory & Cognition,* 1974, *2,* 309–321.

Morais, J., Cary, L., Alegria, J., and Bertelson, P. Does awareness of speech as a sequence of phones arise spontaneously? *Cognition*, 1979, *7*, 323–331.

Morton, J. Interaction of information in word recognition. *Psychological Review*, 1969, *76*, 165–178.

Morton, J. Facilitation in word recognition: Experiments that cause changes in the logogen model. In P. A. Kolers, M. E. Wrolstad, and H. Bouma (Eds.), *Processing of visible language, I*. New York: Plenum, 1979.

Natalicio, D. S. *Reading and the bilingual child*. In L. B. Resnick and P. A. Weaver (Eds.), *Theory and practice of early reading, 3*. Hillsdale, N.J.: Lawrence Erlbaum, 1979.

Neisser, U. *Cognitive psychology*. New York: Appleton-Century-Crofts, 1967.

Newman, A. Later achievement study of pupils underachieving in first grade. *Reading Research Quarterly*, 1972, *7*, 477–508.

Nickerson, R. S. Binary-classification reaction time: A review of some studies of human information-processing capabilities. *Psychonomic Monograph Supplements*, 1972, *4* (17, Whole No. 65).

Oates, W. J. (Ed.) *Basic writings of Saint Augustine, 1*. New York: Random House, 1948.

Onmacht, D. D. *The effects of letter-knowledge on achievement in reading in the first grade*. Paper presented at the American Educational Research Association. Los Angeles: 1969.

O'Regan, K. Moment to moment control of eye saccades as a function of textual parameters in reading. In P. A. Kolers, M. E. Wrolstad, and H. Bouma (Eds.), *Processing of visible language, I*, New York: Plenum, 1979.

Owen, F. W. Dyslexia—Genetic aspects. In A. L. Benton and D. Pearl (Eds.), *Dyslexia: An appraisal of current knowledge*. New York: Oxford University Press, 1978.

Perfetti, C. A., Goldman, S. A., and Hogaboam, T. W. Reading skill and the identification of words in connected discourse. *Memory & Cognition*, 1979, *7*, 273–282.

Pitman, J., and St. John, J. *Alphabets and reading*. Pitman: New York, 1969.

Rayner, K. Eye movements in reading and information processing, *Psychological Bulletin*, 1978, *85*, 618–660.

Rayner, K., and McConkie, G. W. Perceptual processes in reading: The perceptual spans. In A. S. Reber and D. L. Scarborough (Eds.), *Toward a psychology of reading*. Hillsdale, N.J.: Lawrence Erlbaum, 1977.

Rayner, K., McConkie, G. W., and Ehrlich, S. Eye movements and integrating information across fixations. *Journal of Experimental Psychology: Human Perception and Performance*. 1978, *4*, 529–544.

Rayner, K., Well, A. D., and Pollatsek, A. Asymmetry of the effective visual field in reading. *Perception and Psychophysics*, 1980, *27*, 537–544.

Reicher, G. M. Perceptual recognition as a function of the meaningfulness of the stimulus material. *Journal of Experimental Psychology*, 1969, *81*, 275–280.

Resnick, L. B., and Weaver, P. A. (Eds.). *Theory and practice of early reading* (3 volumes). Hillsdale, N.J.: Lawrence Erlbaum, 1979.

Rourke, B. P. Neuropsychological research in reading retardation: A review. In A. L. Benton and D. Pearl (Eds.), *Dyslexia: An appraisal of current knowledge*. New York: Oxford University Press, 1978.

Rozin, P., Bressman, B., and Taft, M. Do children understand the basic relation between speech and writing? The mow-motorcycle test. *Journal of Reading*, 1974, *6*, 326–334.

Rozin, P., and Gleitman, L. R. The structure and acquisition of reading II: The reading process and the acquisition of the alphabetic principle. In A. S. Reber and D. L. Scarborough (Eds.), *Toward a psychology of reading*. Hillsdale, N.J.: Lawrence Erlbaum, 1977.

Rozin, P., Portisky, S., and Sotsky, R. American children with reading problems can easily learn to read English represented by Chinese characters. *Science*, 1971, *71*, 1264–1267.

Rubin, A. A theoretical taxonomy of the differences between oral and written language. In R. J. Spiro, B. C. Bruce, and W. F. Brewer (Eds.), *Theoretical issues in reading comprehension*. Hillsdale, N.J.: Lawrence Erlbaum, 1980.

Rubenstein, H., Lewis, S. S., and Rubenstein, M. A. Evidence for phonemic recoding in visual word recognition. *Journal of Verbal Learning and Verbal Behavior*, 1971, *10*, 645–657.

Rutter, M. Prevalence and types of dyslexia. In A. L. Benton and D. Pearl (Eds.), *Dyslexia: An appraisal of current knowledge*. New York: Oxford University Press, 1978.

Sakitt, B. Iconic memory. *Psychological Review*, 1976, *83*, 257–276.

Sanford, A. J., and Garrod, S. C. *Understanding written language: Explorations in comprehension beyond the sentence.* Chichester: Wiley, 1981.

Satz, P. Laterality tests: An inferential problem. *Cortex*, 1977, *13*, 208–212.

Satz, P., and Sparrow, S. S. Specific developmental dyslexia: A theoretical formulation. In D. J. Bakker and P. Satz (Eds.), *Specific reading disability: Advances in theory and method.* Rotterdam: Rotterdam University Press, 1970.

Schank, R. C. Conceptual dependency: A theory of natural language understanding. *Cognitive Psychology*, 1972, *3*, 552–631.

Schank, R. C., and Abelson, R. P. Scripts, plans, goals, and understanding. Hillsdale, N.J.: Lawrence Erlbaum, 1977.

Shadler, M., and Thisson, D. M. The development of automatic word recognition and reading skills. *Memory & Cognition*, 1981, *9*, 132–141.

Simons, H. D. Black dialect, reading interference, and classroom interaction. In L. B. Resnick and P. A. Weaver (Eds.), *Theory and practice of early reading, 3.* Hillsdale, N.J.: Lawrence Erlbaum, 1979.

Smith, E. E., and Kleiman, G. M. Word recognition: Theoretical issues and instructional hints. In L. B. Resnick and P. L. Weaver (Eds.), *Theory and practice of early reading, 1.* Hillsdale, N.J.: Lawrence Erlbaum, 1979.

Smith, E. E., and Spoehr, K. T. The perception of printed English: A theoretical perspective. In B. H. Kantowitz (Ed.), *Human information processing: Tutorials in performance and cognition.* Hillsdale, N.J.: Lawrence Erlbaum, 1974.

Smith, F. *Understanding reading.* New York: Holt, 1971.

Sperling, G. The information available in brief visual presentation. *Psychological Monographs*, 1960, *74*, 1–29.

Sperling, G. A model for visual memory tasks. *Human Factors*, 1963, *5*, 19–31.

Sperling, G. Successive approximations to a model for short-term memory, *Acta Psychologica*, 1967, *27*, 285–292.

Spiro, R. J., Bruce, B. C., and Brewer, W. F. (Eds.). *Theoretical issues in reading comprehension: Perspectives from cognitive psychology, linguistics, artificial intelligence, and education.* Hillsdale, N.J.: Lawrence Erlbaum, 1980.

Steinberg, D. D. Phonology, reading, and Chomsky's optimal orthography. *Journal of Psycholinguistic Research*, 1973, *2*, 239–258.

Sternberg, S. High-speed scanning in human memory. *Science*, 1966, *153*, 652–654.

Sternberg, S. The discovery of processing stages: Extensions of Donders' method. In W. G. Koster (Ed.), *Attention and performance II. Acta Psychologica*, 1969, *30*, 276–315.

Stewart, W. A. On the use of Negro dialect in the teaching of reading. In J. Baratz and R. Shuy (Eds.), *Teaching Black children to read*. Washington, D.C.: Center for Applied Linguistics, 1969.

Sticht, T. G. The acquisition of literacy by children and adults. In F. B. Murray and J. J. Pikulski (Eds.), *The acquisition of reading*. Baltimore: University Park Press, 1978.

Sticht, T. G. Applications of the audread model to reading evaluation and instruction. In L. B. Resnick and P. L. Weaver (Eds.), *Theory and practice of early reading*, 1. Hillsdale, N.J.: Lawrence Erlbaum, 1979.

Stroop, V. R. Studies of interference in serial verbal reactions. *Journal of Experimental Psychology*, 1935, *18*, 643–662.

Taylor, I. The Korean writing system: An alphabet? A syllabary? A logography? In P. A. Kolers, M. E. Wrolstad, and H. Bouma (Eds.), *Processing of visible language*, 2. New York: Plenum, 1980.

Taylor, I. Writing systems and reading. In G. E. MacKinnon and T. G. Waller (Eds.), *Reading research: Advances in theory and practice*, 2. New York: Academic Press, 1981.

Taylor, S. E. Eye movements in reading: Facts and fallacies. *American Educational Research Journal*, 1965, *2*, 187–202.

Taylor, S. E., Frackenpohl, H., and Pettee, J. L. *Grade level norms for the components of the fundamental reading skill*. EDL research and information bulletin, no. 3. Huntington, N.Y.: Educational Development Laboratories, 1960.

Thompson, M. C., and Massaro, D. W. Visual information and redundancy in reading. *Journal of Experimental Psychology*, 1973, *98*, 49–54.

Tulving, E., and Gold, C. Stimulus information and contextual information as determinants of tachistoscopic recognition of words. *Journal of Experimental Psychology*, 1963, *66*, 319–327.

Tzeng, O. J. L., Hung, D. L., and Wang, W. S-Y. Speech recoding in reading Chinese characters. *Journal of Experimental Psychology: Human Learning and Memory*. 1977, *3*, 621–630.

Vellutino, F. R. Toward an understanding of dyslexia: Psychological factors in specific reading disability. In A L. Benton and D. Pearl (Eds.), *Dyslexia: An appraisal of current knowledge*. New York: Oxford University Press, 1978.

Vellutino, F. R. *Dyslexia: Theory and practice*. Cambridge, Mass.: MIT Press, 1979.

Wheeler, D. D. Processes in word recognition. *Cognitive Psychology*, 1970, 1, 59–85.

Williams, J. Reading instruction today. *American Psychologist*, 1979, 34, 917–922.

Wingfield, A., and Byrnes, D. L. *The psychology of human memory*. New York: Academic Press, 1981.

Wolford, G., and Fowler, C. A. The perception and use of information in good and poor readers. In T. Tighe and B. Shepp (Eds.), *The development of cognition and perception* (tentative title). Hillsdale, N.J.: Lawrence Erlbaum, 1982.

Woodworth, R. S. *Experimental Psychology*. New York: Holt, 1938.

Young, A. W., and Ellis, A. Asymmetry of cerebral hemisphere function in normal and poor readers. *Psychological Bulletin*, 1981, 89, 183–190.

Index